Sogobujutsu
Psychology, Philosophy, Tradition

iUniverse books may be ordered through booksellers or by contacting:
iUniverse
1663 Liberty Drive
Bloomington, IN 47403
www.iuniverse.com
1-800-Authors (1-800-288-4677)

www.LehighValleyWarriorArts.com
www.Bumon.net

ISBN: 978-1-4759-3634-6 (sc)
ISBN: 978-1-4759-3636-0 (hc)
ISBN: 978-1-4759-3635-3 (e)

The cover's digital design, drawing and artistic rendering, was done by A.R.T. Productions. www.artproandgraphics.net .
The artistic talents of Nichol Benner provided some of the drawn figures used in this cover. All rights reserved. Copyright 2009-2012

Thank you to our photographers: Barry Thomas, Eric Miller, Chris DePrimeo, Terri Schuon, Ken Miller, Carl Engelke, Oreste Jimenez, Adam Temple, Lehigh Valley Photo Group, and "the ages."

Thank you to our Edtior: Mike Valentino

Printed in the United States of America
iUniverse rev. date: 7/12/2012

Sogobujutsu

五大　心道場　捻子撃劍流　総合武術

Psychology Philosophy Tradition

David C. Falcaro

五大　心道場　捻子撃劍流　総合武術

I loved my journey into the warrior science of **Sogobujutsu** *Integrated warrior science*. To share in that journey with you is to know a kind and loving God. I am grateful and thankful.

When I was a little boy who had trouble learning to read and write. I was broken of all confidence. I was labeled and called learning disabled, dumb, slow, and lazy. I was made an example of, punished in front of the class for not keeping up with the others, and outcasted; no teacher had time for me. Finally, someone came along who changed my life, a very special teacher, Sue Vanic. She took me under her wing and spent time getting me to smile. She found out how to reach me and then spent years teaching me the distinct way I learned.

Completing my book, and thinking through my progress, I came to think of that little boy. The kid who, in a million years, would never believe he could read and understand a book such as this, never mind be the author of one. I thought of how a few had the job before you, Ms. Vanic, but you were my first teacher.
I am an author because of you and I am so grateful.

Dedication

I dedicate this work to all of my **Kyu** *Martial arts student* and **Dan** *Black belt*. It is for my family, for my friends, for my brothers within this **Ryu** *Martial arts family tradition*, and for me that I train in **Kobudo** *Classically derived martial arts*. It is for all of you that I strive to bring about the true essence that was passed to me. I ask that you embody these teachings, personify **Sogobujutsu** *Integrated warrior science*, and add all that you can to the already strong **Ryu** *Martial arts family tradition* that is our Martial Family and become a strong link in an already strong chain.

To the students now beginning with the **Godaishin Dojo** *Spirit of the five elements martial arts school*, I hope that this work will help to impress what an important thing it is to become a part of the **Neji Gekken Ryu** *Martial arts family of the spiraling combative edge*. The education one receives is unmatched; beyond this, the experiences felt and encountered are unlike anything else. It is commonly said that the most precious commodity we possess is time and knowing this to be true, I urge you to enjoy your time with us. Appreciate each class; take in the experience of being a whitebelt, the awkwardness, the feeling of sometimes being overwhelmed with information. You don't want to miss out on what you are seeing and feeling now by looking too much toward the future. You are only a whitebelt in our art once; enjoy each step of the way, grabbing hold of as much as you can along the way.

To my senior students:

It is time to take the reins. I have prepped you to become leaders, so lead. All of these teachings of **Sogobujutsu** *Integrated warrior science* enriched my life as they are now enriching yours. Remember to not be selfish.

Do not rob the future **Bugei** *Warrior* of their destiny; do not allow this art to die with you. It will be tempting at times to dumb things down, and not pass on everything you were taught. You must let it flow freely through you as it flows through me. Try not to give too much too soon. Give the gifts as they were given to you. Do not ever betray our beloved traditions. Keep them whole and strong. Lead and pass on the qualities of leadership. As you teach, take this advice with you: Lead from your **Hara** *Bodies center of intuition and motion* and love your students. I have loved and do love all of you; do not teach those incapable of sharing love. They may be good students, but would be undeserving of this beautiful and powerful, yet destructive, art. Please allow this book to stand throughout time. It is meant to inspire, explain, enrich, and help in governing our **Ryu** *Martial arts family tradition*.

Table Of Contents

2009 The beginning of my son's training. Liam David **Takeda** Falcaro and David C. Falcaro **Sensei**.

Acknowledgments

To my family, to my beautiful and intelligent wife, who provides me with love, understanding, support and daily lessons in humility. I am honored to share my life with such a wonderful person.

To my son and daughter, this is your legacy. Follow the path, live **Sogobujutsu**. Let my advanced be your basics. Remember that there is no greater love in this world than that of family. Always be there for each other; this art will help you with that.

To my Gram, you are the glue that binds this family together. Your wisdom impresses me. You are the single greatest cook on Earth. You are so many things to all of us and I love you for all that you are.

To my stepfather, your strong part in our family has always brought me solace. Thank you for your backing and love.

To my brother, Mike, when I was a little boy, I prayed and prayed to God for a little brother. I now pray that I am worthy of such a gift.

To my sister, Jen, everyone loves you, but very few people know you at your core. To know that person is to be truly blessed. You are wonderful, Jenny.

To my mother, there is too much to thank you for. I could write a book entitled "More than what a mother should be" and it would not do you justice. Saying "thank you" is a gross understatement.

To my father, an insightful teacher of life. You never put limits on where and how I could dream. You taught me how to build my dreams, no matter how big or small, you have helped them become tangible. You have given years of your work, a dedication to me of countless hours; the **Hombu Dojo** *Headquarters of all of the martial arts schools within the Ryu* could not exist without you. Your spiritual guidance is unmatched.

To my first success, Jacob B. Fouts **Sensei** *Instructor*, You know how I think and I have told you many times how I feel, so that everyone else knows, "If this **Bugei** *Warrior* is your **Sensei**, consider yourself blessed by the heavens".

To my senior **Kyu**, all of you will be remarkable teachers. The well you draw from is deep, delve into its depths. Stay in the **HA** *The second state of martial development* as long as you can; be forced into **RE** *The third state of martial development.*

To the **Neji Gekken Ryu** *Martial arts family of the spiraling combative edge*, don't just read this book, employ it and embody its teachings and try to learn more than your **Sensei** can teach you.

To the **Sensei**, you are never done learning, nor am I, let us continue together.

2007 Taken during a class on **Kata Garuma**. I am teaching with **Fuku** Jeremy Hochrine.

To the future of our **Ryu**, appreciate your foundation. You stand in line with truly great men. My favorite saying of **Tanemura Katsumi Sensei**'s is "If I am in fact this great master, it's for one reason, I have had the honor and privilege of standing on the shoulders of giants".

To my second success, Eric P. Fichter **Sensei**, My goal has been to make you a great **Bugei** *Warrior*, I am happy to have succeeded. Your impressive dedication breathes life into the art. You are an example of the strength of this **Ryu**.

2011 Taken at our annual **Ryugi** *A concept meaning wearing the brotherhood and respectful aspects of the martial family like a uniform* celebration. These are many of my advanced Students.

To Tia, thank you for your efforts and dedication to the success of our **Ryu**.

To one of my first teachers Stan Triplett, who began my studies into **Nihon Bujutsu** *Japanese derived warrior arts*. You inspired me in more ways than you wanted to. I appreciate you. Thank you for you efforts.

And to my **Sensei**, Edward J. Smith, who provided me with my struggle, and married me to a lifestyle. You stand as the most impressive Martial Artist I have ever seen. You are the inspiration to never stop learning and growing. I hope to make you proud.

Preface

There is a lot of information that has the potential of taking up class time on the mat. Every student, in my view, must

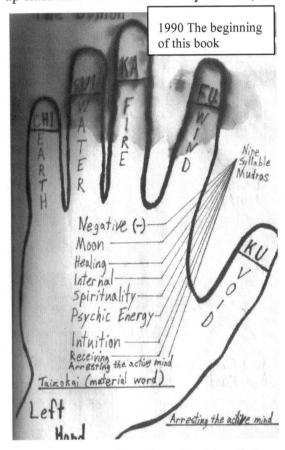

1990 The beginning of this book

possess this knowledge. At the very least, have access to it. After a class of lecturing, I am left wondering how much of what I have just said I will have to repeat. The thought of a textbook for the study of **Sogobujutsu** *Integrated warrior science* was an image I could not escape. I found myself often daydreaming about its content. I got to the point of writing little notes for myself throughout the day on topics I wanted covered. I became a bit obsessive for a while there, trying to cover every possible avenue and answer every question before it could be asked. I wanted something tangible. A mental foundation in our history, psychology and philosophy that I could convey verbally did not seem to be enough anymore. It was too time consuming and a strain mentally to remember how much or how little information each student received.

It became apparent that I could reach the world with a

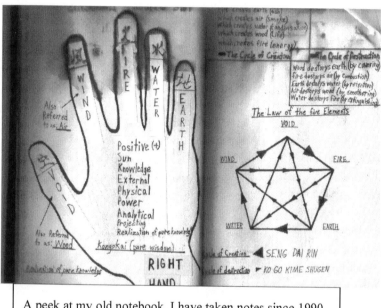

A peek at my old notebook, I have taken notes since 1990

textbook and this work could stand for generations. It consumed much of my time but it had to be as in-depth and complete as I could make it. The art deserved representation and I desired documentation. Cognizant that so many books have been written about other forms of martial arts and yet nothing so far has broached the topic of **Sogobujutsu**, I realized that it was time for me to make every attempt to honor the art I am so honored to possess.

Introduction

In this text, we delve into what is behind the warrior art of **Sogobujutsu** *Integrated warrior science*, taking a deep look into its roots and rich history. It establishes a clear view of the basis from which the art of **Sogobujutsu** was derived. This text attempts to present a full and concise picture of the vast range of study that **Sogobujutsu** encompasses. This is explained through an in-depth outline of the warrior arts and their sub-arts. Also, I have given a unique explanation of the 9 principle concepts of my martial family. I spent time writing about codes of conduct that are found in a traditional **Dojo** *Martial arts school* setting. This text reveals a level of

2011 My son and I on a family vacation in North Carolina. While teaching him about **Zanshin** from **Seigan No Kamae.**

importance behind warrior mindset and traditions never before explained in a book.

Furthermore, the book explores different aspects often overlooked and perhaps never covered in the martial arts. Many martial artists openly claim to "live the life of **Budo** *Martial arts*" or **Bujutsu** *Warrior arts*. When asked what that means to them, they often lack the education to match their desired commitment to living the martial way. The information uncovered in this book will inspire, while impressing you with a sense of the scope of the warriors' philosophies of life. Readers are provided a personal look into our Martial family, our home, and our art to share how we interpret these truths that were passed to us and how we gladly keep these traditions alive today. I have been very open about myself, sharing many photos and details of my training to convey the truth about my credentials.

Over ten years ago I started on a quest to write down everything a student would need that may not be covered in a regular class. After over a decade of adding to my work, only now do I feel confident that I am done. Having birthed this text out of a lifetime of labored experiences, I am providing what I know to be invaluable information.

I am honored that you have chosen this book to further your knowledge of **Budo** *Martial arts*. My hope is that it inspires you to get everything you want out of martial arts. After you have read it over a few times, if you feel a calling to this martial art and its teachings, please feel free to contact me directly in order to get involved.

Chapter 1

Sogobujutsu

The Forging of a Martial Science

Sogobujutsu is a modern term for what has been birthed from hundreds of years of martial history. Forged in battle during Japan's feudal age, it is considered the birthplace from which all Japanese martial arts sprang. **Sogobujutsu** presents itself as the total view of all Warrior Sciences. There are no areas untouched or not covered. I understand this is quite a statement. If we come to understand its origins, only then will we be able to see how this comprehensive study came to be. The warriors of old were motivated by fear of death, dishonor, honor, life, family and many pressing outside influences. This constant pressure forced them to develop and hone their science of war. They were educated from childhood to become warriors. They were learned men who could read and write and they documented their triumphs and their struggles. Through centuries of trial and error, this science was birthed out of the victories in war. **Sogobujutsu** was documented in **Densho** *scrolls* and altered toward

18

refinement by each surviving generation. Every warring **Gumi** *samurai clan* developed **Sogobujutsu** during the many hundreds of years of Japan's feudal age. During this time period, warriors were given a stipend. Their entire lives were

2011 Jacob B. Fouts **Sensei** demonstrating **Hanbojutsu** Jack Toole during a **Shihandai** class at the Hellertown **Godaishin Dojo.**

dedicated to the study and practice of war. The surviving **Bugei** *warriors* of their **Gumi** instructed **Bugei** throughout their lives. **Bugei** learned little outside of every known way to kill and how to survive against the same. They learned not just to survive, but to prevent, reverse, counter and recover from a seasoned battleground tested warrior's attack. These **Bugei** were taught to face multiple attackers at once. The use of another's force was a necessity because an attack from **Samurai** *noble warriors* could most often not be stopped. A **Bugei** did not wait his turn, they all attacked at once. This was how most of the art was forged, out of the necessity to cope with the effective and advanced skills of the opposing warriors. It was an arms race that lasted over a thousand years. Fueled by a governmental and social set caste system, a national budget geared toward maintaining civil war, seemingly endless multi-generational family feuds, every preceding generation's documented knowledge of success and how to triumph in combat, and by countless human lives. Any method that did not work died with the men who attempted it. This stands as the most extreme Darwinist approach to the development of a science ever. No other study in human history comes close. The result is a proven true science of war, **Sogobujutsu**.

2011 Jacob B. Fouts **Sensei** demonstrating **Shotojutsu** with Nevin Moyer Jr. during a **Shihandai** class at the Hellertown **Godaishin Dojo**.

The Warrior Science of our **Ryu**

The martial art form that we practice is derived from many sources. We use the term **Sogobujutsu** as an umbrella term to encompass all of the old Japanese warrior arts. If we look at the **Kanji** *Japanese characters* that make up the term

Locking up four men during a class in 2009 at the Northampton **Godaishin Dojo.**

"**Sogobujutsu**", we see the depth of its meaning. The **Kanji** for **So Go** 総合 translates to: the amalgamation of many into one, total, integrated, consolidated, brought together, and comprehensive. It is Japanese for E-pluribus Unum. The meaning behind the **Kanji** for **Bu** 武 translates to: war, military, warrior, weapons, and chivalry. The **Kanji** for **jutsu** 術 means: skills, science, art form, and technology. Simply put, **Sogobujutsu** can be translated as "the integration of all warrior sciences".

For us, this integration is depicted inside of every **Waza** *technique*; the same motion we use in cutting with a sword or knife is the same motion we use to strike with our hands and arms as well as in throwing a person. For instance, any single **Waza**, can be used with a **Tanto** *knife*, **Hanbo** *3ft staff*, **Kobo** *2ft staff*, **Tanbo** *9in. stick*, **Kama** *sickle*, **Kusari Fundo** *weighted chain*, as well as empty handed.

This ideology was developed over many centuries for the purpose of efficient and effective movement. The **Bugei** *warrior* learns principles that are unified for the purpose of governing all actions; every movement in his/her life is fashioned in accordance with this way. We refer to this as "proper movement". And by this, I am only referring to the developed pinnacle of martial form.

Why learn multiple martial arts forms? Many martial arts have a different form for each weapon. In my opinion, this would be a difficult study; it would prove to be even more difficult when attempting to recall the appropriate form for each given weapon in the middle of combat. Instead, **Sogobujutsu** teaches one efficient and effective movement developed to maximize power and minimize the use of effort.

Bukijutsu *the weaponry arts*, **Jujutsu** *the **Samurai** derived art of hand to hand combat*, **Aikijujutsu** *the higher order of **Jujutsu***, as well as **Ninjutsu** *the art of the **Ninja***, to most people are considered different entities, to us they are merely pieces from the same pie.

Throwing Erin O'Neil during a class in 2008 at the Bethlehem **Godaishin Hombu Dojo.**

Our art includes hundreds of weapons, throws, joint-locks, chokes, many different kicks and punches, hundreds of pressure and nerve points, and also muscle attacks and bone breaks. In addition to all of these teachings (and more) there are **Hanka** *variation techniques*, and these are almost limitless. Without the common principles that are used to tie the art together, one would get lost in technique. The practitioner would spend their training time on "collecting" **Ho** *methods*, **Waza** *technique*, and **Gata** *forms*. It would take decades just to get a working understanding of all of the older Japanese derived martial forms. When training **Bujutsu** *warrior arts* and holding the unifying principles of **Sogo** *integration* in constant mind during training, one quickly notices the inherent synchronistic "proper movement" that occurs within each technique--this is the basis behind our art. When "proper movement" (empowered by principles) becomes the focus in training, no longer is the warrior practitioner training one thing at a time. Instead, for every one **Waza** *technique* the practitioner trains, he/she is invariably training a larger body of the martial art's teachings.

Teaching a class on reversing an attack with a rifle. Jack Toole is working as my **Uke**. Taken in 2011 at the Hellertown **Godaishin Dojo**.

Menkyo vs. Dan
How our curriculum took shape

The first system of codifying warrior arts is now
referred to as the **Menkyo** *teachers certification* system. The
Menkyo system is made up of levels of knowledge
transcribed in books and scrolls. Each **Ryu** *martial tradition*
has their own order of scrolls. The names and documents
differ greatly from tradition to tradition. In the **Tagakishin
Ryu**, the different **Ryu** *traditions* were added to the same
Densho *scrolls* and kept in separated sections. For instance,
the **Daito Ryu** transmissions were a section called **Takeda
No Maki** *the scroll of the **Takeda** family*. The transmissions
of the **Yoshin Ryu** were marked on the **Densho** as **Yoshin
No Kata** *the forms of the **Yoshin** family*. This is the order
and names of **Densho** that are transmitted from the
**Tagakishin Ryu: Okueri, Hiden, Mokuroku, Hiden
Mokuroku, Menkyo, Kaiden, Menkyo Kaiden.** These
were the main levels of the syllabus but they do not include
all of the teachings. There were secondary scrolls
transmitted to me. These were separate weapon arts and
fields of study covered in other non-required **Densho**. I
strived to learn them all.

By the time I was learning under my **Sensei, Akahisa
Tanemura Sensei,** I had eight years of prior experience in
the martial arts. This experience helped me greatly in
understanding and absorbing the information in the
Tagakishin Ryu syllabus. As I started, it was exciting to
work toward the attainment of scrolls. This feeling faded
away after years of struggle. By the time I attained my first
Densho *scrolls*, the desire to have them was lost. This might
sound strange but the journey was so long and difficult that

25

by the time I received it, my mind was focused on the next material. After you have an understanding of the material, having it in a scroll is nice but not very helpful.

With years set between each scroll and no achievement of any sort of ranking that came with it, it was difficult to relate to the **Gendai Budoka** *modern martial artist*. Twelve years into martial arts and four years into training under my **Sensei**, I had a fun conversation. Pushed to converse with a fellow **Budoka** during a party with friends, I gained new perspective. He described how good he was at **Karate**, having attained his **Shodan** *black belt* in just under two years. He, in turn, asked my rank. I began to describe all I had learned, the many fields of in-depth study, and the knowledge attained. I was interrupted with the same question, "Yeah, but what rank are you?" I went back to explaining how long I was training for and how hard the training was. He responded, "Look, what color belt do you wear on your uniform?" I answered that I wore a white belt. He quickly replied, "What? You suck! Twelve years and you are still a white belt? God, you suck!" As he laughed and walked away from me, the experience inspired me. At first, the inspiration brought me to appreciate humility. After a little while though, I got the feeling that the lesson was not just a good shot to the ego. The feeling became an idea. I thought if it were ever my turn to lead, I would transmit this wealth of knowledge differently. As I continued through my training, the concept grew. I thought about how much further I would be if I had learned this piece back then as it directly relates to something taught years ago. And I questioned why this knowledge was not all systematically grouped together. It became the subtext to my note taking during, between and after classes.

The **Dan** *rank level* system presented a new platform for organizing and conveying **Bujutsu** *warrior arts*. No longer would I separate knowledge into the groups named after the places where they were derived from. Instead, I would break up the entirety of the study into its parts and subparts. Then, I categorized everything into its logical place; integrating each warrior tradition together. Where different **Bujutsu** were taught, now **Sogobujutsu** was birthed. For instance,

Nevin Moyer Jr. applying **Kata Garuma** to Eric Coderly during class in 2009 at the Hellertown **Godaishin Dojo.**

every kick from every **Ryu** *martial tradition* makes up our **Keri Waza** *group of kicking techniques*, and every entanglement from every **Ryu** now makes up our **Karamae Waza** *group of entanglement techniques*. I integrated every lesson from every source into one study. What I was left with was a huge amalgamation of parts. So, to simplify for the means of convenience, I split each part into three groups. The three groups for each part are **Okuden** *hidden advanced* *transmissions*, **Chuden** *intermediate transmissions* and **Kihon** *fundamentals*. This was an easy thing to do because this material was most often originally organized this way in the **Densho** *scrolls*. Even after the division, each part was quite extensive, fifty **Kihon Gatamae Waza** *basic limb locks*, one hundred and fifty **Kihon Nage Waza** *basic throwing techniques*, thirty-seven **Kihon Ate Waza** *basic upper body striking techniques,* forty **Kihon Shime Waza** *basic strangulation techniques* and so on. When I laid it all out in front of me, it was a huge, organized mess.

Then, through reviewing the notes I took as I learned, remembering the journey and thinking in terms of logical progression, I started to outline a **Kyoka** *curriculum*. The inspiration was to have a commonsensical succession to the order of things taught so that each teaching would expound on the last learned. The **Dan** system provides twenty ranks. Ten of these ranks are **Kyu** *student ranks* and ten are **Dan** *graduate student ranks*. For much of **Budo** *martial arts*, many of the **Kyu** stages are not used; many martial forms only use seven or less stages of **Kyu**. I thought about how **Gendai Budo** *modern martial forms* package all of their teachings into seventeen ranks. I would need to use all twenty ranks to get it all in; truly, I thought I would need nine times more than that. That much material, I thought, would be too much for a martial arts school. The problem was that I could not cut out any of it; all of it was essential. So, I would think of the **Godaishin Dojo** not as a school, but as a university. In order to earn a degree, a **Kyu** must have attained all nine required credits toward that degree. Things really took shape and the **Kyoka** was born.

28

Mike Affatato Locking Eric Coberly and Zack Edgett during a class in 2009 at the Northampton **Godaishin Dojo.**

Jukyu *white belt* begins the journey by laying the strong foundation. Included in the **Jukyu** syllabus are nine distinct areas of study worth one credit toward the **Kukyu** *yellow belt* degree. Each of the nine can be learned in any order. After attaining a basic understanding of them, a stripe is placed on the blank side of the **Obi** *belt* to signify the attained knowledge, ability and therefore credit. When the **Obi** has nine stripes on it, the **Sensei** *teacher* and **Kyu** *student* set a time for the belt test. The belt test is less a test and more of a demonstration, a quick review of all of the nine credits. That cycle is the same for each degree or each belt earned. Every proceeding belt rank builds on and fortifies the preceding rank.

For each rank earned, a new custom colored belt is presented. These are unique to our **Dojo**. It is embroidered with **Kanji** *Japanese calligraphy* stating **Godaishin Dojo, Neji Gekken Ryu**. Above the **Kanji** is also embroidered our **Ryu Mon** *family crest*. A custom certificate is presented written in **Kanji** and in English. Our certificates are of the highest quality. They were translated and made by the same man that created the certificates for the **Dai Nippon Butoku Kai** *greater Japan Martial Virtue Society*, the most prestigious martial arts organization of Japan. Each are personalized, signed, dated and affixed with **Hanko** *personal seal* by your instructor and by myself. Also, a belt rank booklet is given. The booklet is a detailed outline of every credit needed for your next belt degree. This includes the Japanese terms of every **Jutsu** field of study, **Gata** *form*, **Ho** *method*, **Waza** *technique*, **Undo** *drill* and their English translation. Each booklet is personalized with your name, signature, and the date it was received. Every promotion is documented in our log books, the rank promotion log, as well as publicly to all **Fuku** *members* on the **Nafuda Kake** *rank board indicating hierarchy of the Dojo*. All of this is done with no monetary cost to the **Kyu** student. There is also no charge for all tests. The **Dojo** eats the cost of all of this to impose and to uphold an ideal. The ideal that in no way can rank be bought in the **Neji Gekken Ryu**.

So as not to lose any of the nostalgia surrounding our roots in tradition, **Densho** are also awarded in the **Dan** ranks. These are also at no cost to the **Fuku** *member*.

Sogobujutsu No Kyoka
Our Curriculum from Mukyu to Shodan

Outai *belt rank* is never given out. It cannot be bought. It is not a reward for contributions to the **Sensei** *instructor*, **Dojo** *martial arts school*, or **Ryu** *martial arts family tradition*. To be attained, it must be achieved by the passing of ten separate evaluations. The only way to pass is through work and dedication.

MuKyu (No belt)

-**Reigi Saho:** Methods of proper **Dojo** etiquette

JuKyu (White belt)

-**Reiho:** Methods of bowing

-**Taihenjutsu No Tobi Waza:** Techniques of leaping and jumping of the martial art of supple movement

-**Shintaiho:** Methods of body/spirit movement

-**Taijutsu No Kamae:** Transitory positions of the martial art of unarmed combat

-**Dakentaijutsu No Uke Waza:** Techniques of reception of the martial art of striking and kicking

-**Rokushakubojutsu No Uchi Waza:** Techniques of striking of the martial art of the six-foot staff

-**Rokushakubojutsu No Kaeshi Gata:** Forms of spinning of the martial art of the six-foot staff

31

-**Rokushakubojutsu No Kamae:** Transitory positions of the martial art of the six-foot staff

-**Rokushakubojutsu No Uke Waza:** Techniques of reception of the martial art of the six-foot staff

KuKyu (Yellow belt)

-**Taihenjutsu No Kaiten Waza:** Techniques of rolling and flipping of the martial art of supple movement

-**Dakentaijutsu No Ate Waza:** Techniques of upper body striking of the martial art of striking and kicking

-**Dakentaijutsu No Geri Waza:** Techniques of lower body kicking of the martial art of striking and kicking

-**Fukidakejutsu:** The martial art of the blowgun

-**Hanbojutsu No Kamae:** Transitory positions of the martial art of the three-foot staff

-**Hokojutsu:** The martial art of stealth running

-**Kenjutsu No Kamae:** Transitory positions of the martial art of the sword

-**Taisabaki No Muto Dori:** Unarmed body evasions against the sword

-**Rendori:** The practice of random movement focusing on striking attacks on a heavy bag

HachiKyu (Orange belt)

-**Tehodoki:** Wrist escapes

-**Taihenjutsu No Ukemi Waza:** Techniques of receiving falls of the martial art of supple movement

-**Shinobi Aruki Waza:** Techniques of ninja stealth walking

-**Metsubushi:** Blinding powders

-**Hanbojutsu No Uchi Waza:** Techniques of striking of the martial art of the three-foot staff

-**Shoten No Jutsu:** The martial art of running up and/or over surfaces

-**Iaijutsu No Iai Gata:** Forms of drawing of the martial art of the sword

-**Junan Taiso:** Flexibility and stretching

-**Rendori:** The practice of random movement focusing on wrist and arm escapes with one or two attackers

ShichiKyu (Blue belt)

-**Taihodoki:** Body escapes

-**Shimehodoki:** Choking and strangulation escapes

-**Jutaijutsu No Osaekomi Waza:** Techniques of holding a person down of the martial art of grappling

-**Yobai Waza:** Techniques of night sneaking and stalking

-**Godai No Meisoho:** Methods of meditation of the five universal moods

-**Shurikenjutsu No Kamae:** Transitory positions of the martial art of the throwing weapons

-**Kenjutsu No Giri Waza:** Techniques of cutting, stabbing and

33

slicing of the martial art of the sword

-**Katon:** The use of fire

-**Rendori:** The practice of random movement focusing on wrist, body, choking/strangulation escapes with one or two attackers

RokuKyu (Red belt)

-**Jutaijutsu No Kansetsu Waza:** Techniques of locking and twisting restraints of the martial art of grappling

-**Jutaijutsu No Gyakute Waza:** Techniques of wrists and forearm locks /throws of the martial art of grappling

-**Jutaijutsu No Shime Waza:** Techniques of choking and strangulation of the martial art of grappling

-**Kyujutsu:** The martial art of archery

-**Taihojutsu:** The martial art of unarmed arresting

-**Fundojutsu No Uchi Waza:** Techniques of striking of the martial art of the weighted chain

-**Kenjutsu No Uke Waza:** Techniques of reception of the martial art of the sword

-**Tantojutsu No Kamae:** Transitory positions of the martial art of the knife

-**Rendori:** The practice of random movement focusing on wrist, body, choking/strangulation escapes and deflection and countering of upper body attacks with one or two attackers

GoKyu (Purple belt)

-**Somoho:** Methods of wrestling

-**Seiho:** Methods of healing.

-**Hanbojutsu No Waza:** Techniques of the martial art of the three-
foot staff

-**Rekishi:** History research

-**Shoku Waza: Kyusho/Tsubo/Koppo/Koshi:**
Nerve/Pressure/Bone/Muscle-points

-**Jutaijutsu No Katame Waza:** Techniques of joint locking of the
martial art of grappling

-**Tantojutsu No Kiri Waza:** Techniques of cutting, stabbing and
slicing of the martial art of the knife

-**Irimi Waza:** Techniques of entering an enemy's attack

-**Rendori:** The practice of random movement focusing on wrist,
body, choking/strangulation escapes and deflection and
countering of upper/lower body attacks with one or two
attackers

YonKyu (Green belt)

-**Hojojutsu No Waza:** Techniques of the martial art of rope tying
restraints

-**Jojutsu No Kata:** Techniques of the martial art of the four-foot
staff

-**Toamijutsu No Waza:** Techniques of the martial art of the net

-**Tantojutsu No Waza:** Techniques of the martial art of the knife

-**Koshijutsu No Waza:** the martial art of muscle, organ and ligament

35

destruction

-**Koppoujutsu No Waza:** Techniques of the martial art of bone
breaking and bone destruction

-**Nobori Gata:** Forms of climbing poles, walls, fences, trees, and
buildings

-**Teppojutsu No Kamae:** Transitory positions of the martial art of
firearms

-**Rendori:** The practice of random movement focusing on wrist,
body, choking/strangulation escapes and deflection and
countering of upper/lower body attacks with one to three
attackers

SanKyu (Grey belt)

-**Jutaijutsu No Karame Waza:** Techniques of limb entanglements
of the martial art of grappling

-**Shurikenjutsu No Uchi Waza:** Techniques of throwing attacks of
the martial art of the throwing weapons

-**Kokyuho:** Methods of breathing

-**Dakentaijutsu No Daken Gata:** Forms of striking combinations of
the martial art of striking

-**Inpoho:** Methods of hiding

-**Teppojutsu No Gyaku Waza:** Techniques of reversing of the
martial art of firearms

-**Kenjutsu No Ninjakenpo:** Techniques of the higher-order of the
ninja sword of the sword art

-**Jutaijutsu No Nage Waza:** Techniques of throwing of the martial art of grappling

-**Rendori:** The practice of random movement focusing on knife attacks with one to three attackers

NiKyu (Maroon belt)

-**Jutaijutsu No Kaeshi Waza:** Techniques of reversing throws of the martial art of grappling

-**Jutaijutsu No Gyaku Waza:** Techniques of reversing joint locking and joint twisting of the martial art of grappling

-**Ningu:** Specialized ninja weapons and tools

-**Sojutsu:** The marital art of the spear

-**Kujin:** The nine interplexing/interlacing meridian meditations

-**Saiminjutsu:** The martial art of hypnotism, mesmerism, mind-direction, mind-control and mind-manipulation

-**Teppojutsu No Uchi Waza:** Techniques of discharging a firearm of the art of firearms

-**Kusarifundojutsu No Waza:** Techniques with the weighted chain of the martial art of the weighted chain

-**Rendori:** The practice of random movement focusing on knife, unarmed, sword, bat and stick attacks with one to three attackers

IkKyu (Brown belt)

-**Taijutsu Shodan Ouyou:** Demonstrate a combination of all forms of hand-to-hand combat

-**Nandemo Buki Ni Nareru:** Demonstrate how anything can be used

as a weapon

-**Sensei Ni Naru Shikaku:** Explanation of what it means to be a

Sensei

-**Mikkyo:** Secret and esoteric teachings

-**Tanbojutsu No Waza:** Techniques of the 6in. to 9in. stick of the art

of the 6in. to 9in. stick

-**Kamajutsu no Waza:** Techniques of the art of two sickles

-**Senjutsu Dokyo:** Teachings from mountain sages

-**Bushido:** The warrior's code

-**Rendori:** The practice of random movement focusing on the circle

of death

<u>ShoDan (Black belt)</u>

Our curriculum is not shared openly after this point. Black belts are asked to choose nine areas of study within the art. A set amount of material on each topic is given. The black belts are promoted after showing required levels of proficiency in each of the nine areas.

Eric, Ed, Kyle and I Displaying my **Densho** in 2010 at the Hellertown **Godaishin Dojo.**

Sogobujutsu Outlined

For over a decade my students have asked me to show them a chart explaining the breakup of **Sogobujutsu**. After I explain that no such chart exists, the next comment is always, "Let's make one!" "I'm working on it, it's not ready yet," has always been my response. Well it is still not ready, but I'll share what I have so far. I have outlined most of the arts, arts and subarts, subparts, categories, and classifications. I did not dare get into listing the individual techniques, methods, forms, drills, and teachings. These will be covered during classes and throughout the curriculum. In the centuries it took to develop this art, many things were forged, found out, explored, trained, attained, created, adapted from other cultures, refined, constructed and integrated into one Martial Science that is **Sogobujutsu**. It has been said that "no martial art has it all". Although this may be true, this one is darn close! As you read this, it may be easy to become overwhelmed; instead try to become excited! The study is huge, let's dive in.

Sogobujutsu: This art has been called many things; originally, the art was called **Yawara**, then **Yawarajutsu**. We have used the term **Sogobujutsu** for generations for all that it implies.

I.   Bukijutsu: The weaponry arts
A. Bikenjutsu: The art of fighting with a blade

1. Kenjutsu: The art of the sword
a. Battojutsu: Fencing techniques (defensive)

b. **Gekkenjutsu**: Alive spirit sword art

c. **Giri Waza**: Cutting, thrusting and slicing techniques with   a sword

d. **Iaijutsu**: The art of sword drawing

e. **Kenjutsu No Kamae**: Positions in sword fighting

f. **Kumitachi**: Sword partner training

g. **Ninjakenpo**: Fighting with the **Ninja** sword

h. **Ukenagaeshi Waza**: Deflection and/or countering with a sword

2. Shotojutsu: The art of the short sword

a. **Battojutsu**: Fencing art form (defensive)

b. **Gekkenjutsu**: Alive spirit sword art

c. **Giri Waza**: Cutting, thrusting and slicing techniques with a short sword

d. **Iaijutsu**: The art of sword drawing

e. **Kumitachi**: Sword partner training

g. **Shotojutsu No Kamae**: Transitory Positions for the short sword

h. **Shotojutsu No Waza**: Techniques of the martial art of the short sword

i. **Ukenagaeshi Waza**: Deflection and/or countering with a short sword

3. Tantojutsu (also called Kaikenjutsu): Knife fighting art form

a. **Giri Waza**: Cutting, thrusting and slicing techniques with a knife

b. **Tantojutsu No Kamae**: Positions in knife fighting

c. **Tantojutsu No Waza**: Techniques

of the martial art of the knife
d. **Uke Waza**: Deflection and/or countering with a knife

B. Bojutsu: Staff fighting art form

    1. **Bisentojutsu**: Battlefield halberd art form

    2. **Hanbojutsu**: Short stick fighting art form with a **Hanbo** (also called **Sanjakubo**) *(3 ft. staff)*

        a. **Hanbo No Kamae**: Positions with **Hanbo**
        b. **Hanbojutsu No Waza**: The grappling and locking techniques with the **Hanbo**
        c. **Uchi Waza**: Striking techniques
        d. **Kansetsu Waza**: Ground restraints; Immobilization; Joint locks and twists with the **Hanbo**
        e. **Uke Waza**: Deflection and/or countering with a **Hanbo**

    3. **Jojutsu**: Stick fighting art form with a **Jo** (also called **Shinbo** and called **Shishakubo**) *(approx. 4 ft. staff)*

        a. **Jojutsu No Gata**: The forms of the **Jo**
        b. **Jojutsu No Kamae**: Positions with the **Jo**
        c. **Kansetsu Waza**: Ground restraints; Immobilization; Joint locks and twists with the **Jo**
        d. **Uchi Waza**: Striking techniques with the **Jo**

e. **Uke Waza**: Deflection and/or countering

4. **Juttejutsu**: The art of the Truncheon

    a. **Juttejutsu No Waza**: Truncheon fighting techniques

5. **Naginatajutsu**: Fighting art form with a **Naginata** *Halberd*

    a. **Giri Waza**: Cutting, thrusting and slicing techniques with a **Naginata**

    b. **Naginata No Kamae**: Positions with the **Naginata**

    c. **Uke Waza**: Deflection and/or countering with a **Naginata**

6. **Rokushakubojutsu**: Stick fighting art form with a **Rokushakubo** (also called **Bo** and called **Kenbo**) *6 ft staff*

    a. **Rokushakubojutsu No Kamae**: Positions in **Rokushakubo**

    b. **Rokushakubojutsu No Waza**: The grappling and locking techniques with the **Rokushakubo**

    c. **Kaeshi Gata:** Spinning forms of the **Rokushakubo**

    d. **Kansetsu Waza**: Ground restraints; Immobilization; Joint locks and twists with the **Rokushakubo**

    e. **Uchi Waza**: Striking techniques with the **Rokushakubo**

    f. **Uke Waza**: Deflection and/or countering with a **Rokushakubo**

7. **Tanbojutsu**: Stick fighting art with a **Tanbo** (also called **Tanjo**, **Yubibo** and called **Kubotan**)

approx. 6 to 9in. stick

a. **Tanbojutsu No Waza**: The grappling and locking techniques with the **Tonbo**

b. **Kansetsu Waza**: Ground restraints; Immobilization; Joint locks and twists with the **Tanbo**

c. **Uchi Waza**: Striking techniques with the **Tanbo**

d. **Uke Waza**: Deflection and/or countering with a **Tanbo**

8. **Tessenjutsu**: Art of the iron fan

a. **Tessenjutsu No Waza**: The grappling and locking techniques with the **Tessen**

b. **Kansetsu Waza**: Ground restraints; Immobilization; Joint locks and twists with the **Tessen**

c. **Uchi Waza**: Striking techniques with the **Tessen**

d. **Uke Waza**: Deflection and/or countering with a **Tessen**

9. **Sojutsu** (also called **Yarijutsu**): Martial art of the **Yari** *Spear*

a. **Giri Waza**: Cutting, thrusting and slicing techniques with a **Naginata**

b. **Uchi Waza**: Striking techniques with the **Tonbo**

c. **Uke Waza**: Deflection and/or countering with a **Yari**

C. **Kagebukijutsu**: **Ninja** weapon arts

1. **Ashiko**: Spiked foot bands

2. **Bakuhatsugama**: Short handled **Kusari Gama** with a container of explosives, poison or blinding power

3. **Ben**: Whip

4. **Gyokagi**: A **Hanbo** with a chain or cord with a hook on the end hidden inside

5. **Kama:** Sickle

6. **Neko Te**: Metal fingertip claws

7. **Shinobi Zue:** Staff which held chain inside with a weighted end

8. **Shobo**: Metal rod with a ring

9. **Shuko**: Metal hand claws

10. **Tekken**: Metal hand band (like brass knuckles)

D. **Kayakujutsu**: The art of fire and explosives

1. **Bakuhatsujutsu**: The art of using explosives

2. **Dokuenjutsu**: The art of smoke and gas poisoning

3. **Katonjutsu**: The art of using fire

    a. **Katon**: Using fire

      1). **Noroshi**: Making signal fires

E. **Kusarijutsu**: Chain weapon fighting art form

1. **Fundojutsu**: Fighting art form with the **Kusari Fundo** (also called **Manriki Kusari** and

called **Kusari Tundo**) *weighted chain*

    a. **Fundojutsu No Waza**: The grappling and locking techniques with the **Fundo**

    b. **Kaeshi Gata:** Spinning forms of the **Fundo**

    c. **Kansetsu Waza**: Ground restraints; Immobilization; Joint locks and twists with the **Fundo**

    d. **Uchi Waza**: Striking techniques with the **Fundo**

    e. **Uke Waza**: Deflection and/or countering with a **Fundo**

2. **Kusari Gama**: Chain and sickle

3. **Kyoketsu Shoge**: Chain and blade combination weapon

F. **Ningu**: **Ninja** tools and weapons

1. **Hishi Bishi**: Natural cal trop

2. **Kagi Nawa**: Grappling hook

3. **Kakute**: Iron ring or rings with spikes

4. **Kiri**: Single pointed pick

5. **Kunai**: Digging and leverage tool

6. **Shikoro**: The **Ninja** saw

7. **Shikomi Zue**: Hollowed out staff or cane

8. **Tetsubishi**: Caltrops

9. **Tsubute**: Clubbing throwing missiles

G. **Toamijutsu**: The art of the Net

1. **Toamijutsu No Waza**: Net techniques

2. **Uchi Waza**: Striking techniques with the net

H. **Torinawajutsu**: Restraining rope tying art

1. **Hobokujutsu:** Restraining rope tying grappling art

a. Irimi Waza: entering techniques

2. **Hojojutsu:** Restraining rope tying arresting art

a. **Hojojutsu No Waza**: Techniques of the art of tying restraints

I. **Totekijutsu**: The projectile arts

1. **Fukidakejutsu** (also called **Fukiya**)**:** The art of blowguns

a. **Fukidake**: Blowgun

b. **Fuki Ya**: Darts

2. **Kyujutsu**: Archery, skill with a bow and arrows

a. **Do**: Crossbow

b. **Dokyu**: A rapid firing crossbow; one that continuously reloads

c. **Hankyu**: A half bow used to send messages and fight

d. **Hikime:** An arrow with a muffled tip

e. **Hiya**: A flaming arrow

f. **Kiyumi**: Wooden bow

g. **Kyu**: Bow

h. **Oyumi**: Giant bow

i. **Ya**: Arrows

j. **Yumi**: A small bow

3. <u>Shurikenjutsu</u>: Blade throwing art

a. **Arare Shuriken** (also called **Ingadama**): Three dimensional spiked balls

1) **Chuarare**: Medium hailstone

2) **Joarare**: Large hailstone

3) **Koarare**: Small hailstone

b. **Bo Shuriken**: Throwing one or two pointed rods

1) **Embi Gata**: Triangle shaped

2) **Hari Gata**: Needle shaped

3) **Ryo Tanken Gata**: Double edged

4) **Tanto Gata**: Knife shaped

5) **Yari Gata**: Spear shaped

c. **Shaken Shuriken** (also called **Hira Shuriken**): Throwing stars

1) **Goho Shuriken**: Five sided

2) **Happo Shuriken**: Eight sided

3) **Juji Shuriken** also called **Shikaku Ho**: X shaped

4) **Jupo Shuriken**: Ten sided

5) **Kumi Awase Shuriken** also called **Tatamijuji Shuriken** and called **Shiho**: Folding cross shape

6) **Manji Shuriken**: Swastika shaped

7) **Nasare En**: Throwing coins

8) **Ropo Shuriken** also called **Roku Hoshi**: Six sided

9) **Sampo Shuriken** also called **Sanko Gata** and called **Sanakuho**: Three sided

10) **Shiho Shuriken** also called **Sankaku Sukashi**: Four sided

11) **Tekkan Shuriken** also called **Roku Hoshi Sukashi**: O shaped with six outer edges

d. **Shuriken No Kamae**: Positions for throwing weapons

47

e. **Uchi Waza** (also called **Shuriken Nage**): Throws

4. **Teppojutsu**: The art of firearms

    a. **Hojutsu**: Martial art of the shooting arts

    b. **Jukenjutsu**: Bayonet techniques

    c. **Teppo** (also called **Ju**): Gun

        1) **Ishibiya**: Small cannon

        2) **Tanegashima**: Firearms

        3) **Taiho**: Cannon

    d. **Teppojutsu No Kamae**: Positions for firearms

II.   **Heiho**: Study of military strategies

  A. **Aizu Teigi**: Motion Signals

  B. **Batsu**: Raids

  C. **Dangai Kagai**: Cliff Assault

  D. **Fukuzei**: Ambush

    1. **Satsuhako**: The killing box

  E. **Shinjun Heiho**: Infiltration Strategies

  F. **Sokai Heiho**: Deployment Strategies

    1. **Yokoai**: Flanking, Right wing/left wing

  G. **Tekkyo**: Withdrawal

  H. **Yotei Naito**: Night Operations

III.   **Mikkyo**: secret knowledge

  A. **Omyojutsu**: The art of divination, science, and astrology.

1. **Junishijutsu**: Killer astrology art
a. **Godai**: The five elements
1) Attributes of the **Godai** *The five elements*

    a) See **Shinpi** *Concepts of Mysticism*

    b) See **Meso** *Meditation techniques* which is also under **Shinpi** *Concepts of Mysticism*

2) Finding out one's **Godai** *The five elements* sign

3) The beasts of the **Godai** *The five elements*

b. **Kemono Juuni:** The Twelve Beasts
1) **Sadoku**: Finding out one's Beast sign

2) **Zokusei**: Attributes of the beasts

2. **Seishin Teki Kyoko**: Spiritual refinement
a. **Kunin Seishin**: Nine faces

B. **Saiminjutsu**: The hypnotic art, mesmerism; the power of mind directing

C. **Shinpi**: Concepts of mysticism
1. **In O Musubi**: Making hand signs
2. **Inyoho**: The methods or concepts of **In** *Yin* and **Yo** *Yang*
a. **In**: Positive
b. **Ho**: Interaction
c. **Yo**: Negative
3. **Godai**: The five elements
a. **Chi**: Earth
b. **Fu**: Wind
c. **Ka**: Fire

   d. **Ku**: Void

   e. **Sui**: Water

4. **Kiaijutsu**: Art of the spirit shout directing psychic/ telekinetic force through the voice

   a. **Kiai**: Focused shout

   1) **Eh:** "Eeeeeehh"

   2) **Ya:** "Eyyaa"

   3) **Toh:** "Toooohh"

   4) **Ha:** "Hhhha"

5. **Kokyoho**: Deep breathing methods

   a. **Niho**: Seated method

   b. **Suwariho**: Lying method

   c. **Tachiho**: Standing method

6. **Kuji In**: Energy channeling meditations

7. **Kuji Kiri**: Balancing electromagnetic power fields or "nine cuts"

8. **Meso**: Meditation techniques

   a. **Godai Meso**: Element meditation; Meditation techniques that put one in touch with the varying moods of this plane.

9. **Ten Mon**: Meteorology

IV. **Rekishi**: History's message and traditions of significance

   A. **Genron No Neji Gekken Ryu**: Principles of our martial family

   B. **Gishiki**: Ceremonies

1. **Kotodama**: Spiritual lecture
2. **Mokuso**: Preparatory meditation
3. **Ninniku Seishin**: Spiritual code
4. **Shi Rei**: Good Will bow
5. **Shinzen Rei**: Spiritual bow

C. **Keppan**: The blood oath

D. **Reigisaho**: methods of appropriateness

E. **Ryuha**: Different families or traditions

F. **Senjutsu Dokyo**: Teachings of mountain sages

V. **Shinobijutsu**: The martial art of stealth

A. **Choho**: Espionage the act of spying

1. **Bo Ryaku**: Strategy
2. **Chikairijutsu**: The infiltration of enemy lines during a battle

a. **Chakuzen no jutsu**: infiltration through entering rooftops

3. **Gotonpo**: Five principles/ natural elements of escape

a. **Gisou**: Camouflage and concealment tricks

b. **Kankyo Yaku**: Using the environment

c. **Kichi Gawa**: Understanding surroundings

51

d. **Kousaku**: Blending in

e. **Sakuran**: Distraction tricks

4. **Hensojutsu**: Disguise and impersonation

a. **Hengenkashi No Jutsu**: The study and knowledge of each disguise assumed

5. **Kakurejutsu**: The art of stealth

a. **Dobutsujutsu**: The art of using animals for diversion

b. **Inpojutsu**: The art of hiding

1) **Amegakurejutsu**: The art of hiding in the rain

c. **Intonjutsu**: Escape and concealment/ camouflage

1) **Gotono**: Using natural elements for evasion

d. **Joei No Jutsu**: Training in moving without making sound or shadows

1) **Aruki Waza**: Stealth walking techniques

2) **Hoko No Jutsu**: Stealth Running techniques

3) **Kaiten Waza**: Rolling and flipping techniques

4) **Tobi Waza**: Jumping and leaping techniques

5) **Yobai Waza**: Night sneaking and crawling techniques

e. **Shinobi Iri**: Stealth and entering

1) **Nyudaki no Jutsu**: Discovering a guard's shortcomings in order to break in

6. **Onshinjutsu**: The art of invisibility

a. **Metsubushi**: Art of blinding

1) **Kinton**: Using metal objects for

distraction

> 2) **Chigi Riki**: **Ninja** mace

7. Tonpo: Escaping techniques

    a. **Chitonjutsu**: Using water, fire, wood, earth, or metal for escape

    b. **Tejyonukejutsu** (also called **Nawanuke No Jutsu**): Loosening or escaping from bonds by dislocating joints

B. Genjutsu: Illusion art form

    1. **Gisho Giin No Jutsu**: The art of forgery

    2. **Kyonin No Jutsu**: The art form of taking advantage of one's fears and superstitions

C. Sekkojutsu: Scouting art form

    1. **Chi Mon**: Geography

    2. **Jissensekko Gijutsu**: Scouting in actual battle art

    3. **Ninki**: Specialized **Ninja** gear and tools

    4. **Nobori Gata**: Climbing buildings, fences, walls, poles, or trees

    5. **Noboriki**: Climbing tools

        a. **Ashiko**: Spiked foot bands

        b. **Hojo** (also called **Nawa**): Rope

        c. **Kagi**: Hook

        d. **Kagi Nawa**: Grappling hook

        e. **Kama**: Sickle

        f. **Kamayari**: Sickle spear

        g. **Kasha**: Pulley

        h. **Kiri**: Single pointed pick

        i. **Kuda Bashigo**: Tube ladder
        j. **Kusari**: Chain
        k. **Musubi Basigo**: Single cable loop ladder
        l. **Ninja Ken**: The Ninja sword
        m. **Shuko**: Spiked hand bands
        n. **Taka Bashigo**: High ladder
        o. **Tobi Bashigo**: Throwing ladder
        p. **Tsuri Bashigo**: Hanging ladder

    6. **Sacchijutsu**: Art of strategy of taking advantage of the natural features of the land

    7. **Shoten No Jutsu**: Running up surfaces art

    8. **Tobikomi**: Leaping

        a. **Tobiori**: Leaping and landing from heights

        b. **Tobi Waza**: Jumping and leaping techniques

D. **Yogen**: Chemistry

    1. **Ninyakujutsu**: Medicines and drugs art

    2. **Doku**: Poisons

    3. **Haretsu**: Pyrotechnics

VI. Taijutsu: Unarmed combat art form

A. **Dakentaijutsu**: The art of striking

    1. **Atemijutsu**: Striking art, striking with the limbs

        a. **Ate Waza** (also called **Datotsu Waza** and called **Atemi Waza**): Upper body striking techniques

b. **Keri Waza**: Lower body striking techniques

c. **Uke Waza** also called **Uke Nagashi**: Reception techniques; deflection and/ or trapping strikes

2. **Daken Gata**: Formulated sets of striking forms

3. **Koppojutsu**: Art of striking bone breaks, displacement

    a. **Koppo Gata**: Formulated sets of bone breaking forms

    b. **Koppojutsu No Waza**: Techniques of striking bone breaks, displacement

4. **Koshijutsu**: Art of striking muscle, organ or ligament attacks and/or displacement

    a. **Koshi Gata**: Formulated sets of organ and muscle attacking forms

    b. **Koshijutsu No Waza**: Techniques of striking muscle, organ or ligament attacks and/or displacement

5. **Rendori**: Fighting practice

6. **Shiokujutsu**: Touching art

    a. **Koppo**: Bone points

    b. **Koshi**: Muscle, ligament, and organ points

    c. **Kyusho**: Pressure points

    d. **Shubo**: Nerve points

B. **Hajutsu**: Escaping art form

    1. **Gyaku Waza**: Reversal techniques

55

2. **Kaeshi Waza**: Spinning techniques
3. **Taihodoki**: Body escapes
4. **Tehodoki**: Wrist escapes
5. **Shimehodoki**: Choking/ strangulation escapes

C. Jutaijutsu: Art of locking, throwing and strangling

1. **Aikijutsu**: The higher understanding art

    a. **Aiki No Jutsu**: Techniques of **Aiki**

    b. **Aiki Myoden**: Esoteric transitions of **Aiki**

    c. **Aiki Inyoho**: Philosophical understanding of the application of **Aiki**

2. **Gyakute Waza**: Wrist techniqes
3. **Happo No Kuzushi**: The eight directions of off balancing

    a. **Hidari Koho Naname No Kuzushi** (also called **Hidari Ushirosumi No Kuzushi**): left backward diagonal way of off balancing

    b. **Hidari Yoko No Kuzushi** (also called **Hidari Mayoko No Kuzushi**): Left side way of off balancing

    c. **Hidari Zenpo Naname No Kuzushi** (also called **Hidari Maesumi No Kuzushi**): Left forward diagonal way of off balancing

    d. **Migi Koho Naname No Kuzushi** (also called **Migi Ushirosumi No Kuzushi**): Right backward diagonal way of off balancing

e. **Migi Yoko No Kuzushi** (also called **Migi Mayoko No Kuzushi**): Right side way of off balancing

f. **Migi Zenpo Naname No Kuzushi** (also called **Migi Maesumi No Kuzushi**): Right forward diagonal way of off balancing

g. **Koho No Kuzushi** (also called **Maushiro No Kuzushi**): Backward way of off balancing

h. **Zenpo No Kuzushi** (also called **Mamae No Kuzushi**): Forward way of off balancing

4. **Irimi Waza**: Entering techniques

5. **Kansetsu Waza**: Ground restraints, immobilization, Joint locks and twists techniques

a. **Ni Waza**: Seated techniques

b. **Suwari Waza**: Lying techniques

c. **Tachi Waza**: Standing techniques

6. **Kakuto Waza**: Grappling standing/seated/lying position

7. **Nage Waza**: Throwing techniques

8. **Osaekomi Waza**: Hold-down techniques

9. **Shime Waza**: Choking and strangulation techniques

10. **Somoho**: Wrestling for positioning methods

11. **Taihojutsu**: Unarmed arresting art

D. **Kogeki Waza**: Attacking techniques

E. **Suietjutsu**: Swimming and fighting in water art form
> 1. **Sui Ren**: Water Training
>> a. **Suiton**: Using water

F. **Taihenjutsu**: Body movement art
> 1. **Junbi Undo**: Drills for warming up and loosening up
> 2. **Kaiten Waza**: Rolling and flipping techniques
> 3. **Shintaiho**: Body movement stepping or pivoting methods
> 4. **Tai Sabaki**: Body evasions
> 5. **Junan Taiso**: Yoga-type stretching and training
> 6. **Tobi Waza**: Jumping and leaping techniques
> 7. **Ukemi Waza**: Break falling techniques

G. **Taijutsu No Kamae**: Transitory positions of unarmed combat

This depth of study is why we often call our **Dojo** a university, instead of a school.

Godai No Heiho

In classes, we try to focus on continuing with students' understanding of the **Godai** *five elements*. The five elements have everything to do with our training. The **Heiho**, or warrior strategy, behind our combat consists of these five forms.

Chi No Heiho: The strategy of earth. This strategy consists of little movement centered around the thighs and hips. The movement consists mainly of up and down motions. Its methods are intercepting in nature with bulldozing effect. The feeling behind the movement is one of confidence backed with strength to overcome. To understand the earth mindset, one might look to the stereotypical construction worker. "There's a right way to do things and there's a wrong way to do things."

Sui No Heiho: The strategy of water. This strategy consists of large movements centered around the legs, they are mainly angular movements. Its methods are avoiding in nature, splashing out of the way of an oncoming attack and tidal waving back to consume one's enemy with a deluge of a drowning effect. The feeling behind the movement is one of cautious intention, often fear-based. To personify the water mindset, one would look to the profession of the scientist: cautious with every step, studying and steadily figuring things out.

Ka No Heiho: The strategy of fire. This strategy consists of expedient, short to long bursts of movement involving the heart chakra. The movement consists mainly of straightforward, circular advances. Its methods are consuming in nature, burning around and through everything it comes in contact with. The feeling behind the movement is intense passion or pure rage, both of which fuel the fire. To understand the fire mindset, one could look to the Marine Corps drill sergeant, "You will move up that front line! You will kill everything that moves! If it is your time to die, then you will die!"

Fu No **Heiho**: The strategy of wind. This strategy consists of roundabout, circular movement involving the neck and arms. The movement consists of encompassing and surrounding for the purpose of evasion and control. Its methods are tornado-like; floating out of the way, spinning around and under, and uprooting objects and tossing them. The feeling behind the movement can be compassionate or resilient in intention. To personify the wind mindset, one could think of an entrepreneur: open-minded and able to create situations where he can take advantage of and exploit opportunity.

Ku No **Heiho**: The strategy of void. This strategy consists of the expression of the other four elements through the expression of life force. The movement can be expressive of any individual element but is often looked at as the culmination of the many understandings of the combination of all four elements. The movement also includes the transcendence of the four elements. Its methods are described as the expression of all life and the absence of life itself. The Chinese often refer to this element as wood instead of void, as the properties of wood consist of a dead inside surrounded by the life on the outside. A tree's inside can be hollowed out by an animal and the outside still lives. The death on the inside of the tree serves the life; the death supports the structure of life. Other Chinese teachings refer to the void as metal, for metal is birthed from all four elements. Metal is mined from the earth, forged with fire and wind (the bellows are used in every forging process to superheat the flame in order to extract the metal from the rock), cooled and tempered with water. The feeling behind the movement is true soul expression; it is the internal becoming the external. To personify void, one would look to the samurai; possessing the power and the tools of life and death at his disposal at any second of the day.

Through the better understanding of these strategies, we will find the freedom of natural expression. We will utilize any emotion to fuel our appropriate combative strategy, working off of the normal reactions of man to sift through the confusions of emotion and to find the solace of expression in the conflict of warring chaos. This is done prior to working toward transcendence of these unavoidable human emotions. Expression comes through the understanding of the self and how these strategies, the **Godai** *five elements*, can better accommodate the human condition.

The teachings of the **Godai** go far deeper than mere martial strategy. To open your view into the depth of the **Godai**, I have created the chart on the next page.

David C. Falcaro **Sensei** posing with his father, Brian Falcaro, in 2000 shortly after they constructed the first stand made to attract public interest. From humble beginnings, and with a ton of hard work, we built something of substance. Looking back now it seems like an impossible task for my younger self to take on. It is a good thing I did not know how hard it would be.

Things that correspond	Chi	Fu	Ka	Ku	Sui
English term	Earth	Wind / Air	Fire	Void / Wood	Water
Direction	Center	West	South	East	North
Compatibly with **Chi**	Compatible Element	Compatible Element	Compatible Element	Incompatible Element	Incompatible Element
Compatibly with **Fu**	Compatible Element	Compatible Element	Incompatible Element	Incompatible Element	Compatible Element
Compatibly with **Ka**	Compatible Element	Incompatible Element	Compatible Element	Compatible Element	Incompatible Element
Compatibly with **Ku**	Incompatible Element	Incompatible Element	Compatible Element	Compatible Element	Compatible Element
Compatibly with **Sui**	Incompatible Element	Compatible Element	Incompatible Element	Compatible Element	Compatible Element
Color	Yellow	White	Red	Green	Black
Season	Early Fall	Autumn	Summer	Spring	Winter
Attitude	Stability	Benevolence	Aggression	Creativity	Adaptability
Finger	Little	Index	Middle	Thumb	Ring
Sense	Taste	Smell	Speech	Vision	Hearing
Flavor	Sweet	Pungent	Bitter	Sour	Salty
Ideas	Fear Nothing	Compassion	Pure Rage	Joy / Peace	Defensive
Source	Strength	Resiliency	Energy	Insight	Power
Core Focus	The Body	Wisdom	Intellect	Communing	Emotions
Planet	Saturn	Venus	Mars	Jupiter	Mercury
Animals Of The Zodiac	Dog And Oxen	Chicken And Monkey	Horse And Snake	Tiger And Rabbit	Pig And Rat
Movement Of The **Hara**	Up And Down	Circular Rotation	Forward And Backward	All And No Movement	Side To Side
Physical Center	Thighs And Butt	Center Of Chest / Heart	Solar Plexus	Felt Vibrations	Navel / Low Abdomen
Action	Crossing	Splitting	Pounding	Crushing	Drilling
In Personality	Secure	Avoidance	Confrontational	Experienced	Easy going
Yo Personality	Stubborn	Unapproachable	Oppressive	Know it all	Careless
Combat Footwork Movements	Immovable / Meeting Dead On	Sidestepping / Circular Evasion	Shuffling Or Running Forward	Any Type But None Needed	Zig Zaging Backward And Forward
In Responses	Judgmental	Agreeable	Excited	Understood	Give/take
Yo Responses	Board	Distant	Bothered	Unaffected	Take/give
State	Solid	Gas	Chem-reaction	Life	Liquid
Other Name	**Ji**	**Kaze**	**Hi**	**Sora**	**Mizu**
Kanji	地	風	火	空	水
Charka	Root	Throat	Stomach	3rd eye/ crown	Heart
Body System	Skeletal	Respiratory	Digestive	Katra	Circulatory
In Organ	Spleen	Lungs	Heart	Liver	Kidneys
Yo Organ	Stomach	Colon	Triple heater	Gall bladder	Bladder
Destructive cycle	From earth to water	From fire to void	From fire to wind	From void to earth	From water to fire
Constructive cycle	From earth to wind	From wind to water	From fire to earth	From void to fire	From water to void
Feeling	Dry	Cold	Hot	Comfortable	Wet
Chinese	Tu	Jin	Huo	Mu	Shui
Body limb	Left arm	Left leg	Head	Right arm	Right leg
In Emotions	Confidence	Compassion	Passion	Mastery	Logic
Yo Emotions	Arrogant	Absentminded	Rage	Domination	Fear
Thoughts	Resistance	Open-minded	Forceful	Spontaneity	Suppleness
Working	Sureness	Carefree	Energetic	Inventiveness	Growing
Storm	Avalanche	Tornado	Lightning	All / None	Hurricane
Dimension	Width	Height	Time	Field of possible	Length

Setting standards

There are a great many statements made within the martial arts community.

- "Each martial art has something to offer."
- "All martial arts are the same."
- "It does not matter which martial art you train in, as long as you train hard in it."
- "Each martial art can bring you to the same place."
- "There is no wrong way, just different applications."

All of these statements promote dismissive behavior. Statements like these are recited to convey caring, acceptance, and openness. They have great intentions behind them, but as many say, "The road to hell is paved with good intentions." In my opinion, it is important to dissolve this type of thinking. We need not worry about people's feelings, merely switch our intention to what is real. We need to study everything and ask ourselves: Does is work? How often will it work? We don't want to fall into judgment like so many others. Instead, let us be on a fact-finding mission in search for the amount of truth that can be seen behind each method. We need to not become self-righteous and make judgments, placing ourselves above what anyone else is doing with their martial arts. The fact is, learning **Sogobujutsu** definetely sets us apart from others. To remain humble, we need to understand that our knowledge is not a result of our efforts. The possession of a deeper understanding of martial application is not because we train hard. Many **Budoka** train hard; we are no different in that respect. It is about what material is being absorbed and how we are training it. We can thank the origins of the **Sogobujutsu** for that gift.

Instead of feeding our egos and attempting to debunk everyone's claim to effective martial arts, we will concentrate our efforts on something constructive. Before looking at what others are doing, we need to be concerned with ourselves. This book is all about looking into ourselves, but what I am decribing is a more personal evaluation. What I ask of myself and the descendents of this art is simply stated and not easily done. Maintain a scrutinizing, nonjudgmental approach to the evaluation of all martial arts. Setting fair standards for the classification of **Budo** *martial arts* is necessary for accomplishing said goals.

To say "ours is better than yours" is more dismissive behavior that does not promote learning. It is far too easy to look at the other guy and point out all they are doing wrong or what they are missing. Instead, I take it upon myself, as a mental training exercise to evaluate what is there, and to view everything that each group is displaying. There are separate goals within martial arts. I break down all martial study into four martial categories. These are Martial Skills, Martial Sports, Martial Systems and Martial Sciences.

Martial Skills
The standards set forth for Martial Skills are quite open, as they should be. Martial Skills have the luxury of being expressive. One who practices a Martial Skill can express their art any way they deem fit. Martial Skills can be difficult to perform, flashy, ineffective, effective, complicated, unrealistic, dramatic, dangerous, or even silly. Instead of moving like a man, one can strive to mimic animals and insects' movements. A telltale sign of a Martial Skill is the disinterest in the effects of physics, such as training to make impact with a kick while the supporting leg

is standing up on the ball of the foot or on the tips of the toes. Martial Skills often leave out essential aspects of combat, such as punching, ground fighting, weaponry, kicking, or even striking altogether. Counterintuitive training can be stressed, such as twirling weapons around and tossing them into the air and then catching them, sinking to absorb the impact of an enemy's attack, or training to move a different way while wielding each weapon or tool. We often see difficult movements trained only because it is difficult to do them. There are many instances in Martial Skills in which it can take a great deal of control of balance to do a maneuver. Some groups train to take hits to the vitals, such as the groin and throat. They are often loose with their lack of detail toward goals that are spoken of and promised, but never realized. Phrases such as this are thrown around:

> "One day you won't have to move."
> "Enlightenment is just around the corner."
> "The most advanced moves can't be seen, only felt."
> "Mastery is found outside of each technique."

This is said as if the perfection of punching and kicking patterns will somehow grant one entry into some outer-worldly ability. In Martial Skills, we find a great deal of ego-based entitlement and grand titles. Titles like triple grandmaster, guru-shaman-grandmaster, god-master, or 15th degree black belt (as a possible point of interest, I did not make up any of these titles, I saw or personally met people using them). Making outrageous claims such as, "I can strike you without touching you." And also, "When one reaches this stage, they can float in the air." These must be allowed in Martial Skills. Throughout time, many have enjoyed making such claims and many defend and believe in them.

Martial Sport
A Martial Sport is about competition. One characteristic of a
Martial Sport is placing rules on competing. A great deal of
strength, coordination, flexibility, and speed are trained and
relied on. The Martial Sport trains to dominate over the
opponent while curtailing their training and application to the
confines of the competition. This covers everything from
Karate point sparring to cage fighting. Restrictions can be
placed on attacking and defending. A few examples of
Martial Sports are: **Judo, Sumo,** fencing, wrestling, **Kendo,**
boxing, kickboxing, MMA, and tae kwan do.

Martial System
The defining characteristics of a Martial System set them
apart from others. This is a systemic approach to martial
training for combat. Their common focus is simplicity.
They present a curriculum that does not need questioning
because it is straightforward and basic. Martial Systems are
most often seen as a military style designed to be quickly
absorbed by the masses. They are easily taught with not
much focus on anything but the physical. The thought
behind a Martial System revolves around use of muscle
structure, size of opponent, weapons offense and defense.
Many Martial Systems choose to incorporate hard and soft
movements. The taking of partial movements from many
styles are incorporated for quick takedowns and take-outs. A
few examples of Martial Systems are: krav maga, systema,
defendo, Navy SEALs combat, and sambo.

Martial Science
The standards set forth for establishing a Martial Science
must remain the strictest. To qualify as a science, we must

adhere to logic first and foremost. Logic is the purpose behind all actions. Martial Sciences train the body, mind and spirit equally. Everything is trained in a simple, decisive manner to develop reaction. The spiritual and emotional side is intensive. Development of this side of the training promotes transcendence toward the point of enlightenment. In the beginning of training, there is exploration into the core roots of each emotional reaction utilizing each emotion as fuel to empower thought and action. Decisions are worked out as a point of training the mental side so that nothing is left to contemplate. In this way, reaction is not hindered by thought, rather it is complemented by it. All physical motions are applied in the same way. The way one slices with a knife is the same motion used to throw a projectile weapon. It is this ability that is developed and applied in the same manner. Cutting with different sized blades, swinging chains or locking and throwing men are all done with the same trained, decisive action. In training, cutting with two knives resembles closely the striking with staffs no matter their length. The model for proper movement is the human body's natural movement that is never interested in strenuous actions, rather comfortable, unarguable ease in motion. The mental reasoning is to develop different neurological pathways in the brain that is trained hard in the physical to hone muscle memory. These pathways start at many different points, knife, gun, stick, chain, and enemy's limb. From different mentally written beginnings, the engrained physical motion brings the trained man to the same end. This creates a reactive application to any scenario. The result is a trained warrior. Much work goes into training the conscious and subconscious mind. This mental and physical training allows for mental and physical freedom. The mental freedom is seen in a captured mind. It is natural for a mind to wander away from the point. Even if one were scatter brained in the arena of combat, one was thinking the mind would come to the same point. As the old saying goes, "All roads lead to Rome." This training presents a physical freedom within the confines of the strictest form. The form needs to remain strict because it follows function. The functionality of a Martial Science is concise, efficient, and effective. Amassing the most powerful attacks toward the most vulnerable areas. Anything on the body that is known to be a nonvital point is not considered a target. Every movement is simultaneously offensive and defensive. The power behind an attack is derived from **Tai Ate** *unified body motion,* **Koshi Mawari** *the twisting of the midsection,* **Haragae** *the expression of the body's center,* **Aiki** *stealing the force of the enemy's attack while using his body's structure against him.* Muscular strength and flexibility are not relied on. One does not rely on the effectiveness of any aspect of the technique in order to accomplish the technique. This type of training allows for a huge margin of failure while maintaining a successful outcome. **Sogobujutsu** is a Martial Science.

There are many instances in which people start with one martial form and work to changing it into another. For example, sport sambo is a Martial System that decided to limit their form and go for the glory of competition, becoming a martial sport. Combat **Aikido** breaks from what **Aikido** is, for instance, not striking, to strive to become a Martial System. Things can get a bit blurry at times. The deciding factor in classifying which martial art falls into which martial category I'll attempt to make easy. Where does their focus lie? A martial artist cannot effectively train in more than one martial form. Imagine trying to explain to a professional baseball player that he needs to spend half of his time training to move in a way that will not be effective on the playing field. Asking a man training in a Martial System to compete in a Martial Sport will result in a disqualification.

Terri Schuon and I displaying a tie from **Hojojutsu** in 2009 at the Northampton **Godaishin Dojo.**

The point that I am trying to make is to notice, define, and to celebrate the differences in the martial forms. We commonly use others for self-reflection. When we come to understand how we are different from others, the inevitable result is we get to know ourselves. We need our differences. As **Budoka**, we need to convey caring, acceptance, and openness to all other martial artists. The thing that stands in our way of doing this is our need for a strong definition of self-expression. We also desire the correct understanding of that expression from others. When I am asked if all martial forms are the same, I enjoy explaining how the Cub Scouts and the Army Rangers are the same because they both wear green outfits and hangout in the woods. This can be a way in which we grow to resent others because on an unconscious level their actions in their own martial study reflects on every **Budoka**, and somehow this promotes the common social ignorance of martial arts. We can blame ourselves for this ignorance. I have been in the room and kept quiet while friends gathered to hear the expert opinion of a **Karate** guy explaining how Filipino martial arts works. Proficiency in one area of study does not equal proficiency in others. Many people believe that all martial arts are the same.

It is important to set standards. It makes us accountable, forcing us to live up to the standards we claim. With a fair and just assessment of each martial study, the student will know what they are signing up for and what they are getting into. If we can promote these standards, we will be better understood. With this understanding will come a much greater mutual appreciation of everyone's efforts within the different martial forms.

Buhei
Combative Concepts

Over the years, I found myself trying to convey the same important lessons to each generation of students. These "Combative Concepts" are the summation of a great many thoughts and ideas concerning the motive behind our combative strategy. These lessons should act as guidelines to govern all our movement within **Sogobujutsu**. The importance of these concepts should not be underestimated.

1. Move out of the way while simultaneously putting something in the way.
2. Keep the technique between yourself and the enemy's weapons.
3. Strike to attain positioning.
4. Work to occupy the enemy's mind/spirit.
5. Move first from the point of connection.
6. The point is, to move to a place of dominance.
7. Superior positioning is key.
8. The proper angle for attack must be stressed.
9. Move around the strength or force.
10. Cut the angle, set the barrier.
11. Closest weapon to the closest target.
12. Remain behind the blade.
13. Everything is a weapon.
14. There are three points to our training; one must train Prevention, Reaction and Recovery.
15. When he compensates, he commits.
16. There are eighty-one variations per technique.
17. Limbs are interchangeable.
18. The arm is the gateway to the neck.
19. Distance equals time.

20. Rotation, Rotation, Hyperextension and Compression.
21. Apply every aspect, yet rely on none to complete the attack.
22. Before transcendence, emotions provide the motivation behind the attack.
23. Power stems from **Tai Ate**, **Koshi Mawari**, **Haragei** and is stolen with **Aiki**.
24. The angle of pressure, while applying force to the **Waza**, must be projected across the **Chushin**.
25. "A" moves around "B" as "B" moves around "A".
26. Pulling is pushing against yourself.
27. The angle of pressure is applied to make the enemy fly or dig.
28. Duplicate your hands/ fists, then steal more of them from the enemy.

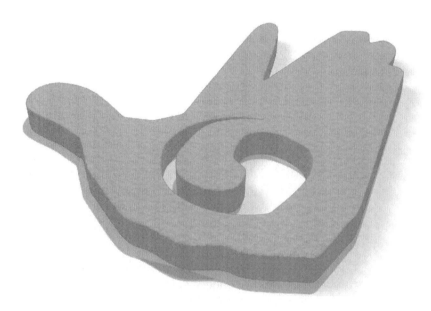

Chapter 2

Neji Gekken Ryu

The birth of our martial arts family

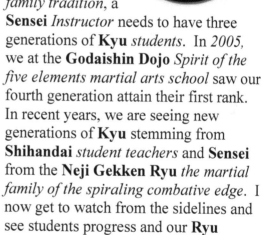

It is said that in order to become a **Ryu** *martial arts family tradition*, a **Sensei** *Instructor* needs to have three generations of **Kyu** *students*. In *2005*, we at the **Godaishin Dojo** *Spirit of the five elements martial arts school* saw our fourth generation attain their first rank. In recent years, we are seeing new generations of **Kyu** stemming from **Shihandai** *student teachers* and **Sensei** from the **Neji Gekken Ryu** *the martial family of the spiraling combative edge.* I now get to watch from the sidelines and see students progress and our **Ryu** flourish.

An aspect that was traditionally needed to become a **Ryu** was for the **Sensei** to earn the position of **Menkyo Kaiden** *keeper of the scrolls.* This meant that the

Sensei inherited a martial tradition; he became a **Soke** *inheritor*. The second way was to become a **Sodenke** *scroll inheritor or keeper*. This was different from a **Soke** in that a **Soke** carried on the mainline tradition whereas a **Sodenke** carried on an offshoot of the tradition. In 2005, I became a **Sodenke**. It wasn't until 2009 that my **Sensei** gave me permission and requested that I officially start the **Neji Gekken Ryu.**

Many people (most all) do not go the traditional route, but for me it was worth doing. I felt that it gave more credence to what I wanted to accomplish. I also wanted to stick with my **Sensei** forever to learn as much as I could; because of this, the **Sodenke** *scroll inheritor/ keeper* became my chosen destiny.

Our **Ryu** is a **Ryuha** or a **Ryu** that came from the delineation of many older **Ryu**. It is not an art form in and of itself; our art form is **Sogobujutsu**. Instead, it is a different outlook on the teachings of many other **Koryu** *ancient martial families*. I did not, would not, dare not combine these teachings into my own art form; I have too much appreciation for these **Waza** *techniques*, **Ho** *methods*, **Gata** *forms*, **Undo** *exercises/ drills*, in their evolved purist state. My goal with our **Ryu** was, and will remain, to learn and pass on these teachings unaltered while seeing within them the unifying ideals and principles and to keep our focus there as the guiding force of the **Neji Gekken Ryu**. So we are not so much a blend of many **Ryu**; we strive to be the expression of each of them. In my view, the individual strengths of each **Ryu** are important and must remain intact. An attempt to blend them together is not warranted. Make no mistake, the teachings and concepts become applied interchangeably between the techniques from each **Ryu**. This is the resulting factor with our training.

When people ask if I created a system, I must say "no" because I am not a founder. What did I find? I did not find anything that has not already been practiced. I would sooner claim to have found and invented the Moon.

The birth of our **Ryu** was from pure intent. The name

1999
Fudoza Gatamae, Teaching out of my parent's backyard.

itself was picked to convey a sense of depth of knowledge and importance. Our name is a true expression of importance for the **Ryu Fuku** *members of the martial family*. Also, the name of our **Ryu** is a tool to remind us all of our mindset as modern **Bugei** *warriors*. The importance (the credit) should not be placed on our **Ryu**, it should be given to the **Koryu** *Classical martial arts family traditions*, the developers of the ancient martial ways. Too many modern **Ryu** place importance on themselves and not enough on what they are doing and where it comes from. What they are missing is the respect and appreciation of our ancestors in the arts. This is what my **Sensei** understood to be necessary, then and now, to acknowledge. He made it a point to instill this while he was teaching me, as his **Sensei** did with him, as I will do with each of you.

I formulated the **Sogobujutsu No Kyoka**, *our curriculum of the integrated warrior science* to pass on these arts more freely with ease. Even my teaching style was influenced partially by my teachers so I cannot and would not say I invented much; invention is not the goal of a **Bugei** *warrior*. What I did do, while I was a **Kyu** *student* rank under the tutelage of my **Sensei**, was learn and train. The breakup of degrees (colored belts or **Kyu Outai** *student ranks*), the nine credits (9 stripes on the belts) for each **Kyu**-- that part was me--the rest was from the ages. Our **Ryu** came about through people focusing on a likeminded intention to bring about a rebirth into the study of the older ways of **Sogobujutsu**.

Why then not remain a **Koryu** *a classical martial arts family tradition*? Although we have ties to these traditions, we are not remaining strict to the confines of any one **Ryu** *Martial arts family tradition*. If one is to be **Daito Ryu**, then one may only study **Daito Ryu** and train in only **Daito Ryu** methods. My **Sensei**'s **Sensei, Katsumi Tanemura Sensei,** trained in many **Koryu** and brought these teachings to the West as his understanding of the warrior arts. In the olden

1997 **Za No Kamae** Training in my parents backyard.

days, one was not permitted to openly learn the arts of different **Ryu**. When the opportunity for **Tanemura Sensei** to learn from **Ryu** such as the **Takeuchi Ryu** opened up, he took it. **Tanemura Den** *transmissions of Tanemura Sensei* became known today as **Tagakishin Ryu.**

I am a part of this **Ryu**, it is where all of my understanding of the **Samurai** Arts stem from. The proclamation of individuality is important to the **Tagakishin Ryu**; it must separate itself as its own entity. This is done for many reasons, most being wrapped up in the definition of a pure **Koryu**. The **Tagakishin Ryu** is not strictly any one **Ryu**; therefore, it does not make any such claim.

I have a profound love for Smith **Den** *the transmissions from my **Sensei***. I want nothing more than to continue learning and growing under my **Sensei**'s guidance. As his student, I instruct the traditions as they were passed to me. This is what is asked of me as a **Sodenke** *scroll inheritor/ keeper*.

I have had other teachers and as a result have learned the arts of **Ninpo** *higher order of ninjutsu* and **Ninjutsu** *the martial art of the ninja*. I see validity in these arts and would like to pass on the knowledge of this to my **Kyu** *students*. Because of my previous years of dedicated study of **Ninpo** *higher order of ninjutsu*, I was permitted to continue training in this art by my **Samurai Sensei,** Smith **Sensei**. My **Sensei** even asked me to find further (outside of our training) validation within the **Ninpo** arts. This proved very difficult for me and, for years, finding someone with a wealth of understanding in the **Ninja** *assassin* arts seemed impossible. Then in 2002, I met Jaime Ellerbe **Sensei** of the **Nagano**

Ryu. This relationship was one of **Buyu** *warrior brotherhood*; it proved a pleasant exchange of knowledge, methods and inspiration. This is just another example of why our **Ryu** cannot fit into the confines of any other. Although we must remain separate for the purpose of correctness of

Eric Coderly applying **Kubi Ori Nage** to Nevin Moyer Jr. during class in 2009 at the Hellertown **Godaishin Dojo.**

defining our **Ryu**, we must also have the freedom to train in all that is attained from alternative sources. The birth of the **Neji Gekken Ryu** was done for this liberty, not for the promotion of a new entity. Many of the ideas, and most of the curriculum, of our **Ryu** were formulated in 1998. By that time, I was eight years into my study (obsession) of **Ninjutsu** *the martial art of the ninja* and was documenting everything I could so as not to forget anything. In 1998, I was also two years a **Kyu** of Smith **Sensei** and meticulously studied his art. In late 1999, under the supervision of my **Sensei**, I started with my first real students. From that crop came Jacob B. Fouts **Sensei**. Fouts **Sensei,** having seen me instruct from the beginning, was witness to the beginning of **Sogobujutsu** as taught by our **Ryu** and the **Godaishin Dojo** *the martial home of the intentions behind the five universal elements of creation.* In the beginning, **Ninjutsu** was stressed more as I had a longer history with it and a deeper understanding of it at the time. **Jujutsu** *the martial art of grappling*, then **Aikijujutsu** *the higher order of jujutsu*, became the mainstay of my teaching as time went on and I attained teaching licensing from Smith **Sensei** in 1999. From 1999 to 2009 we called ourselves the **Kakureta Ryu** *the martial family of the big secret.* As far as anyone outside of our **Dojo** at that time was concerned, we were not a **Ryu** *families.* Within our first ten years, there was focus on the promotion of the **Godaishin Dojo** and of **Sogobujutsu** but not of the **Ryu**. The name **Kakureta Ryu** was not found on anything, no websites, flyers, shirts, or bags. Our **Dojo** name was placed on most things. This was done for many reasons. When asked what **Ryu** we train in, we respond with a list of **Koryu** *classical martial families* that our methods came from. One of the largest reasons for the "secret family" was to avoid having to deal with the politics that would most certainly be brought up. For the past fifteen years, many martial arts groups within the U.S. make it a point to search out and attack other groups in an attempt to uncover false claims. It seems that most groups who spend their time in a willful pursuit of questioning others are the same groups who have trouble providing proof for their own claims in the martial arts. It's a silly thing but it is the same tactic that insecure grade school children use: "If I put others down, then I'll look good." We live in a day where everyone is accused of being a fake. It is because of these trends in the martial arts that we refrained from making any claims. By keeping quiet about our **Ryu** *families*, we did not have to waste time proving who we were to those people. It should be noted that they were never interested in the truth, for their goal is self-gratification in an attempt to expose people; much as their predecessors did during the Salem Witch-Hunt Trials. All of the most notable and knowledgeable martial artists I know of have been wrongfully placed under the thumb of their scrutiny.

Tossing two 2010
Ed Hall and Jacob
B. Fouts **Sensei**
Hellertown
Godaishin Dojo.

As in all things, there is an **In** (yin) and **Yo** (yang).
Something great did come from the nonsense of martial
artists attacking one another. It became increasingly
important to me to research, discover and document our
roots. I knew the truth, but the thought that my students may
become wrongfully ridiculed by other martial arts groups
provided me with the motivation to write this book. Proof of
where we came from would give each **Fuku** *member* the
confidence and security to make a rightful stand against
anyone who states we were just made up or mixed together
pieces of many arts. Our **Ryu** *families* came from the
knowledge of countless thousands of documented warriors'
life experiences--trained, refined and passed through our
martial lineage to us. They lend years of refined research,
crosschecked and examined to make sure things are as

2007 Taken during a class on **Kata Garuma**. I am teaching with
Fuku Jeremy Hochrine and Eric P. Fichter **Sensei**. This is a
combination technique one applied right after the other, then at the
same time. This is one of my **Sensei**'s favorite, he often uses
images of this **Waza**.

accurate as possible. This book is a testament to that work, as it proudly displays the true story of our history.

In 2009, my **Sensei** backed the idea that we go public with our **Ryu**. Under his guidance, I outwardly named our **Ryu** the **Neji Gekken Ryu**. There is no longer a need for secrecy. In an attempt to establish ourselves before moving public, we researched and documented the proof of our history. We have also, for many years now, gone through our **Kyoka** *curriculum* documenting and formulating training manuals for each rank. This was done to further establish the **Neji Gekken Ryu** and aid in our growth. We wanted to become ready to move into a public forum with the awareness that you get one chance to make a first impression. For this reason, it was important that we became knowledgeable about our history so that we could answer any questions of legitimacy. I have always been confident in our physical martial ability. We needed that same confidence in every aspect of our **Ryu** before witnessing the scrutiny of the public eye. I have worked for five years on creating a website for public consumption. I put many aspects of our history, philosophy, and technique on the World Wide Web.

The point that I am attempting to make is that our lineage is traceable; we know who we are and where we came from. The real proof of who we are, as my **Sensei** put it, "is in how we move". I urge all of you, in the future, to spend time learning our history and lineage so that you may better represent it as you become a part of it. Learn it, represent it, but never feel as if you need to prove it to anyone. Within this book, I have presented many aspects so that when you feel inclined to, you will be better equipped to present this knowledge.

The birth of the **Neji Gekken Ryu** and the choosing of this term was important to me; it brought about the essence of what our **Ryu** was to be about. **Neji** means

Twentieth year Demonstration celebration 2010 my top guys

"spiral", which is the principle of our martial movement. It is the principle of flow reflected in our universe. It is seen in everything. It is also called the golden-mean. **Gekken** is an old term meaning "live sword combat". The essence implies a readied blade; one that was forged and honed with a prepared warrior that was trained and able to wield it. **Gekken** also means "living blade" or "combative edge". Our **Ryu** name, then, can have many meanings. A simple translation is: the martial family of the spiraling combative edge. Along with our new name, we bring an old identity. We remain a **Ryu** for the **Ryu**--not for a name, but for the expression of the teachings; and not merely for the leader, but for each other. We are living the life of **Budo** *martial arts* and finding true expression as we learn to be free to do so. In my vision, we are becoming a strong **Ryu** and "**Neji Gekken Ryu**" is a fitting title. The understanding of our martial arts movement is not based on linear or circular configuration, but on a spiral. This spiral is what lends us our combative edge.

<u>Neji Gekken Ryu Mon</u>
Our Family Crest

The **Mon** *warrior family crest* is the family symbol of a **Ryu**. This was traditionally placed almost everywhere. It is the mark of the **Ryu**, something the practitioners of the **Ryu** would hold in high regard. It was seen in the **Tsuba** *sword guard*, as well as in their flags, clothing, training gear, on their  **Kimono** *formal attire* five times and displayed at the **Dojo** and in their dwellings. For this reason, a **Dojo** and a **Ryu** were known by their **Mon**. Older **Mon** were usually derived from a flower or a geometric shape. The **Mon** was always passed from teacher to student, as were the teachings of that **Ryu**.

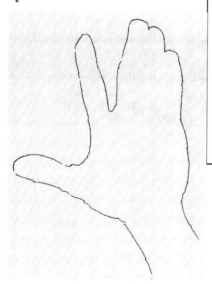

In 2000, After two years of thinking about some how combining all of the **mon** of the **ryu** we are derived from into one elaborate **mon**. I traced my hand, scanned in into the computer and thought of, something that would represent us well, a neoclassical depiction.

In modern days a **Ryu Mon** *warrior family crest* is often found on t-shirts, jackets, and **Gi** patches. One glance at a

Mon *warrior family crest* will teach us much about the
history, philosophy and methodology of the **Ryu**.

The left hand was chosen to be the symbol of our
Ryu for what it represents. During the feudal age in Japan,
one's right side represented the warring side and the left side
represented the peaceful side. The palm of the left hand is
displayed in our **Mon** as if the hand is extended outward.
This is done to show that we will always, as a **Ryu**, first
extend peace to the world.

The index finger is shown separated to imply an
understanding of **Ki** flow and the expression of **Ki** within our
art. The middle, ring, and pinky finger are grouped together
in remembrance of the **Samurai** teaching of primary gripping
fingers. Another reason the pointer finger is extended is to
express the **Shinobi**'s *ninja* knack for utilizing the pointer
finger in combative technique much like a second thumb.

The hands are each universal poles of inner and outer
forces. The right hand represents: analytical, external, gods,
knowledge, **Kongokai** *pure wisdom*, physical, positive,
power, projecting, realization of pure knowledge, sun,
ultimate actuality, **Yo** *yang*. Whereas, the left hand
represents: arresting the active mind, healing, **In** *yin*, internal,
intuition, moon, negative, psychic, receiving, spirituality,
Taizokai *material world*, temporal reality, worldly beings.

The fingers of the hand represent the elements of the
五大 **Godai** *five universal elements of creation*. The index
finger represents the element of 風 **Fu** *air*, the little finger
represents the element of 地 **Chi** *earth*, the middle finger
represents the element of 火 **Ka** *fire*, the ring finger

represents the element of 水 **Sui** *water* and the thumb finger represents the element of 空 **Ku** *void*. This understanding is used in **Kuji-in** *many forms of advanced meditation*, healing and many other forms of **Mikyo** *secret teachings*.

It was important to choose a **Mon** *warrior family crest* that showed the history of where our **Ryu** *family* came from, and that also depicted where we were headed as a **Ryu** and how we planned to get there. For us, the **Godai** *five elements of universal creation* has always been a very important lesson, as well as a true expression of the teachings of our **Ryu** *family*.

The **Godai** is the key to the universal realm in which all things were created. From this existence, came the understanding of the **Godai**, which means "comprehending the total workings and outcomes of all instances". This triggers a spark; if one is to feed and follow that spark, one can leap forward toward **Satori** *enlightenment*. For this reason, we included the **Godai** in the naming of our **Dojo**. In fact, the **Dojo** name stems from the same importance as the **Ryu Mon**. The **Godaishin Dojo** name was made from two Japanese terms, one being the **Godai** and the second the phrase "**Shin**". **Shin** has a great amount of meaning in Japanese. Often, it means heart but for us, it was picked to convey spirit or essence. When "**Shin**" is combined with "**Godai**", "**Godaishin**" means the essence, or spirit, of the five universal elements of creation.

In the **Mon**, the **Shin** is represented by the **Inyo**. The **Inyo** (a.k.a. yin-yang) is a symbol of the understanding of **Inyoho**. **Inyoho** is the dualism that is the nature of our reality: dark and light, negative and positive--the complementary opposites that give us freewill and choice. "**In**" would, in simple terms, be the good, and "**Yo**" would be the bad. This is **Inyo**. **Inyoho** implies a greater understanding of these works. "**Ho**" refers to the method in which the two interact. Altogether, they are the methods of interaction which lay the ground rules for our universe. **Inyoho** is the map of this world; when read, it defines detailed directions.

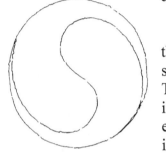

The teaching depicts many things. One is to see the white and see the black, but realize the gray. The physical universe that we live in is made up of both sides, each exists within the other. It is so integrated, that every action has an equal and opposite reaction. The Chinese depiction of the **Inyo**, or the yin and yang, depicts a swirled circle with a white side and a black side, each with a small amount of the other within it. Less well known, is the Japanese version which is a black circle within the white circle.

One must express **In** and yet have the balanced expression of **Yo**. A difficult thing to remember, that is often overlooked, is that **Yo** need not be the expression of anger, madness, sadness or wrongdoing. This is not efficient expression. Rather, think in ones and zeros--101010101011110000--expression of true love and the absence of it. For example, the balance of light and dark is where light and the absence of light makes up the darkness. **In** and **Yo** and all that is perceived is the **Ho** or the interaction of In and Yo is the expression of reality. This part may be left up to someone else.our perceptions limited

88

to what has already been created. Manifestation of the melding of polar forces to the in yo is every side has an equal and opposite side that make up a whole.makeup of everything breakup of everything. Front & back =side where they come together, an expression of interaction. Expression of all three is creation. That whole has an equal and opposite side. There are two sides to a coin, which represents the whole. If it attracts then it repels.

    The **Inyo** that exists within our **Mon** is purely **In** and

2009 Posing with my family, my daughter was just a baby at the time.

Yo. Although we agree with and attempt to understand the greater importance of its teachings, we remain hopeful that in at least one instance, the state of **In** could be purely **In** and the state of **Yo** (although swirling around with the **In**) could remain purely **Yo**. The *concept* of pure intention, neither the action nor the ripples it creates in the world, may be pure. As we journey through our art, we strive for spontaneous right action. This is found through attaining pure intention. For this reason, we have left the **Yo** out of the **In**, and in turn left the **In** out of the **Yo**. This stands as a constant remembrance to hold the ideal of pure intent in mind.

The importance of this is defining the roots and preferred roads taken by the warriors who came before us. The path has been cleared for us by so many and they have become landmarks along the way. This journey is about pure truth.

The Fibonacci Sequence.

Our **Inyo** also shows an exaggerated swirl. This is to remind us that we cannot escape the confines of our reality. If one could reach a purely good intention, they would invariably find that the purity would be enveloped inside of its opposite. The exaggerated swirling is a depiction of the universal counterbalance.

Therefore, we can--and we cannot--escape the confines of our reality; this is just another teaching of **Inyoho**. There is an old saying in the West, "The answer is in the palm of your hand." This is the reason for placing the **Inyo** within the palm of our **Mon**; it is to signify that the teachings of the universe, or **Inyo**, are *in the palm of our hands*.

90

The swirling **Inyo** also represents the spiral. Spiraling movement exists at the basis within our art. Sometimes, this is referred to as the "golden-mean". It is an example of the peak in proper movement within each and every movement of our martial art. Some martial arts are linear in nature, some are circular, and our art, **Sogobujutsu**, is spiral in nature.

Posing with just acquired **Densho** 2005. This photo displays two of the seven scrolls earned from many years of training.

The background of the **Mon** is black and the hand is white to signify that in dark times, as in times of war, the members of the **Ryu** will be able to rely on one another. The palm of the extended hand is reaching out of the darkness and pointing toward the way of the code. The white represents the purity of the warrior code: honor, respect and loyalty. This code shines the way of brotherhood, appreciation, knowledge, compassion, understanding, wisdom and love.

With its substance and detailed representation, our **Mon** is very descriptive and stands as a true example of the depth of our **Ryu**.

<u>Neji Gekken Ryu</u> Model of Operations

To understand the way things work, I have compiled short descriptions of the different organizations that run things on behalf of the **Neji Gekken Ryu**. The desired result of each of these independent organizations is the maintenance, growth and prosperity of the **Neji Gekken Ryu**.

LEHIGH VALLEY WARRIOR ARTS, LLC.

This is the independent business that controls and maintains all operations of business. LVWA LLC. controls the following:
*Recruitment of new students

*Promotion of the **Dojo, Budo,** and **Ryu**
*Paying overhead expenses
*Accounting and taxes
*Collecting of tuition/**Dojo** dues
*Advocating funds for projects
*Outsourcing (A.M.S., **Godaishin Dojo, Godaishin Hombu Dojo** Productions)
*The sale of any and all items
*The leasing of any and all items
*Trademarks

GODAISHIN DOJO

This is the chain of martial arts schools, the first was established in 1999. It maintains the highest standards of teaching. It holds ownership of all training equipment. It is rightful owner of the **Sogobujutsu No Kyoka**, which is the curriculum of martial knowledge taught to the **Neji Gekken Ryu**. This is an independent learning institution. The **Godaishin Dojo** is also in charge of the awarding and stripping of rank, belts, certificates, scrolls, positions, and titles within the **Ryu**.

GODAISHIN HOMBU DOJO

This is a part of the **Godaishin Dojo** and, as such, is in charge of the same instruction as the rest. Also, as the **Hombu**, it is the main headquarters of the **Neji Gekken Ryu**. This is a place of training, congregation and recreation for the **Ryu**.

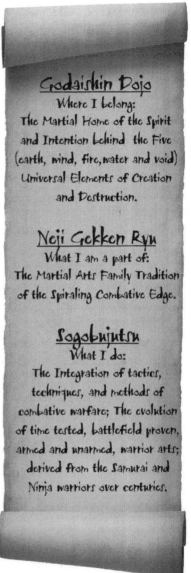

Godaishin Dojo
Where I belong:
The Martial Home of the Spirit and Intention behind the Five (earth, wind, fire, water and void) Universal Elements of Creation and Destruction.

Neji Gekken Ryu
What I am a part of:
The Martial Arts Family Tradition of the Spiraling Combative Edge.

Sogobujutsu
What I do:
The Integration of tactics, techniques, and methods of combative warfare; The evolution of time tested, battlefield proven, armed and unarmed, warrior arts; derived from the Samurai and Ninja warriors over centuries.

GODAISHIN HOMBU DOJO PRODUCTIONS

This is an organization that holds the copyright on all productions. It is made up of volunteers that give of their time and efforts freely in order to produce equipment, training materials, educational products, and many forms of media. Its main goal is one of documentation. Some of the items it has produced are dvds, websites (www.LeighValleyWarriorArts.com www.bumon.net www.jbkai.com and many other online pages), **Dojo** newsletters, books, booklets and training manuals (one for each rank), patches, clothing designs, and advertising materials (flyers, brochures, postcards, pamphlets, ads). They have also been responsible for the construction of the **Hombu Dojo** and the interior of each **Dojo**.

GODAISHIN KAI

It is our **Yudansha Kai**. This is a group made up of all of the **Yudansha** *black belts*. Their goal is to comment on the current state of operations. The **Godaishin Kai** also helps in taking lead of the organizations. Their purpose is to push for advancement in all areas. Their main task is planning for the future, setting goals and accomplishing them. They do this by leading the rest of the **Ryu**, when needed, through example. The **Godaishin Kai** takes advisement continually from the **Shihandai** as well from any and all **Fuku**.

JIHI BUJUTSU KAI

This is an organization of martial artists outside of our teachings and our martial family. It is our outreach program. It is designed to bind

94

together an extended brotherhood of martial artists from different backgrounds under one common home. The JBK is intended for the promoting of mutual appreciation and building **Buyu**. One of its underlining goals is to provide mutual support in times of need.

Mushado

This our martial arts equipment label. It is the creation department in charge of the design and branding of our martial arts gear. This includes uniforms, suits, jackets, equipment bags, weapons, training gear and anything else we can dream up.
The goal is to produce the highest quality products.

95

Chapter 3

Godaishin Dojo

Our martial home

This School was started in October of 1999 in Ambler, Pennsylvania, outside of my rented apartment in a small wooded grove. Along with the support of Jacob B. Fouts **Sensei**, one of my first students, I organized the first **Shibu** *training group*. From these meek beginnings, and a lot of help from family, friends and the support of students' involvement, we pushed forward. It was my intention to bring to life this vision of the perfect training school, the ideal **Dojo**. This **Dojo** is the materialization of a life dream for me. Unlike other **Dojo** in America, it belongs to the **Ryu** *our martial arts family*. We are giving new life to the old ways of warrior tradition. We must break through the prejudice of the layman and other artists, start as they did and eventually live the life of **Budo**. As a member, this is your school. It is our time to learn, grow and hold true to the warrior traditions. Since we began, we have had great success in building our **Ryu** and making this **Dojo** a strong force in the martial arts community. We have had great help by our **Ryu** members and their friends and family, and as a result of that help, we have spread to multiple locations. As we grow and expand by opening more **Dojo** and promoting more **Shihandai** *student instructor* and **Sensei**, it is up to each and every one of us to uphold the morals, values, ethics, and combative standards of this **Dojo**. Our **Dojo** is unlike any other and if we can hold true to its essence, then it will give way to future success. It has always been the standpoint of our **Dojo** to provide the best overall training experience to each and every one of our students, while never letting anyone slip through the cracks and never forgetting to provide for each person's individual needs. Maybe, it is for this reason that our **Dojo** has so often through the years been referred to by its members as a "sanctuary from the outside world". This has never been an easy thing to provide, but we, as a **Dojo**, have always held each other up--remaining steadfast to our goal to pass on everything we were so thankful to receive ourselves. As this knowledge enriches the next generation, the lineage chain gets longer and the **Godaishin Dojo** grows stronger. This strength helps everyone grow. This is *our* **Dojo**, *your* **Dojo**, take good care of it.

Our **Dojo** Patch

The patch has a unique responsibility. It is the defining part of the martial arts uniform. It has the responsibility of defining the **Dojo**, **Ryu**, and style of martial art all at the same time. This is a difficult task, as well as quite the undertaking when trying to encompass great meaning within a four-inch sewn circle. My plan was to convey what was most important, as well as to attempt to keep a somewhat simple design so as not to look cluttered. Our patch is comprised of two parts. I wanted straightforward and direct artwork for the patch. Following this line of thinking, the first piece, our **Ryu Mon**, was placed in the patch. For the second piece, **Kanji** was chosen. I chose **Kanji** partly because our art originated in **Japan**, but mainly because one can convey a great deal of meaning with very little writing. In some of our early original patch designs, we used the **Kanji** *Japanese calligraphy* for **Ai**, **Nin**, **Sogo**, and

Jujutsu. This was picked to express the rest of what was not already said by the **Ryu Mon**. Then, in the second generation patch, we added the **Kanji** of each of the **Godai** *five elements* placed within the corresponding fingers. The design for the third patch never made it to production. The plan was to no longer display the **"nin" Kanji** (not very ninjaesque to tell everyone right on your patch). We added the **"ki" Kanji** in its place and also

replaced the **Kanji** we originally were using for **"sogo"** as it could have been read as **"sugo"**, depending on who was reading it. We used a much more accurate **Kanji** for **"sogo"** and removed the elemental **Kanji** in the hand. The fourth design (third patch) displayed the kanji for the **Dojo, Ryu,** and the art. The hope was to simplify things. As of 2009, we changed the patch quite a bit. Our hope to simplify things went out the window. In the most recent design, we display the name of the **Budo** *martial art*, **Ryu** *martial family*, and the name of the **Dojo** *martial home*. The current patch (as of 2009) reads: **Godaishin Dojo, Neji Gekken Ryu,** and **Sogobujutsu** in **Kanji**. The **Kanji** is read traditionally, from top to bottom and from right to left. We added a bit more because our martial art's movement is a spiral; we added a depiction of the Fibonacci sequence. What else needs to be said? The future will dictate. No matter how our patch may change in the future, we are still the same **Dojo, Ryu,** and **Budo**.

The Velcro on our patch

Unlike most other schools, our patch is fastened with a Velcro backing so that it can be easily removed from the **Keiko Gi** *practice uniform.*

The main reason behind this is anonymity. We can accomplish this by easily exchanging our patch with other patches. This is a form of **Hensojutsu** *disguise and impersonation.* We then have the opportunity to switch to other patches when we represent other groups. We would not do this for just anyone; we only represent the **Ryu** that we are closely related to

This is the original **Hokushin Kai** patch. The **Kanji** in the center reads **Budo**. The **Kanji** over the top reads from left to right **Nihon Budo Hohushin Kai**.

such as the **Takagshin Ryu** or the **Kai** that we are members of (i.e. **Jihi Bujutsu Kai** or **Hokushin Kai**).

The Velcro patches are also useful on occasions where, for example, Smith **Sensei** has changed the name of his **Ryu**. It has been called the **Tanemura Ryu**, the **Hokushin Ryu**, the **Shindokoden Ryu** and most recently, the **Takagishin Ryu**. For practicality and avoiding seam ripping and re-stitching, Velcro is helpful.

When in a public setting, under the supervision of other martial artists, we use this "patch switching" so that we may blend in with the other groups. No one need ask about our affiliations and no one would think anything more than what they see on our **Gi**.

Another reason is that when perceived by others as an outsider for wearing a different patch, sometimes rivalries spring up. I have heard many stories about this. Actual fights were started because of the "you are not one of us" attitude. Stan Triplett **Sensei** got his knee back-warded in the mid 1980s by a member of the **Genbukan** for showing up to a seminar (which he was invited to and paid for) while wearing the patch of his own **Ryu**. The most likely scenario of that event is that others believed Triplett **Sensei** was attending the seminar in order to steal methods for himself that he could later claim to have invented. He also received some comments in the locker room such as, "What the heck is up with that patch?"
Even though I can understand both perspectives in a situation like this, we attempt to avoid conflict where we can. There are two main schools of thought. The first is that a martial artist should always represent their **Ryu** by wearing the **Mon** and patch on everything (this is a **Samurai** way of thinking). The second is to never tell anyone anything about oneself, one's training background, or one's **Ryu** while maintaining complete anonymity whenever training with other **Ryu** (of course, this is more of a **Ninja** mindset).

We must walk the line between these two concepts.

When it is time for us to take the lead, then we represent our **Ryu** and where we stem from. This would be done in demonstrations, lectures, and seminars in which we are featured as instructors. When it is time to learn, we take a backseat to who is teaching. We wear the appropriate patch to blend in, such as the **Takagishin Ryu**

This is our current patch. The **Kanji** reads **Godaishin Dojo, Neji Gekken Ryu, Sogobujutsu.**

patch or the **Jihi Bujutsu Kai** patch, or we remove our patch and wear nothing on our **Gi**. When asked who we are and what we do, we respond, "It's not pertinent." Our goal is to learn and "empty our cup" as the old saying goes, not to make a name for ourselves.

The Purpose in Wearing the **Jihi Bujutsu Kai** Patch
For some time I have observed my students while cross training. Each time I noticed that when attempting to learn about another **Ryu**'s methods, they got confused and things did not flow well. This is expected. When it was my turn instructing at an event, they did wonderfully as they are trained to do.

Still, I thought about proper movement and how, because of photos and video, untruths could become documented as facts. If people see documentation of members of our **Ryu** training other methods and wearing our patch, what are they to think? What if

This is the original **Jihi Bujutsu Kai** patch. The **Kanji** reads **Bushido Buyu** *Warrior brotherhood by the warrior code.*

outsiders see this without knowing our **Ryu** personally? They will make assumptions and draw conclusions. How often during our classes do people take photos or video? Almost never. How often are vidoes or photographs taken at other group's events? Very often. This could pose a problem. If we want to continue enjoying events and cross training, we must think about the effect it could have on our future as a **Ryu**. We must preserve our way. To do this, we wear the **Jihi Bujutsu Kai** patch when training techniques that are not our own. Although we wear it to make a statement of brotherhood, unity, and appreciation for others, we also wear it to confirm that we are training outside of our own art.

The purpose behind wearing the **Takagishin Ryu** Patch:
Takagishin Ryu Patch is worn when we are training in
strictly the **Samurai** arts that are Smith **Den** *derived through*
the delineation of
*Smith **Sensei**.* We
wear this patch
where others may
not. This is done
because of the direct
lineage-link that we
hold to the
Takagishin Ryu
traditions. We must
remain careful while
wearing this patch;
careful to represent
the **Takagishin Ryu**
properly. If we wear
this patch while
doing any
techniques, methods,
forms, or drills that came from any other source, then we
would be misrepresenting the **Takagishin Ryu**. This would
be a disgraceful act.

> This is the **Takagishin Ryu** patch. The **Kanji** reads **Aiki Budo**.

All of these points illustrate why it is so very
important that we developed a patch that would serve the
cause of our **Ryu**. As members of the **Neji Gekken Ryu**,
you must understand why our Patch is so different and you
must understand the meaning behind it.

104

Common **Dojo** Phrases and Commands

Domo Arigato Gozaimashita: (Douh-Moe Adee-Ga-Toe Go-Zai-Mosh-Tah) Thank you very very much

Arigato Gozaimasu: (Adee-Ga-Toe Go-Zai-Mosh-Tah) Thank you a lot

Arigato: (Adee-Ga-Toe) Thank you

Domo: (Douh-Moe) Thanks

Do Itashimashite: (Doe E-Tah-She-Mash-Teh) You are welcome

Chaku za: (Cha-Koo Zah) Sit down (in **Seiza**)

Dozo: (Douh-Zoh) Please, By all means

Keiko Shu Ryo: (K-ko Shoo Row) Class is over

Kiretsu: (Key-Ree-tsss) Stand up

Kiotsuke: (Key-O-Tsss-Kay) Attention

Tancho: (Tan-Ch-O) Start

Hajime: (Hah-Je-May) Begin

Yame: (Yah-May) Finish

Kamiza ni rei: (Ka-Me-Zah Knee Ray) Bow toward the **Kamiza** *center of respect*

Shomen ni rei: (Show-Men Knee Ray) Bow toward front wall of the **Dojo** floor

Matte: (Ma-Teh) Wait

Matte Kurasai: (Ma-Teh Koo-Dah-Sigh) Wait please

Chotto Matte Kurasai: (Cho-Toe Ma-Teh Koo-Dah-Sigh) Wait just a moment please

Matte: (Ma-Teh) Stop!

Mawatte: (Mah-Wah-Teh) Turn around

Mokuso: (Mue-Koo-So) Meditate
Otagai ni rei: (O-Tah-Guy Knee Ray) Bow to each other

Sensei ni rei: (Sen-Say Knee Ray) Bow to **Sensei**

Yoi: (Yoee) Get ready!

Batsu: (Bahh-tsss) Attack!

Daijabu: (Die-Jah-Boo) Are you ok?

Ohayo Gozaimasu: (O-Hi-Yo Go-Zai-Mass) Kindly have a Good morning

Ohayo: (O-Hi-Yo) Good morning

Konnichiwa: (Ko-Knee-Chee-Wah) Hello, Good afternoon

Konbanwa: (Koun-Ban-Wah) Good evening

Oyasuminasai: (O-Yah-Sew-Men-Na-Shy) Good night, Have good sleep

Soyonara: (Sa-Yo-Nah-Da) Goodbye

Dewa Mata: (Dee-Wah Mah-Tah) Well then, see you again

Ja Mata: (Jah Mah-Tah) See you tomorrow

Ja Ne: (Jah Nae) See ya

Gomen nasai: (Go-Men Nah-Shy) I am sorry

Sumi masen: (Sew-Me Mah-Sen) Please excuse me

Wakari masen: (Wah-Ka-Dee Mah-Sen) I don't understand

Wakari maska: (Wah-Ka-Dee Mah-Kah) Do you understand?

Wakari mas: (Wah-Ka-Dee Mahsss) I understand

Mo Ichido Onegaishimasu: (Moe Each-E-Doe O-Neh-Guy-She-Mahsss) Please show it once more

Yukkuri Onegaishimasu: (You-Ku-Dee O-Neh-Guy-She-Mahsss) Please show it slowly

Hajamae Mashite Dozo Yoroshiku Onegaishimasu David Falcaro **Sensei Desu:** (Hah-Je-May Mash-Teh Douh-Zoh Yo-Doe-Shh-Kooo O-Neh-Guy-She-Mahsss David Fal-care-o Sen-Say Desss) From our first start please let us have a nice meeting, I am the teacher David Falcaro

Attire for Our **Dojo**

Kimono

Formal attire is worn at formal demonstrations,

banquets and meetings, and during formal classes. Formal dress consists of a **Hakama** *large pleated pants* and **Kimono** *formal top consisting of elongated*

sleeves. **Hakama** can be of any color or design. Some are very decadent with stripes or cross patterns. Although there are many accepted designs, certain things are unacceptable for formal wear. **Hakama** *large pleated pants* consisting of zebra

108

stripes, the American flag, camouflage, denim, and any sewn-on patches are becoming popular. These are modern trends that are growing and this is a nice way to stand out for other groups, but it not acceptable dress for representing our **Budo**, **Dojo**, and **Ryu**. Another modern trend that is unacceptable is to wear a **Keiko Obi** *training belt*, whether it is on top of or under the **Kimono** *formal top consisting of elongated sleeves*.

  The **Kimono** is a formal robe having exaggerated long upper sleeves that begin at the elbow and end at the armpit. These sleeves hang off of the arm six or more inches. This robe is worn extremely loose around the body and fits comfortably around the torso. The **Kimono** consists of a **Soto Kimono** *Outer formal top* and **Uchi Kimono** *Inner formal top*, which are outer and inner **Kimono** as well as a **Kanjuban** *under shirt*. The outer **Kimono** displays the **Mon** *warrior family crest* three times, sometimes as many as seven. The size of the **Mon** *family crest* is about the size of a half dollar, any bigger is considered tacky. The placement of the **Mon** *crest* is over each pectoral muscle and centered on the back high between the shoulder blades. The **Mon** can also appear an additional four times, centered on the front and back of the hanging part of each sleeve. The **Kimono** can be any color, but is kept uniform in each **Ryu** *martial arts tradition*. A **Hanjuban** *under shirt* resembles a **Kekogi Kesa** *practice uniform top*. They are worn purely white and made of a fine fabric for the purpose of absorbing sweat so that it does not penetrate and reach the **Kimono**. A **Kimono Obi** *formal dress belt* is worn under the **Hakama** *large pleated pants* and over all three layers to straighten and keep each layer of the **Kimono** straight. A **Tasuke** *top shoulder/sleeve tied sash* can be worn to hold back the sleeves of the inner **Kimono** or the outer **Kimono**. A

Hajimaki *headband* is acceptable for formal attire. Indoor **Tabbi** *split toe mat slippers* are worn. For outdoors, they are worn in combination with **Getta** *wooden sandals*, or **Zori** *straw sandals*. **Jika tabbi** *split toe outdoor shoes* may be acceptable in rare instances. Feet are never bare. In ancient times of war, usually in periods after the **Majiin** restoration, this uniform was sometimes worn. In these cases, the **Hakama** was tucked up in one of two fashions. The first was the middle of the side folds pulled up and tucked behind, down and through the side straps of the **Hakama** *large pleated pants*. The second fashion was done by gripping the material on the outsides of the ankles and drawing it up under and through the ties on the hips. This version resembles poofy shorts.

Hakama

Semiformal attire is worn at formal classes, and with permission from the **Sensei,** can be worn for informal classes as well as at **Taikai** *culmination seminar*, seminars, and gatherings. Semiformal wear consists of a **Joba Hakama** *this type of large pleated pants with a separation of pants legs* (once derived from **Samurai**

undergarments), **Hajimaki** *headband*, and the **Kesa** *practice uniform top* of a **Keikogi** *practice uniform*, proudly displaying the **Ryu**'s patch. This **Hakama** can only be solid black with no markings or patches. It is unacceptable to wear a **Keiko Obi** *practice belt* over or under the **Hakama**. An **Obi** *belt* is not worn with this uniform. Either **Tabbi** *split toe mat slippers* or **Jika Tabbi** *split toe outdoor shoes* are worn.

Keikogi

Keikogi *practice uniform*, also called **Dogi**, is considered informal attire and is worn during classes or with permission of **Sensei** during formal classes. It should not be worn to formal functions, such as formal demonstrations, banquets, and meetings. Informal wear is called **Keikogi**, which is made up of **Keiko Kesa** *practice top* and **Zubon** *pants*, also called **Keiko Hakama**. Other **Ryu** accept bare feet but we do not. Either **Tabbi** *split toe matt slippers* or **Jika Tabbi** *split toe outdoor shoes* are worn. **Hajimaki** should be worn, but are not necessary unless **Sensei** specifies. The color of the **Keikogi** differs from **Ryu** *warrior family* to **Ryu**. Within our **Ryu**, we all wear the color black. This is done to promote unity; no matter your rank, we all wear the same uniform. In other **Ryu**, the color of your uniform often signifies status. The only time we would wear a different color **Keikogi** *practice uniform* would be for photos to more easily show off the mechanics of a technique.

Shozuku

Shozuku *uniform of stealth* is sometimes called the

cloak of darkness or the uniform of war. This uniform was used by the **Ninja** when going into battle. They wore a **Gi** *uniform* consisting of **Kesa** *top* and **Zubon** *pants*. The **Gi** *uniform* was a plain color either black or blood red for males, black or dark purple for **Kunoichi** *female Ninja*. The **Kesa** *top* was plain with no markings of a **Mon** *family crest* or patches. The **Zubon** *pants* was worn over top of the bottom of the **Kesa** *top* and was equipped with four straps, two binding the material at the knees and two binding the material before the ankles. In the **Zubon** *pants*, there was a harness sewn into the seat of the pants, once around the top of each thigh and once around the waist. These three circles were connected and provided the **Ninja** the ability to repel as well as propel himself into the air. The **Jika Tabbi** *split toe*

outdoor shoes were worn over top of this bound material.
Kote *gauntlets* were worn over the top of the sleeves of the
Kesa *top.* Some **Ryu** wore them under the sleeves of the
Kesa *top.* They were worn beginning at a ring around the
base of the middle finger, over the back of the hand, over the
arm, and ending at the elbow. They did not cover the palm
of the hand. In more modern times, black gloves are worn
under the **Kote** *gauntlets.* **Uchizu** *facemask* was worn over
the entire head ending at the pectoral muscles and the
shoulder blades. It had a small slit to expose the eyes. It is a
common misconception that the **Ninja** wore a mask that
resembles our ski masks with holes for each eye. This type
of mask would inhibit their ability to have peripheral vision
and put them at great risk. The base of the **Uchizu** *facemask*
was worn under the **Kesa** *top.* The **Uchizu** could also consist
of a long wrapped sash. This sash was dipped in antibiotics
and dried. If in trouble, the **Uchizu** *facemask* sash became a
tourniquet or a bandage. The **Sotozu** *hood* was worn over
the **Uchizu.** It had two main shapes. One peaked all the way
down along the center of the top of the head. The other form
was quite large and stood a foot above the top of the head. It
then extended and angled out from the head on both sides,
bowed in from the sides and peaked outward at the middle.
This was worn to intimidate the enemy because it was a sight
that he was not used to having run at him. Many weapons
were hidden in the **Shozuku** *uniform of stealth.*

Yoroi

      Yoroi was a samurai's armored uniform for war.
Yoroi *armor* consists of **Kabuto** *helmet,* **Maedate** *helmet
crest,* **Watagami** *shoulder strap,* **Shikoro** *nape guard,* **Do**
chest plate, **Sode** *shoulder/ sleeve armor,* **Hitatare** *patted
under robe,* **Kote** *forearm armor,* **Tekko** *hand guard,*

Kusazuri *upper thigh plating,* **Haidate** *lower thigh plating,* **Hakama** *under pants,* and **Suneate** *lower leg armor.* The **Do** was a chest plate displaying the **Mon** *warrior family crest.* Depending on the period of time and the **Ryu**, it could be solid metal or sewn in metal plates resembling the scales of a fish or reptile. These scales were found  over the arms as well. The helmet consisted of two parts: the headdress and a scary mask. The mask often depicted a gruesome face with hair and teeth showing. The helmet sometimes displayed large horns or protruding metal shapes. **Hachigani** were **Hajimaki** with an armored plate sewn into them at the peak of the forehead; these were sometimes worn.

Keiko Yoroi

Keiko Yoroi is a practice uniform that mimics the mechanics of **Yoroi**. The uniform consists of a **Men, Do,** **Kote**, and **Hakama**. **Sune** *shin guards* are also sometimes worn with this uniform. **Sune** are often also worn by **Naginatadoka** *Naginatado practitioners*. The rest of the uniform is also used as one of the uniforms worn by **Kendoka** *Kendo practitioners*.

Titles and Positions

Ryu *martial arts family*
The **Giri** *duty* for a **Ryu** is to grow in numbers as well as individual and personal growth. The **Ryu** is to get stronger through training and interpersonal relationships. It is to maintain a brotherhood that loves, protects, and cares for each and every member. By being a member of the **Ryu,** you are committing yourself to the moral and ethical values set forth by your "martial family".

Sensei *teacher or "One who has gone before"*
A **sensei** must hold the rank of **Shodan** *first degree black belt* or above, be awarded a **Menkyo** *teaching license,* and

1997 David C. Falcaro **Sensei** Training **Hanbojutsu** with my classmate Martin Rivera **Sensei.**

must be an adult. The role of the **Sensei** is to teach, to develop closeness with each and every member of the **Dojo**, and to present himself as a best friend and confidant. To be the embodiment of the principles and ideals of the art, a **Sensei** must follow the warrior code. A **Sensei** is to be supportive, trusting, caring, appreciative, guiding, motivational and a guardian of the **Ryu**. The **Sensei** should never have to take the role of a disciplinarian (this is a **Sempai** *student leader* job). The reason being that there must never be allowed any distance between the **Sensei** and the **Kyu**. The **Kyu** and **Sensei** are the best of friends and nothing may come between them. A **Sensei** takes the side of the **Kyu** in all matters, whenever possible. The only time the **Sensei** takes the role of a disciplinarian is when he is forced to do so. In the instance a member of the **Ryu** makes a direct move against the **Sensei**, only then is his hand forced.

A **Sensei** must be respected and held in high regard. It is considered proper to treat all **Sensei** with a strong sense of dignity and loyalty. The old saying is, "**Sensei** is the well from which we all drink". If the **Sensei** is tarnished in any way, the drinking water may become poisoned. If overlooked, unappreciated or taken for granted, the well may dry up. "Never bite the hand that feeds you" points out the same idea of how not to treat those who give of themselves. A **Sensei** is looked at as the "source". The "source" is the beginning and ending of the **Ryu**. With the **Sensei**, there is a beginning; without the **Sensei**, there is no **Ryu**. As the source, the goal is to create more beginnings. More **Sensei** means an even greater beginning, a greater source. This also creates less of a chance of an ending to the **Ryu**. Gain from the source and, in time, pass that knowledge onto the rest of the **Ryu**. Then, return to the source for more. This is the **Giri** *duty* of a good **Deshi** *dedicated student*.

Shidoin *assistant instructor*
This is a term given to a **Sensei** who is a member of the **Ryu** that holds a rank under the head **Sensei**. It is an in-house term in that the classmates of the assistant instructor would only use it. Everyone else would call that person **Sensei** or

his last name then **Sensei.**

Uchideshi *live-in disciple*
This position was once very common in the martial arts, but
no longer. It is now very uncommon; in fact, it is almost
unheard of. The role of an **Uchideshi** is to have a life
devotion to the art as well as one to the **Ryu**, **Sensei**, and
Dojo. An **Uchideshi** focuses mainly on his own training and
caring for his **Sensei**. He is an apprentice that has given his
heart to the warrior arts. To be an **Uchideshi**, one must be
hand picked by the **Sensei** to live with the **Sensei**. This
person holds a unique position with the **Sensei**. Not only
does this person live in the same house as the **Sensei**, but
they also train every day with the personal guidance and
teachings of that **Sensei**. The training of an **Uchideshi** is
quite different than that of a **Kyu**. There is not a point during
the day where the **Uchideshi** is not in training from when he
awakes to when he falls asleep at night. Even while he
dreams, all things are said to aid him in his journey; all things
are training. Also, the teachings are passed much more
rapidly and more frequently, over three times that of a
normal **Kyu**. Training that would normally take nine years
to complete; the **Uchideshi** *live-in disciple* must do in three.
The **Uchideshi**'s **Giri** *duty* is to more than just keep up with
the training; it is to push the **Sensei** to teach him more.
Another aspect of his **Giri** is to care and support the **Sensei**
in all ways. An **Uchideshi**'s vocation is similar to that of a
knight's page. He lives in the **Sensei**'s shadow. He alone
may speak for the **Sensei**. He is able to demonstrate on the
Sensei's behalf. He is constantly being groomed by the
Sensei to become a **Sensei**. An **Uchideshi** can be as close, or
closer, to the **Sensei** than his own blood family. An
Uchideshi is often considered the next **Sensei** because

becoming one is an oath that seals one's fate. This person holds a **Kyu** ranking and will do so until he graduates past the rank of **IkKyu** *first degree student* and is no longer a **Kyu**, at which point they become a **Dan** *black belt*. After becoming a **Sensei,** this **Dan** may remain an **Uchideshi** as long as he wishes. Some people only become **Uchideshi** after attaining a **Dan** *black belt* rank. An **Uchideshi** may help in the maintaining of the **Dojo**'s log.

Sempai *senior student leader*

A **Sempai** is a "consiglieri" to the **Sensei** as well as an active student teacher. The **Sempai** has the **Kopai** *junior student leader* and **Kohai** *junior student leader* at his disposal to dispatch for any task as he deems fit. **Sempai** is a best friend to each of the **Kyu** as well as their confidant. The **Giri** *duty* of a **Sempai** includes becoming close to each and every student personally and, when that is not possible, using a medium to do so (**Kopai, Kohai** or **Dohai**). He is personally responsible for each student's mental and emotional well-being. He acts as the main reporter to the **Sensei**. His job is to report all wrongful dealings and mishappenings done by the **Kyu**. He is also responsible for reporting updates on the overall students' consensus and his own separate conclusions that are put together through counseling with the **Kopai, Kohai** and **Dohai** *student body leader*. His **Giri** is to the **Kyu** as a disciplinarian. He deals in all matters of discipline. He maintains the **Dojo**'s log. He keeps order through verbal discussions and physical action. A **Sempai** handles the making up and the handing out of assignments to the **Kyu** when they have fallen short of their own **Giri**. He deals with all violations of code and ethics. A wrongdoing or an offense perpetrated by a member of the **Ryu** is considered by all to be a self-imposed dishonor. It must be known and made

118

clear to the **Kyu** that the **Sempai** hands out tasks and assignments NOT as a punishment, but rather for the sole purpose of giving the disgraced **Kyu** the opportunity to regain his lost honor. It is important that the **Sempai** takes the full brunt of the shamed **Kyu**'s misplaced aggression. He must shelter the **Sensei** from this misplaced aggression by explaining that it is his job alone to pass out punishments and this punishment has nothing to do with the **Sensei**. The **Sempai** must first and foremost promote a healthy and loving relationship between the **Sensei** and the **Kyu**. Secondly, he must promote that same relationship between each of the **Kyu.** And thirdly, he must have this relationship between himself and the **Kyu**. Although the **Sempai** is considered the leader of the **Kyu**, he is still a member of the **Kyu**.

Taken in the mid 90's at the **Takeshin Dojo** of the whole class

Kopai *junior student leader*
The position of a **Kopai** is filled by an adult. It is improper to give money to or to speak of money with the **Sensei**; this is why all money dealings are run through the **Kopai** as an intermediary. It is the job of the **Kopai** to make all monetary transactions as simplified and as straight forward as possible, while always emphasizing truth and understanding. With money dealings comes a lot of debate and strife. Misunderstandings are a reality of this, giving way to a distressed, displeased, disturbed, or saddened **Kyu**. **Kopai** must shelter the **Sensei** from these dealings by explaining to all persons that they should direct all monetary questions to him alone. Although the **Kopai** is a leader of the **Kyu**, he is still a member of the **Kyu**. The **Kopai** also helps to maintain the **Dojo**'s log. The **Kopai** is in command under the **Sempai** *senior student leader* and is third in command under the **Sensei**. He is a member of the **Kyu**, but this title and position supersedes the rights and privileges of all **Kyu** ranks with the exception of the **Sempai** and the **Uchideshi**. The **Kohai** *junior student leader* shares an equal status to the **Kohai**.

Kohai *junior student leader*
The position of a **Kohai** is filled by a teenager, not an adult. Although the **Kohai** is a leader of the **Kyu**, he is still a member of the **Kyu**. The **Kohai** is in command under the **Sempai** and is third in command under the **Sensei**. He is a member of the **Kyu**, but this title and position supersedes the rights and privileges of all **Kyu** ranks with the exception of the **Sempai** *senior student leader* and the **Uchideshi** *live-in disciple*. The **Kohai** also helps to maintain the **Dojo**'s log. The **Kohai** shares an equal status to the **Kopai**.

120

Dohai *student body*

This title has to do with the person striving toward perfecting skill in the warrior arts. It is because of that achievement that one who is a **Dohai** is looked on as the example of what a student should be. If the **Ryu** was a person, then the **Dohai** would represent the "body" (the strong trunk or torso). Basically, the **Dohai** is the big (because there are many of them) and the strong (because of their continued commitment and accomplishment) part of the **Kyu**. Unlike the **Sensei**, **Uchideshi** *live-in disciple*, **Sempai**, **Kopai** and **Kohai**, the **Dohai** are not referred to by the title they hold in the **Dojo**. Although the **Dohai** help lead the **Kyu**, they are still members of the **Kyu** and their title and position does not supersede the rights and privileges of the **Kyu** ranks. Each **Dohai** is an overseer to a core group of **Kyu** made up of around five members. The **Dohai** are the eyes and ears of the **Ryu**. Their job is to take care of and mentor a group of lower ranked **Kyu**. They are responsible for looking out for them and making sure that the five or so **Kyu** that they are in charge of are doing well. They help their core group continue to progress in the art, while also presenting themselves as one part of the larger "support team" that is our **Ryu**. The **Dohai**'s **Giri** is to make sure that no one is forgotten about, that no one is left behind. Everyone must be cared for. The **Dohai** are there to enforce brotherhood and to lead by example. Another task they must fulfill is to end disputes between **Kyu** and to immediately attain council for the disputing **Kyu**. This is done by reporting to the **Kohai**, **Kopai**, **Sempai**, and always to the **Sensei**. The **Dohai** also has access to the **Dojo**'s log and may be asked to update it from time to time. The **Dohai**'s main job is that of a detective. A **Dohai** keeps his eyes open and asks questions, always remaining aware of the going-ons of the group. The goal is always to maintain a strong and happy **Ryu**.

Kyu *martial student*
The **Kyu** are the largest part of the **Ryu**, encompassing all of the ranks under **Shodan** from **Mukyu** through **IkKyu**. The **Sempai, Kopai, Kohai**, and **Dohai** are all a part of the **Kyu** as well. It should be noted that the rank of **MuKyu** *no rank* is not position gained; it is a position given, therefore a **MuKyu** is not, in the strictest sense, a **Kyu**. Many say that the **Kyu** are the most important part of the **Ryu**. The **Kyu** have different tasks that are asked of them. Their **Giri** is to develop and maintain their honor, to grow in the warrior arts, to learn the warrior's code, to care for their **Sensei**, to honor and respect the teachings, and to appreciate and take care of the **Dojo** and the **Ryu**. Strive to be more than a **Kyu**; strive to be a **Deshi** and a **Dan**.

Dan *level*
The **Dan** are no longer just students, they are also teachers and masters. These ranks are **Shodan** *first degree black belt*, **Nidan** *second degree black belt*, **Sandan** *third degree black belt*, **Shidan** *fourth degree black belt*, **Godan** *fifth degree black belt*, **Rokudan** *sixth degree black belt*, **Shichidan** *seventh degree black belt*, **Hachidan** *eighth degree black belt*, **Kudan** *ninth degree black belt*, and **Judan** The **Dan** are no longer just students, they are also teachers and masters. These ranks are **Shodan** *first degree black belt*, **Nidan** *second degree black belt*, **Sandan** *third degree black belt*, **Shidan** *fourth degree black belt*, **Godan** *fifth degree black belt*, **Rokudan** *sixth degree black belt*, **Shichidan** *seventh degree black belt*, **Hachidan** *eighth degree black belt*, **Kudan** *ninth degree black belt*, and **Judan** *tenth degree black belt.*

There is no such thing as a higher rank then a tenth degree black belt. Tenth degree black belt is not achieved through the acquisition of greater knowledge. It is a position granted to signify the leader of a **Ryu**. All knowledge, no matter how in-depth the curriculum, is passed on by ninth degree black belt in all martial arts. Any rank beyond tenth **Dan** would be pure ego indulgence.

Besides feeding the ego, it has no purpose.

Deshi, Jikideshi *apprentice or disciple*
A **Deshi** is a title given to one who once was first a **Kyu** or **Dan** that has far succeeded the expectations of that role. It is someone who has developed a life devotion to the art as well as one to the **Ryu, Sensei**, and **Dojo**. A **Deshi** is one who is confident that they will one day be the **Sensei**. One who wants more than the normal training, one who has an insatiable need for learning everything he can. The mark of **Deshi** is that they are at the **Dojo** before the **Dojo** is open and they stay to help the **Sensei** close up. They are constantly bugging the **Sensei** and their superiors with countless questions they thought about while doing their own research outside of class. Unlike the **Sensei, Uchideshi, Sempai, Kopai** and **Kohai**, the **Deshi** are not referred to by the title they hold in the **Dojo** because this title holds no other responsibilities (in the way of tasks) than that of a **Kyu** or **Dan**; it is merely a position of greater honor. Of course, with greater honor comes the greater responsibility to uphold that honor. It should be noted that some older **Ryu** do not accept **Kyu**. They expect no less than what a **Deshi** offers to their **Ryu**. This is a difficult thing to reproduce in the United States. Asking an American student straight off the bat for this type of loyalty, commitment, confidence, time,

Jack Toole displays **Kobojutsu** with Nevin Moyer Jr. 2011
Hellertown **Godaishin Dojo.**

appreciation, devotion and respect would be looked down
upon in the U.S. It would often be seen as weakness rather
than strength. To avoid this, we gladly accept **Kyu**. We
attempt to inspire more.

Shihandai *student teacher*
Shihandai is a term used widely in the Japanese-derived
martial arts. This is normally not a spoken title, so this will
not change the way members refer to those individuals who
become **Shihandai**. However, the students who receive
tutelage from a **Shihandai** may refer to them as such. This
position will entail the following:

124

- student teaching under the supervision of the **Sensei**
- watching over the inner workings of the class or classes you are assigned to
- reporting to the **Sensei** on a regular basis about the progress of each student
- reporting to the **Sensei** as a student may be ready to evaluate for stripes or belts
- remaining dedicated to each student's development
- providing a strong unwavering example of **Sogobujutsu**

The criteria one must meet in order to be considered for the position of **Shihandai** is:

* One must attain the rank of **Gokyu** (purple belt, 45 credits) or a level beyond that rank.
* One must be a current member and a dedicated **Kyu** currently making all of their own classes.

Sinban *formal judge*

Sinban are present when a **Kyu** goes through a formal evaluation to receive a credit toward his or her next degree. Another time that they are used is during a formal review or belt test. During this, the evaluation is given to review the nine proceeding credits toward the new degree or new belt. Anyone of higher rank who earned the current credit (represented by a stripe) can act as a **Sinban**. The **Giri** *duty* of a **Sinban** is to give the **Hantei** *judgment*, **Hai** *yes* meaning this person should pass or **Iiya** *no* meaning this person needs more work. One is only a **Sinban** during an evaluation.

Fuku *member*

Fuku is anyone who has joined the **Dojo**.

Eric Fichter **Sensei** displays **Kamajutsu** with Nevin Moyer Jr. Durring his Black Belt test in 2010 at the Northampton **Godaishin Dojo.**

Our **Dojo Kun**
The Oath of our Martial Home

1. I will never forget the true virtue and importance of humility.

2. I will look to my art, internalizing it for wisdom and strength.

3. I will maintain the guidelines of courtesy, respect and loyalty to my family and to my **Ryu**. I will treat others as I would like to be treated.

4. I will train my heart, mind and body for **Fudoshin** *a firm, unshaken spirit*.

5. I will pursue the true meaning of the martial arts way so that, through time, I can work toward perfecting my character.

6. Throughout my life, with the discipline I learn from **Sogobujutsu**, I will seek to find the true meaning of the way.

7. I will refrain from violence whenever possible. When I must, I will be quick to react. I will use every skill earned through my training to dominate over any aggression.

Our <u>Dojo Kiyaku</u>
General Rules of our Martial Home

1. **Kyu** shall refer to head instructor as **Sensei**, assistant instructors as **Shidoin**, senior student leader as **Sempai**, under student leader as **Kopai** or **Kohai**. Any other **Sensei** (either within our **Ryu** or outside of it) shall be referred to by their last name spoken first then the title of **Sensei**, i.e. "Smith **Sensei**".

2. Higher belts will assist lower ranked belts in their understanding and training.

3. Lower belts will follow the instruction of the higher ranked belts in the **Dojo**.

4. No talking during class unless permitted by the **Sensei**.

5. Shoes are restricted on the **Dojo** floor during class or at any time.

6. **Kyu** shall **Rei** *bow or salute* when entering and leaving the **Dojo** (to say hello and goodbye). Everyone must **Rei** when getting onto the **Tatame** *mat*, once to the **Enbusen** *center of the training mat* and a second time to the **Kamiza** *center of respect*.

7. **Kyu** shall not interrupt the **Sensei** while he is teaching or training. Questions are asked by bowing as a salute until acknowledged, unless in emergency cases.

8. While class is in process, no **Kyu** shall enter without the permission of the **Sensei**. Take position to the right of the entrance of the mat, on the outer most edge of the mat in

Seiza No Kamae *seated kneeling position.*

9. **Kyu** must wear **Gi** *proper uniforms* at all times. No half
Gi are permitted, we wear the whole thing or nothing.
Nothing can be added to the uniform, no extra garment, skull
cap, more patches, outer robe, inner robe, colored t-shirt,
pins, buttons, extra embroidered stitching. It is not important
to draw attention to oneself by making some sort of fashion
statement. One should not attempt to wear their **Gi**
differently; there is only one way to tie an **Obi** *belt*, one does
not need to remove the sleeves or tuck the top into the pants.
A uniform is to be "uniform" with the rest of the class. The
only thing that should make you stand out is your
accomplishments (the color of your belt). We are to look
united.

10. No rings, watches or other jewelry may be worn during
class.

2010 Taken during Eric P. Fichter **Sensei**'s black belt test while
he was in the middle of **Rendori**. In the photo you can see him
getting out of the way of Mike Wasko's on coming attack and
placing Nevin Moyer Jr. in the way to shield himself.

Reigi Saho
Methods of Proper **Dojo** Etiquette and Discipline

These lessons concern behavior inside the **Dojo**. Most of them should seem obvious, but we have experienced the need to keep things clear. This list exists in the **Mukyu No Maki** *the scroll of the no ranked student*. This chapter defines the reasons behind each of these methods. It is important to know why we do the things we do and what we plan on getting out of this training. In earlier times, even with my **Sensei**, it was impressed to the **Kyu** that **Reigi saho** was necessary for good training. It was always strictly enforced, but not explained. It may have been explained to a **Sensei** many years later, but because of modernization and cultures changing, most all of these lessons were lost. You almost never see any **Ryu** outside of our own still holding to these traditions. This may be because, after a few years of doing something and not knowing why, you stop doing it since it may seem pointless. Yet our **Reigi saho** reinforces really important training. In our Western culture, it is customary to know why we are doing things; because I never want these lessons to be overlooked, thrown out, or unappreciated, you will be receiving some of the explanations about ten years before what is traditional.

1. **Kyu** shall refer to the head instructor as **Sensei**, assistant instructors as **Shidoin**, senior student leader as **Sempai**, under student leader as **Kopai** or **Kohai**. Any other **Sensei** (either within our **Ryu** or outside of it) shall be referred to by their last name spoken first then the title of **Sensei**, i.e. "Smith **Sensei**". This is done to keep order in the **Dojo** and to give the proper respect to each of the instructors. As this is done, everyone will be self-

impressing the importance of successful completion of levels of understanding, competence, experience and acquired ability.

2. Higher ranked belts will assist lower ranked belts in their understanding and training. There are studies that prove 90% of learning comes from teaching another. When one is asked to explain and convey what they have learned, they will attain a deeper understanding of it. Also, a student who has just learned the material is closer to the confusion that can occur when learning it. A **Sensei** may be decades removed from this confusion and it may be harder for them to relate to having any problems with it. Having said this, be open to the exchange with higher belts, but check everything with your **Sensei**.

3. Lower ranked belts will follow the instruction of the higher ranked belts in the **Dojo**. They are there to help. A higher belt can keep you from making the same mistakes they made.

4. No talking during a formal class unless permitted by the **Sensei**. This is a practice that forces much internal thought.

5. Shoes are restricted on the **Dojo** floor. Respect, cleanliness, and protection of the mat material are necessary.

6. **Kyu** shall bow when entering and leaving the **Dojo**. When entering, bow once to the **Enbusen** *center of the training mat*. Then one steps on with the left foot, then the right foot,

and then bows a second time to the **Kamiza** *center of respect*. When leaving, bow once to the **Enbusen**. Then one steps off of the mat with the right foot, then the left foot, and then bows a second time to the **Kamiza**. The right side represents war and the left side represents peace; stepping on the mat with the left side first reminds each individual of the peace they are bringing to their training, while displaying to everyone the offering of peace. Stepping off with the right side first is a retraction of the war side; which displays to everyone that you leave peace in the **Dojo** where it belongs. The outside world is where war lives--never in the **Dojo**. Bowing is done during the same instances and for the same reasons as a military salute.

7. **Kyu** must wear **Gi** *proper training uniform* at all times during class. A proper uniform consists of **Kasa** *top*, **Zubon** *paints*, **Obi** *belt*, **Tabbi** *mat shoes* and a black undershirt if you are a woman. No partial **Gi**, wear the uniform properly. We should represent the **Ryu** and **Dojo** properly and respectfully care for ourselves. We must also be ready for hard training.

8. The **Gi** may not be altered; no cutoff sleeves, cutoff shorts, no add-ons (scarf, hat, gloves, hidden weapons, etc.) No substitutions; we wear the uniform, uniformly. We adhere to this so as not to stand out or disgrace the uniform or ourselves; it is a representation that we are all one martial family.

9. While class is in progress, no **Kyu** shall enter without the permission of the **Sensei**. Get changed first, then take position to the right of the entrance of the mat, on the outer

most edge, in **Seiza No Kamae** *seated kneeling position.* This position is held until you are bowed in. You are bowed in when you are welcomed to join the class. The **Sensei** or highest ranked **Kyu** acknowledges your presence by saluting you with a bow and then you respond with **Seiza Rei** *formal bow.* This is to keep order so that **Kyu** are not distracted from their training and to respectfully join a session.

10. Before you are bowed into class, you are not to interrupt those training and learning. Refrain from interaction with people in class if you are not yet in class. This shows respect for fellow students.

11. No rings, watches, piercings or other jewelry may be worn during class. Nothing is worn that could bring about outside ideas, such as fiscal superiority, some sort of fashion sense or any other thing that would be distracting to the training. Also for safety purposes, these items can catch on clothing and or skin and cause damage.

12. Never wrongfully criticize other schools or styles of the martial arts. Refrain from drama. Respect logical differences.

13. **Kyu** shall not interrupt the **Sensei** while he is teaching or training. One should bow as a salute until acknowledged, unless in emergency cases. Respect is shown for **Sensei**, the teachings being given and the learning of the **Kyu**.

14. No eating or drinking on the mat. No chewing gum. The mat is to be kept as an honored place of training and

Sogobujutsu

training with something in one's mouth is dangerous.

15. No loud outbursts, raising of voices, clapping or leaving your cell phone on with a loud disruptive ring tone. We wish to maintain a solemn atmosphere on the mat and in the **Dojo**. We don't want disruptive actions that can detract from training.

16. No lounging or sleeping on the mat. The mat is not the right place for this. Part of the training is to increase awareness; this would be counterintuitive and disrespectful.

17. Bow a weapon to the **Kamiza** *center of respect* before using it in training and bow it out when done with it. To understand the importance of this act, we can relate it to the acknowledgement of our flag. When one removes their hat, bows their head and places their right hand over their heart when viewing our national flag, the actions should be committed out of loyalty, honor, appreciation, and respect. Like a country is represented by its flag, the traditions of our martial art, **Sogobujutsu**, are represented by the **Kamiza**. It is a pause to reflect on all of those who gave their lives in the hopes that future generations would survive and, because of the knowledge they passed on, would have it easier.

18. Always pass a weapon properly to another member. Poor practices lead to poor training. In New York City, 2010, an experienced master of martial arts was held up at gunpoint. As a result of his training, he quickly disarmed the assailant. As a reflex of his poor

134

practices in the **Dojo**, he quickly handed the gun back to his attacker! This is so sad, but true. Without a thought, he did what he had always done in the **Dojo** after practicing a disarm, he handed the weapon back. On a side note, a few years prior during a cross-training seminar, a member of this same martial arts group criticized my students for stopping and bowing their weapons back to the attackers. "Forget that traditional stuff, it takes too long, just hand it back quickly," he instructed. I attempted to explain but he thought he knew better. I hope that event has helped in changing some minds.

19. When picking up a weapon off the mat, don't bend over. Instead, step over or on the weapon or tool then twist down into **Za no kamae** to uncover it from under your foot. Reach behind you and grip the weapon and stand back up. Another option is to **Kaiten** *roll* and pick it up. There are many reasons for this. If you are bending over to get the weapon, you are exposing your vitals, giving up your balance, placing yourself in an inferior and weak position that is difficult to defend from, pinning your legs down so that you cannot kick or move well, making your **Shintaiho** difficult to do (thereby making your martial art difficult to do), pinning your **Hara** back restricting its power, and taking the flexibility out of your back, legs and arms.

20. There is to be no money on the mat, although it can be carried across. No speaking of money on the mat. No leaving money around the **Dojo**. For any money concerns, see your **Kopai**. It seems that from the beginning of time money has always come between people, separating or

putting a strain on relationships. It has been best to leave money out of the Dojo as much as possible. This is done to preserve the sanctity of the **Dojo.**

21. No flaunting of money or bragging about material items in the **Dojo.** The same rationale as #20 applies to this rule. This is also done to promote brotherhood. Everyone in the **Dojo** is an equal **Fuku** member. We want everyone feeling that it is one's dedication and training that elevates them in rank. Rank and positions aside, we will always remain equal brothers in the **Ryu**.

22. No expressions of negative intent; no arguing, cursing, smacking, complaining, rolling your eyes, or turning your back to someone. Control yourself. If you cannot, ask the **Sensei** for permission to be excused from the mat. This should not need explaining.

23. No teasing or complaining about people for not following the rules. It is everyone's **Giri** duty in the **Ryu** to support one another, look out for each other and build each other up so that our **Ryu** is as strong as it can be. Anything less would not be working toward our common goal.

24. It is the responsibility of every **Fuku** *member* to help all others to understand the proper way things are done and to remind people when they forget. This is done in a kind and giving manner. As we explain these things to others, we are reminding ourselves of their importance. This is an aspect of training as well, for instance, if you notice a new student hiding their hands, then you are becoming more aware.

25. Carry yourself properly while on the mat. It is traditional to:

> not cross your arms in front of your chest
> not hide your hands (except during a technique)
> not walk behind any member unless you are a **Sensei** (if needed, remain the proper distance away from the person)

The lesson here is to increase everyone's awareness of the location of everyone around them. Also, it is a way to practice keeping track of where other people place their hands. This was taught so that the **Bugei** warrior would be able to tell if a person may be flanking them, attempting to step outside of their vision, arming themselves or drawing out a weapon. It was once commonly known that to have a chance against a trained **Bugei**, one would need the element of surprise. This was about taking away the enemy's chances; removing the option of the element of surprise.

26. When a **Sensei** or **Shihandai** calls "**Yamae**" *stop*, take position at the outer edge of the mat in **Seiza No Kamae**. Do not sit under the **kamiza**, and if you are not a **Yudansha** *black belt* do not sit on the **shomen** *front wall*. The exception to this is when one is acting as a **Sinban** *formal judge*. This is about discipline as well as positioning. When instruction starts, everyone will be able to more easily see. This gives the instructor a chance to face everyone he is instructing. Also, sitting in **Seiza No Kamae** *formal kneeling position* is truly uncomfortable. This is done so that one learns to think through pain. It trains your brain to be able to figure things out as you are hearing the instructor teach all the while enduring

through discomfort. The mind becomes clouded when feeling pain and, unless trained properly, one will not be able to think, respond, react, or even act at all. It is common knowledge in **Budo** *martial arts* that one can, through some sort of attack, occupy the enemy's mind with pain. Pain can daze, startle, and own you. For instance, if someone choked you, without being used to the feelings of distress, without being trained to think, you would not think. Even though you know how to reverse, counter and dominate over the assailant, you wouldn't, you couldn't. Because of this human condition, every time you are being instructed, you are also being trained to think through pain. **Seiza No Kamae** was chosen for many reasons. It is not only uncomfortable, but it is constantly increasingly uncomfortable. This is not something one can easily get used to. The pain is real, but the act is not damaging to the body. It is quite the opposite. This practice increases blood flow and overall circulation. This practice of endurance will prevent varicose veins and blood clotting. No other act is this uncomfortable and at the same time so beneficial. As a beginner, the instructor will not torture you with this. Little by little, you will get better and better at it. One should not sit in this way for over two hours, as this could bring about an adverse effect.

27. When a **Sensei** is instructing, and you are not helping to instruct, take position in **Seiza No Kamae** so as not to stand around and block the view of the other students. Obvious.

28. A white belt can do no wrong; a yellow belt can, so use your time as a white belt to understand our **Reigi Saho**. Get

to know it and ask questions about why it is important. Hopefully, this section will provide you with an understanding that you can later build on. Once again, **Reigi Saho** is about instilling secret training and subconscious teachings. I am covering a lot, but there is even more importance behind these practices. A great deal of it is about ingraining repetitive drilling for a multitude of later applications. **Reigi Saho** is also about discipline, but not about punishment. Often, a higher belt (yellow or orange) will assert himself, intending to help by using a demanding tone or talking down to a member about not performing **Reigi Saho** properly. This is disgraceful in my eyes. People forget, they misunderstand and they get distracted; this is what **Reigi Saho** will fix. We are here as a **Ryu** *brotherhood* to support each other. There is no need for an unkind approach. The yellow belt can do "wrong" because we look for accountability by this point in their training. By this time, you will be expected to be self-governing. If a yellow belt should slip up, we just remind them of the proper way. If an orange belt is slipping often, this must be addressed and stopped. Remember that each **Fuku** represents the whole of our **Ryu**. Each of us must do our best to represent it well.

29. If you are a **Fuku**, you are always welcome in the **Dojo** and on the mat (during a class one must be welcomed on properly and participate). There should be a sense of ownership developed. This is your **Dojo**, care for it as such.

30. When in class and asked to complete a task, one should return to training when the task is completed. Only when the

task can not be completed, take position to the right of the entrance of the mat, on the outermost edge of the mat in **Seiza No Kamae**. This position is held until you are bowed in; being bowed in represents the understanding that the task needs more attention. In this way, you will be communicating without interrupting the class. Obvious.

31. Request to be excused before leaving the mat during class. Walking out on a class can easily get one expelled from the **Dojo**. It was always considered insulting to classmates, as well as to the instructor. If you **Rei** *salute* and ask, then things cannot be misinterpreted.

32. No bare feet on the mat. Traditionally, this was very improper and seen as being unclean. I know in this country everyone goes barefoot, but it is not sanitary. We place our face and hands on the mat. This is not a place for sweaty, stinky bare feet. I like this tradition; we lock people with our legs and feet, I, for one, don't want a bare foot on my neck or under my face. Buy some **Tabbi** *traditional mat shoes* and wear them.

33. No training under the influence. I don't care if you think it would be cool or if you think it would be great training. No, it would not be; it would be dangerous and irresponsible.

34. When injured or sick you may still participate in classes. Participation is self-governed; you should remain in your comfort zone. No one will push you to do anything you can not do, but use wise discretion. Coming while sick may be a great way to pass disease. Pushing yourself when

you are hurt may damage things further.

35. There is no gender on the mat. Treat people the same while respecting anatomical differences. Men sometimes feel the need to take it easy on women. If you fake anything, you are not helping. Instead, you are hurting by instilling a sense of false confidence. On the other hand, women often feel they need to show men up. Doing this may cause injury. We remain equals in our **Ryu**.

36. No creating of rules or etiquette. If it is not a part of this list, it is not a part of **Reigi Saho** and does not exist. Sounds silly, but this one comes up a lot. Before you believe someone who has been here longer, check this list.

A large part of **Saho** *etiquette* is **Reiho** *bowing methods*. This aspect is forever overlooked by modern martial arts practices. Without this proper training, the necessary developed ability is never reached. This is the practice of counter balancing oneself. In a bow, one makes their center of balance small by placing their heels together. This is the practice of a worst case scenario--starting with little to no balance. We then bend at the waist, which is referred to as **Koshi kudaki** *breaking the midsection of the body*. This is practiced to retain **Taiseigo** *proper body alignment* while under duress. In combat, you will be pushed, pulled, and struck. The most common effect is to be placed off balance. With the presence of **Reiho** within training, you will be prepared to quickly regain balance. Even the small points of **Reigisaho** bring with them great understanding.

Important **Kanji**
Dojo to Ryu to Budo Kanji
Important Translation of Japanese Calligraphy

Mon: "family symbol"
- **Go:** "five"
- **Dai:** "big"

(the big five universal elements of creation)
- **Shin:** "Spirit of" or intention

(spirit behind or intention behind)
- **Do:** "way"
- **Jo:** "description"

(martial arts home)
- **Ne**
- **Ji**

(spiraling)
- **Gek** "intensity"
- **Ken** "blade" or "edge"

(live spirit or intense intention, blade or edge)
- **Ryu** "martial arts family"
- **So**
- **Go**

(Integration)
- **Bu** "warrior"
- **Jutsu** "art form"

All together: **Ryumon- Godaishin Dojo-
Neji Gekken Ryu- Sogobujutsu**

Chapter 4

Warrior Ideology

Rank and brotherhood

When you train in the martial arts, you put your trust in your **Sensei**'s hands. This trust includes lending your body up for instructional purposes. In skilled hands, when you are joint-locked, choked, thrown, punched and kicked, you immediately become comfortable having witnessed firsthand what could have happened to you and how the skill of your **Sensei** prevented you from becoming injured.

Training with classmates is normally not as easy.

2011 Nevin Moyer Jr. Displays **Tsuebojutsu** with Jack Toole

This comfort and trust usually takes a bit longer to attain. The beginner is not quick to trust the other students because they may have been training longer. The more accomplished student is certainly not quick to lend his body to the toiling of a novice. This process is not just about getting to know others common reactions and movements. You eventually share a great deal of yourself with your classmates. They learn your hang-ups, fears, and frustrations. They share your desires, drive, and passion for martial study. They are there to lend new perspective, pushing you to go further faster and share first hand in your successes. You learn to draw off of each other's strengths and support each other through forging out weakness. Culture, race, and sex--all of these things fall by the wayside. What you find left is brotherhood.

Brotherhood is something that happens as a result of each individual's own dedication to attaining proficiency in the art. Everyone sees the dedication to **Sogobujutsu**, **Sensei**, and the **Godaishin Dojo** as you continue attending classes. This is done, obviously, so that you may learn and grow. A more selfless side quickly evolves as you find yourself also making classes so that your training partner has you to train with. We often see that within one's own drive to earn rank, something else emerges, a sense of responsibility for your training partner to attain rank. To display rank is a return on a successful investment made by you and those who worked in helping you learn the material.

144

Building Leaders in our **Ryu**

I speak a lot about the differences between what a leader is and what a follower is. I am interested in teaching this art to nothing but leaders.

Taken in 2010 during a class while I was teaching **Ninin Gata**. Erin O'Neil and Nevin Moyer Jr. were **Uke**.

A **Kyu** will have trouble with this and most **Kyu**, at least when starting out, are followers. This is expected, but when a **Kyu** learns (in part) what he knows to be right, this should become something to stand behind; it will become a place to lead from. For instance, a member who has reached the position of **Ku-kyu** should then lead from that position.

The problem is when **Kyu** are confused about their place in the **Ryu**. In a **Ryu**, one's place is earned, not given. One must be leading from this (learned and then earned)

Displaying spine locking three men. Taken during an international martial arts demonstration in 2008. The event was held at the Bethlehem **Hombu Dojo.**

position. Too often in the **Dojo** I see newcomers attempting to correct higher belts, this is a common trait in white belts in any **Shibu** *martial arts training group.* This should push the higher belts to (nicely and caringly) put the younger **Kyu** in their place. I see this as a difficult thing for **Kyu** to do. I see them struggling with what action to take: on one hand I should lead, on the other hand, I must remain humble.

It is simple, by holding a rank in the **Ryu**, you are asked to uphold that amount of stature. This must be

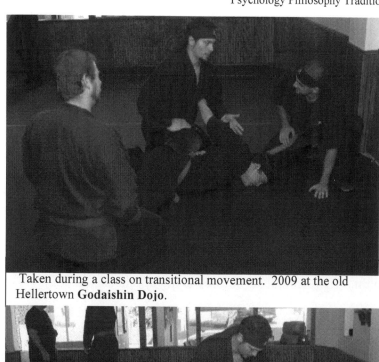

Taken during a class on transitional movement. 2009 at the old Hellertown **Godaishin Dojo**.

balanced with humility, but the search to remain humble must not come between you and that which is expected of the role you play in our **Ryu**. There are a great many roles in a **Ryu**, one for each member. Your job is to play out your role,

147

or as my brother is fond of quoting, "Know your role!" In this way, the power and responsibility is distributed among each of us, which is much better than a dictatorship. A **Sensei** need never become a dictator if everyone upholds their rank and thereby supports their **Ryu**, **Dojo** and **Sensei**. I have seen **Shibu** that were led by his or her **Sensei** and I would much rather have a true **Dojo** that was self-governing in which everyone "toed the line".

I have heard members telling each other, "If you know what needs to be done, do it!" Although I do like this and understand that it comes from good intentions, I would rather you assume that if they are not already doing the task that you know needs to be done, then they need it explained again. Therefore, lead before asking another to do so.

Never forget the meaning of rank. It is not for boasting, it is for leading. As you lead, be just in doing so. I heard a middle-ranked **kyu** during class explaining **Aiki** to another **Kyu**. This was not something learned nor was it earned. Why, then, would you step outside of your role as a middle-ranked **Kyu**? Ego, perhaps? I am not sure. Remember this, to be a good leader it is important to know when to follow.

I worked as a stonemason years ago and my **Uchideshi** was my boss on certain jobs. Of course, I remained his **Sensei**, but as a stonemason it was not my role to lead. Jacob had learned much more about this and earned the position as boss. I know when to follow; I don't have a problem with it and try never to speak outside of my own understanding. I would only ask for my **Kyu** to do the same.

148

I am pushing people to lead, you should know when to follow. This is not humility, it is honesty. Be honest with

Taken during a class on **Ninin Nage** 2007 in the backyard of the Bethelhem **Hombu Dojo**. Erin O'Neil and Justin Hankins were **Uke**.

yourself. Do you have an understanding of the topic? If you can't be honest with yourself, it is only a matter of time until you will be dismissed as a **Kyu** of our **Dojo**. If you are not honest, you cannot lead properly.

Let us build on what we have in order to make sure people are growing into positive new leaders of the art.

Service
The foundation of Samurai nobility

The word "**Samurai**" means to serve. The
Samurai's lives were based in service; service to their
Daimyo *lord of the land*, clan, and family. This was the

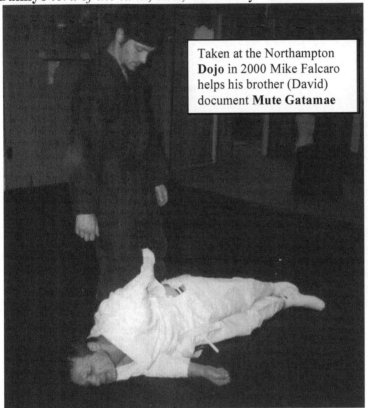

Taken at the Northampton
Dojo in 2000 Mike Falcaro
helps his brother (David)
document **Mute Gatamae**

inner circle that gave them their life's purpose. There was a
reason for selflessness, for caring more for others and their
needs, than for one's own needs. They would gladly do
without if it meant taking care of their family, **Daimyo**, or

150

clan. This was a point of **Giri** *duty and obligation* for the **Samurai**.

A life with purpose was most important. Life was too important to live without meaning. The forging of the self through learning, growing, and training is what encompassed the **Samurai**'s life. The reason for the forging of the self

Taken before we had a **Dojo** in 1999 **Mute Gatamae**

was to create and become a powerful tool to be used in selfless action. To give freely of the self so that the cause will live on was an embraced philosophy. This is what elevated him beyond the common man.

One could debate me in stating that a **Samurai** fought for honor. This is true, and

151

the honor he fought for was his own, but this was not ego. Instead, it was honor to reflect service accomplished.

That was then and this is now. The life teachings of thousands of **Samurai** birthed the ideals of the **Budoka** *martial artist*. **Budoka**, for many generations, have held true to living life with **Samurai** virtues. As it is our time to live, we must embrace these virtues.

A focus on **Giri** has its effects in one's own personal life. When **Giri** is the driving force of one's actions, it can make the trials of life become resolved more easily. Our perception of events in our lives dictates our reaction to them. Perception stems from the self and the self is to be geared toward one's **Giri**.

As teenagers, we rebel because we feel we know

Taken in a class on multiple attackers in 2009. Jack Toole deals with Erin O'Neal attacking while I blind him with the flash of the camera. **Soto Irimi** while applying **Mute Gatamae** at the Northampton **Godaishin Dojo.**

what is right for us and no longer need others' opinions on how we are going to live our lives.

My father is a wise man. To quote him, "It is more important to be loving than to be right."

As adults, many of us make judgments taking into account whose ideas, hopes and dreams matter most in this world--our own.

My **Sensei** once asked me, "Why does your opinion matter so much to you? It should matter least of all to you."

Are you only living this life for yourself? Where is your **Giri**? I ask my students to live this art and not to fake it.

Taken during class at the old Hellertown **Dojo** in 2009 Teaching Joe Pitsko **Shi Te Gata**

Selflessness makes the **Samurai** noble. These ideas are so strange to us in the West. Nobility is something that seemingly does not exist here. In our wonderful land, all men are created equal. Yes, created equal, then we grow into different types of people.

One could argue that we are all fibers from the same thread, all the same in God's eyes, spiritually one, made from one consciousness. Yes, in a spiritual sense, we are one, but

153

remember **Inyoho** *the methods of this reality's duality.* So
we are, so we are not. As physical beings, we are connected
and may be disconnected. In this world of dualism, we must
strive for both. Basically, connect ourselves to our desired
intent and stray away from roles we trap ourselves in which
hinder the expression of our true nature. We may have to
play different roles, but don't let the role alter your intention.

Taken during the **Jihi Bujutsu Kai** 2007 **Taikai** while demonstrating cognitive locking on Jacob B. Fouts **Sensei.**

To be a **Budoka** is to be a noble man. This nobility is earned
as a result of living up to the virtues set forth by one's **Giri**.
One's **Giri** encompasses many things, none so pronounced as
service. As **Budoka**, we must forge ourselves as did the
Samurai to become more powerful tools for the purposes of
breaking through the confines set forth by our own ego, to
find freedom in the expression of selfless action, and to live
the life of a noble man.

154

Meek but not weak

Do not allow your humility to combat your confidence. Humility is used to destroy the ego, but should not get in the way of what is true. Some feel that to become humble, one must downplay what they can do. To talk down one's own ability is not an action of humility, it is merely a distortion of the truth. As a warrior, one stands steadfast and confident in his knowing of what has been accomplished within his life up to this point. This brings to mind the warrior concept of **Fudoshin** *immovable spirit.* This ideology dictates that a warrior remains unwavering in his approach to overcoming adversity. A warrior remains confident in his understanding of the extent of his capability.

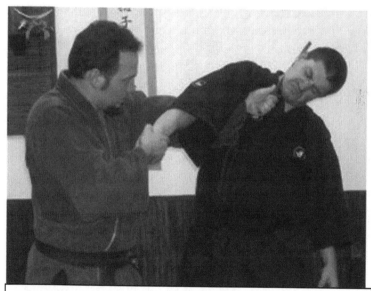

Teaching cognitive rotation and seizing with the **Jutte.** Jack Toole training as **Uke** in 2011 at a **Shihandai** class. Hellertown **Godaishin Dojo**.

To find humility, one must understand the capacity of possibility. Anything is possible. It is said that "sometimes even monkeys fall out of trees". I believe mastery is for the moment and each moment is different. We tend to judge ourselves on what we believe we are capable of doing, the rest of the world tends to judge us only on what we have already done. I personally have survived some nasty spills. When I was 18 years old, I slipped on ice while running outside of a restaurant. As my head speared toward the ground, I saved myself with **Zempo Kaiten** (our forward roll). An example of confidence versus humility is illustrated here:

1) I undoubtedly possess the ability to save myself from falling. I am confident in this ability as a result of years of training and this instance reaffirms the fact that my **Sensei** trained me well. **Here's the confidence.**

2) When looking at the capacity of possible outcomes to this situation, I feel humbled and thankful that I was not injured. Many things could have altered this scenario, changing the outcome to me smacking my head into the ground. **Here's the humility.**

As we develop our warrior-selves, we must remain meek, strong and truthful. We must rely on using true confidence (backed by experience) and true humility (backed by the understanding that there is so much greater than the self) in order to paint an accurate picture of who we are now. We will use this view as a starting block, to push off of so that we may learn from a solid point of reference. From here, we can grow with ease.

Honorific Titles

Titles such as **Shidoshi, Shihan, Soke**, etc. are not spoken terms. They originally served one purpose: to make people outside of the **Ryu** aware of the hierarchy of the **Ryu**. Therefore, one should neither refer to someone by these terms, nor should one ask someone to refer to them by these terms. In older times, the reason it was unspoken was that it was obvious to everyone in the **Ryu**. When you contact someone in another **Ryu** (a **Ryu** you don't know the structure of) it is very important to know exactly who to send information to. This is where it becomes necessary to address the title.

Showing **Suwari Waza** David C. Falcaro **Sensei** and Nevin Moyer Jr., **Mute Hiza Gatamae** at the Hellertown **Godaishin Dojo.** 2012

Imagine you start work at a store. You are new, so you have no title. However, in your store there is a manager, assistant manager, and maybe even a 2nd assistant manager. Also, the district manager stops by frequently, as does the regional manager and once a year you see the president of the company. You would call each of these people "Sir" or "Ma'am". It would be strange to call them by their titles. It would be very strange if a person asked you to call him 2nd assistant manager. Yet, in the martial arts nowadays, this happens frequently. The truth is, "Sir" or "Ma'am" are satisfactory titles, as is **Sensei**.

Nowadays, people forget this cultural phenomenon and insist that others call them **Shihan**, **Reshi**, **O'sensei** or **Soke**. I am unsure of the reason for this. However, if I had to guess, I would say that it was not out of pride that this trend began, rather it was an attempt to make sense of Japanese culture by American military personnel. Military culture is the only culture I am aware of that asks (even demands) that people refer to you by your title. They, of course, were some of the first martial artists to bring Japanese culture to the United States after World War II and the American occupation of Japan. It was seen and taught through a lens of American military protocol. This is an honest mistake, if it is, in fact, the way things happened. However, most martial artists today are not military personnel, nor do they understand the oddness of calling someone **Shihan**. This is a shame because it gives otherwise decent people an opportunity to be prideful, which is, of course, the last thing a martial artist wants to cultivate.

The Martial Arts Experience

David C. Falcaro **Sensei** Taken during **Tamaeshi Giri** practice 2010

In the martial arts today, one finds many things. We, at the **Godaishin Dojo**, offer something different. We are a Neoclassical **Sogobujutsu**. What this means is that we have a new continually evolving approach on the older, **Koryu**, martial arts. This approach comes from the working understanding of the **Oyo** *application* of old martial art methodology.

Our approach is very different from the martial arts commonly seen today. To understand how different, we must examine what is in the public eye, what is being taught and where did it stem from?

To understand **Sogobujutsu**, we will leave it up to you to make a comparative analysis. To help you do this, we must come to an understanding of what martial arts were, what it is currently and where the trends are taking us within the martial arts.

Within the past six decades, we have run into many "**Do**" martial arts that have traveled to the U.S. from Japan. These "**Do**" (pronounced "dough") arts are now found all over, in every state and almost every city. They include: **Karate-do, Aikido, Judo, Iaido, Battodo, Kendo, Fukidakedo, Shurikendo, Kyudo, Naginatado, Yarido, Jodo**, and others. These are the modern fragmentation of the older ideal that was **Sogobujutsu**. In the ancient **Sogobujutsu**, the **Bugei** *warriors* practiced all forms of combat in one art. If we take a look at its components, we can easily see from which these new arts sprang.

160

Arts within the study of **Sogobujutsu**	The break up into modern arts

Dakentaijutsu AKA **Karatejutsu**...................**Karatedo**
Aikijujutsu AKA **Aikijutsu**.............................**Aikido**
Jutaijutsu AKA **Jujutsu**....................................**Judo**
Iaijutsu...**Iaido**
Battojutsu..**Battodo**
Kenjutsu...**Kendo**
Fukiya AKA **Fukidakejutsu**....................**Fukidakedo**
Shurikenjutsu..**Shurikendo**
Kyujutsu..**Kyudo**
Naginatajutsu...**Naginatado**
Sojutsu AKA **Yarijutsu**..................................**Yarido**
Shinbojutsu AKA **Jojutsu**..................................**Jodo**
Tanbojutsu AKA **Tanjojutsu** AKA **Yubibojutsu**..**Kobotan**
Tsuebojutsu..**Tsuebo**

These new arts are a shadow of the old arts. Instead of focusing on everything within the study of the warrior arts, they took a piece and became specialized. Many older arts were overlooked and never became modern studies. With the arts that did become modernized, this specialized thinking became popularized. Many traits have changed from the "**Jutsu**" *martial art of* to the "**Do**" *martial way of.* New ideas formed and new movements; things evolved from arts of "war and peace" into arts of "defense and sport". These new "**Do**" arts are less than one hundred and fifty years old, yet they received greater followings than many of the older arts. The new arts have become so popular that **Koryu**, for a time, was forgotten about. This can be attributed to many reasons:

161

Teaching my student Jacob B. Fouts **Sensei Mute Gatamae** *no handed locks* with the **Hanbo** *three foot staff* when he first began his training. Taken before we had a **Dojo** in 1999.

1) It is a smaller study. What would have taken someone nine years to become proficient, can be two or three years of study now that the art is broken into many pieces. 2) A lot of mystique surrounds many of the "**Do**" arts. **Zen** became a stronger influence for many of them. The focus moved toward enlightened perfection. This is found in arts such as **Aikido, Iaido, Battodo, Shurikendo, Kyudo, Jodo**, and

Naginatado. 3) Sport became the ideal. The goal of competition, trophies, titles, and medals became a strong draw for many. This is found in arts such as **Karate-do, Judo, Kendo,** and **Fukidakedo.** 4) Time became an issue. For many, an art that is a lifestyle became too much to ask. In the modern age, these new artforms created a place for martial arts to be a hobby. Practitioners need not live a certain lifestyle to become a viable martial artist today. 5) In a time of general peace, why train for war? For many, the idea of **Sogobujutsu** became too much to learn. For the modern practitioner, there was seemingly no purpose.

After a little while, Korean practitioners then duplicated many of the modern "**Do**" arts in order to create a Korean martial arts system.

The Japanese "**Do**" Martial Arts	The Korean Counterparts
Karatedo..Tae Kwon Do
Aikido...Hapkido
Judo...Yudo
Kendo...Kumdo
Kyudo...Koong Shi Do
Iaido..Shim Soo Do
Jodo..Jung Bong
Kobotan...Tahn Bong
Tsuebo..Ji Pang E

These Korean martial arts were also blended together to create other Korean martial arts. Hapkido and Tae Kwon Do were blended to found arts such as Tang Soo Do, and Mu Do Kwon. There are many distinctive differences in the

163

Korean martial arts that are completely Korean derived. Some of the obvious differences are much higher kicks and a lot of aerial movements.

The blending together of martial arts is the new thing to sweep the nation. This can be attributed to two main reasons:

1) People are attempting to make a name for themselves. Why remain training under an instructor when you could invent your own style of martial arts and become the "Grandmaster" of it? There are governing bodies of the martial arts that exist to weed through the inventors. Instead of attempting to become legitimate through these organizations, the creators and originators tend to just band together and start their own governing institutions.

Teaching my **Shihandai** a Neck break and shoulder/ spine lock from **Suwari Waza** 2011 Hellertown **Godaishin Dojo.**

2) For some it has again become important to train for more than just hobby. Some modern **Ryu** train for real life and death encounters. Groups like these are attempting to blend the "**Do**" arts back together. The

purpose behind this blending is to be more equipped to deal with an array of combative solutions.

Ed Hall III and Eric Coberly showing some **Kenjutsu** during our New Hellertown **Godaishin Dojo** Grand Opening demonstration in 2010.

There seems to be a growing resurgence back to the old ways. In my opinion, this is what is needed today. If one wants to be equipped to deal with any attack, then one must study all forms of combat. I believe as people find out about the older **Koryu** martial arts, the outlook on martial arts will shift toward the **Koryu** teachings.

As far as our lineage and the **Neji Gekkin Ryu**, there was never a need to shift with trends of the times. The view of **Sogobujutsu** was, and is, a constant and consists of training in all aspects of warrior combat. This is what is focused on and taught at the **Godaishin Dojo**.

Inspirational Sayings

"I always have a weapon as long as the ground remains beneath my feet."
~Common **Jujutsu** saying

"Whether the enemy knows it or not we are working together to kill him."
~David C. Falcaro

"It's not how hard I can hit you, it's how hard I can get you to run into
the hit." ~**Katsumi Tanemura**

"Grab like a man not like a monkey." ~**Katsumi Tanemura**

"Many faces, one art." ~David C. Falcaro

"Don't worry, the ground will always be there to catch you."~ Edward J.
Smith

"I do not look to authority for truth, but look to truth for authority."
~**Kengi Kataro**

"Die a thousand deaths a night (in training) in order to survive the day."
~old **Shinobi** saying

"Interrupt his fall with a throw." ~**Katsumi Tanemura**

"The body will react in the method in which it is trained." ~David C.
Falcaro

"Now that you have grabbed me, I will not let you go." ~Edward J. Smith

(When training outsiders) "If it is something they can get, simplify it.
When it is something they will never attain, over explain it." ~David C.
Falcaro

"First, when beginning, the student makes the technique; then he looks
for the technique; in time, he finds the technique; then he sees the
technique; and eventually, he falls into the technique." ~David C. Falcaro

"Every strength is a weakness and every weakness a strength."
~Common martial arts saying

"First done for love, next for the **Ryu**, then for myself." ~Old **Budo**
Saying

"You don't need the rope and bucket to draw the water from the well,
merely jump in." ~David C. Falcaro

"Weapons away, and now we play." ~David C. Falcaro

"Do the technique fifty times, then ask me that question." ~Jacob B.
Fouts

"Just shut up and train." ~Jacob B. Fouts

"If I am this great master that you say I am, it is because I have had the
distinct honor and privilege of standing on the shoulders of giants!"
~**Katsumi Tanemura**

"Techniques merely point out the direction to the principles." ~**Katsumi
Tanemura**

"The life and death of a technique begins and ends within a breath." ~
Said by many

"If a technique did not work, it died long ago with the man that attempted
it." ~**Yoshida Kataro**

"One man's attack is another man's weapon." ~Eric P. Fichter

"An ant understands **Taisabaki** better than a man." ~**Katsumi
Tanemura**

"An obese man has no option, they all remain aligned as they walk."
~David C. Falcaro

"Move with shoulder, hip, and heel." ~**Sokaku Takeda**

Sogobujutsu

"When a warrior encounters a wall, he moves around it. When he can't, he goes around the other side. When he can't, he climbs over. If he can't, he digs under it. If this proves impossible, he smashes through it." ~Old **Bugei** philosophy

"Hear where there is no sound, see where there is no form." ~**Sokaku Takeda**

"I first see the enemy when I leave the gates." **Sokaku Takeda**

"A warrior without a code is like having a missile without a guidance system." ~David C. Falcaro

"If careless, even a master can lose to an amateur." ~**Sokaku Takeda**

"The secret of **aiki** is to freeze the enemy mentally at first glance, thereby winning without a fight." ~**Sokaku Takeda**

"Dictate terms from a position of dominance." ~Edward J. Smith

"The only thing the enemy decides is how he is going to die." ~David C. Falcaro

"The greater the task, the maker the man must be, the sharper is skill, the humbler is heart." ~**Tanomo Saigo**

Taken in 2003 while teaching a seminar on **Tanbojutsu** and **Kaishi Waza**. Demonstrating with Jacob B. Fouts **Sensei**. In the background, a very young Anthony Rodriguez

168

The **Jihi Bujutsu Kai**

The JBK was formed for the purpose of extending our martial arts family. It is our outreach program of sorts. This is done to find a kinship with others outside of our **Ryu** and also to promote an extended brotherhood. The **Kai** *martial arts organization* consists of many **Ryu** outside of our own. The way it works is that many **Ryu** are members within the **Kai**. If you are a member of one of these **Ryu**, then you are, in turn, a member of the **Jihi Bujutsu Kai**. The meaning of the JBK  translates as the "benevolent warrior arts organization". I have included a great deal of material on the JBK so that everyone may understand its workings. The fact that every one of us are members, and that the **Neji Gekken Ryu** heads our **Kai**, means that each one of our members should possess at least a basic understanding of the JBK's ins and outs.

The **Jihi Bujutsu Kai** was founded in 2002 with one premise--education. Through educating each other about our differences, we find understanding. This understanding translates into appreciation. The organization is geared toward fellowship primarily in the Japanese-derived warrior arts. It is an organization not only for the instructors, but also for the students to experience and enjoy. This brotherhood has grown throughout the years to become what it is today, an example of respect, honor, and camaraderie for today's serious martial artist.

JBK MISSION STATEMENT:

It is the goal as instructors, directors, members and any representative of the **Jihi Bujutsu Kai**, to strive for excellence in ourselves and within the study of our martial art. The main ideals of the JBK are brotherhood, support and the promotion of the martial arts. We also strive to share personal understanding and appreciate differences of opinions on martial arts. The JBK will not provide black belt certificates and certifications, student rank certificates and certifications, black belt promotions, or instructor certification. We will, however, provide organization and **Dojo** charters.

Programs, classes, course content and certification are up the individual instructing members association. Furthermore, the JBK does not get involved in ranking whatsoever. As instructors, directors, members or any representative, we strive for continued growth, expansion and the success of the JBK through our active participation and support of each other and the functions sanctioned by the JBK.

In addition, we seek to perpetuate ethics, morals, and cultural understanding as prescribed in the philosophy of older martial arts. We will combat ignorance, prejudice, and hate. We will accomplish this through acceptance and open mindedness.

JBK MEMBER RULES

All members will conduct themselves in a manner that reflects the philosophy of the JBK and the old ideals of the martial arts. Character, morals, ethics, and humility are all attributes expected and asked of our members.

The head of each **Ryu** reserves freedom to mandate his own curriculum. It must be a quality martial arts curriculum or you will not be accepted as a member; we have a somewhat elitist point of view on this issue. The only time the JBK will supersede is when a particular school is using unsafe or an immoral training practice and when this puts the JBK in some liable, illegal or immoral position.

Certification of rank will not be granted certifying the current rank to those who wish to certify their rank through the JBK. Such certification should be attained through training

under one's own instructor. If you are interested in finding an instructor in order to expand your knowledge, take your pick. All of our instructing members are of the highest caliber and are quite skilled in their fields of study.

Each member may be a member of another martial arts organization of their choosing while still retaining membership with the JBK so long as that organization does not conflict with the moral and ethical code of the JBK.

Expulsion has to be for just cause. Four instructing members in agreement, in accordance with the rules concerning behavior, can determine this. Each board member is equal in their vote and ideas submitted regardless of rank or age. One does not pertain to the other.

171

MEMBERSHIP INTO THE JBK

1. Anyone may apply for membership to the **Jihi Bujutsu Kai** regardless of style, rank or previous or current association affiliation.

2. All applicants must complete membership forms and provide proof of current rank (certificates/scrolls).

3. There is to be no paying of membership fees. Memberships cannot be bought.

4. Members may receive a membership certificate and association patch.

5. Members are eligible to advertise on the **Jihi Bujutsu Kai** website free of charge. Submissions must be made in advance to ensure web publication.

6. Membership entitles the member to discounts on all video training material, seminars, tournaments & training camps sponsored by the JBK. Members are eligible to become State Director or Province Directors.

JBK EXPECTATIONS AND DUTIES

Members are asked to act as ambassadors in their region. This is for the JBK to perpetuate its growth. Members are also asked to act as representatives on behalf of the JBK in their region or local community.

Members are asked to serve as instructors and mentors to members who join the JBK (if needed) in their region under their own direction.

2010 Taken during Eric P. Fichter **Sensei**'s **Menkyo** *teachers certification* test. A depiction of a **Suwari Nage** *ground throw.* One of my favorite photos because a man is being tossed with a concussive throw, and if you look at my students in the background, everyone is paying attention and no one seems surprised. It makes me smile.

Members are asked to help the **Kai** in dispersing any information concerning training and events sponsored by or under the direction of the JBK.

Instructing members are expected to hold lifetime memberships and **Dojo** charters.

173

Members should take it upon themselves to contact each other on a regular basis to discuss updates, changes in policy, delegation of duties, new members and other business matters concerning the JBK.

The goal of the JBK is to serve each other in brotherhood, not to perpetuate status through titles and rank.

JBK EXECUTIVE MEMBERS OF THE BOARD

The Executive Board is made up of many members. These positions are filled with at least one member of each **Ryu**. They would most likely be the highest ranking member of that **Ryu**, the **Soke** *head inheritor of Ryu*, founder or the Chairperson of the **Ryu**. Executive Members may also include someone of high rank (usually master level). This person will act as an executive officer and speak on behalf of their **Ryu**.

JBK MEMBERSHIP FEES

Membership fees are kept at a minimum to ensure everyone wishing to apply and join the JBK will have an opportunity to do so.

Initial Annual **Kyu** (Under Black Belt) Membership - $0.00
Annual Renewal - $0.00
Initial Annual Yudansha (Black Belt) Membership - $0.00
Annual Renewal - $0.00

Dojo Charter - $0.00

Lifetime Membership - $0.00

We don't want your money; we want something more meaningful than that, a lifelong friendship.

174

Chapter 5

Historical Influences

Our historical origins

Special thanks to Jack Toole for helping in the completion of the knowledge found in this section. This knowledge came from many years of **Kuden** *direct transmissions, training and interviews with one's* **Sensei**.

We as a **Ryu**, practice **Sogobujutsu**. We are the integration

Taken in 2010 while teaching a class on **Ninin Gata**. Terri Schuon is training the form on Erin O'Neil and Nevin Moyer Jr.

of the knowledge derived from **Koryu** *Samurai-derived warrior arts family traditions*. From these many **Ryu**, we have attained a number of influences as well as techniques from them. Our **Waza** *techniques*, **Ho** *methods*, **Gata** *forms*, **Undo** *drills*, and **Jutsu** *fields of study* all stem from these **Ryu**. Aside from their uniqueness of each specific **Waza**, **Ho**, **Gata**, **Undo**, and **Jutsu**, they are also the source of our principal conceptual movement and **Zokusei** *attribution* must be conveyed. This is the focus of this section. As I list the **Ryu** who have the largest influences in our art, I will not be focusing on their specific **Waza**, **Ho**, **Gata**, **Undo**, or **Jutsu**, which we have attained from them. Instead, I will primarily be explaining the birthplace of our principle-based conceptual movement.

Throughout the progression of this section, we will list the **Ryu** in order of the amount of influence we have received from them. Attributing credit where credit is due is an important thing to note. The list of our primary influences is as follows: **Tagakishin Ryu**, **Daito Ryu**, **Muraha Yoshin Ryu**, **Tàkenouchi Ryu**, **Kukishin Ryu**, **Kosin Ryu**, **Koto Ryu**, **Fusin Ryu**, and the **Gyoko Ryu**. Our secondary influences are **Ono Ha Itto Ryu**, **Yagu Ryu**, **Esshin Ryu**, **Shindo Muso Ryu**, **Shin No Shindo Ryu**, **Pheonix Ninpo Ryu / Genbukan**, and **Nagano Ryu**. These are the **Ryu** that have influenced and inspired how we move today.

Tagakishin Ryu, Gendai Aikibudo

The **Tagakishin Ryu** is the main source of our knowledge. It is through our lineage with them that we find transmission of most all of the **Koryu** knowledge passed through to us. Other than these facts, the **Tagakishin Ryu** uniquely influences our **Ryu**:

176

- **Goho No Oyo** *the harsh combative application of martial practices*
- Principle-derived movement
- Competent combat training methods
- The passing of one **Ryu**'s principle toward the application of another **Ryu**'s technique
- The melding of many understandings
- A translating of application from **Ryu** to **Ryu**
- Applying **Hara**, **Tai Ate** and **Koshi Mawari** to everything
- Angle of applied pressure in locking, breaking, throwing and so on
- Much of our understanding of what **Sogobujutsu** is
- An up-to-date application for very old time tested methods

Daito Ryu, Aikibujutsu

Daito Ryu is a large influence on our **Ryu**. As well as a vast amount of technique, **Daito Ryu** is the main source of our **Taijutsu Tachi Waza**, **Ne Waza**, **Katame Waza**, **Kensetsu Waza**, and **Soden waza**.

Aside from **Waza**, **Daito Ryu** gives us many things.

Among them are:
- **Nagiri** *proper grip*
- A large influence in our **Shintaiho**
- General **Kazushi** *using direction to off balance*
- Cognitive rotation
- Cognitive locking
- Cognitive pressure
- **Aiki**
- **Aiki No jutsu**

177

- **Aiki Meioden**
- **Hando No Kazushi** *using the enemy's natural reaction to off balance*
- Sending the **Uke** over the barrier
- Drawing the **Uke** to the barrier
- Making the **Uke**'s body his own barrier
- Making the **Uke**'s body a barrier for another **Uke**
- Overall form in application

Muraha Yoshin Ryu, Koden Jujutsu

We have a great deal of influence from the **Yoshin Ryu**. Aside from many **Waza**, the **Yoshin Ryu** gives us many traits.

Among them are:
- Applied motion of directed falling from **Tori** into **Uke** for the purpose of positioning, **Koshi Kudaki**, **Nage**, and **Kazushi**
- Some entangling application of **Shiko**
- Accents on our **Jutaijutsu**
- Transitional throws from our **Tachi Waza** into **Ne Waza**
- Influence of **Ne Waza Nage Waza** and **Suwari Waza**

Takenouchi Ryu, Koden Bujutsu

The **Takenouchi Ryu** is fourth in the list of our primary influences. We received many **Waza** from them. For instance, they are the main source of our **Tantojutsu** and **Kikenjutsu No Waza**. They have had influence on our **Nage Waza**, **Bojutsu No Waza**, and **Kenjutsu**. They also influence us in our **Taijutsu**. The **Takenouchi Ryu** allows us other influences as well.

178

Among them are:
- Stabilization of the body
- Application of reversing the **Koshi**
- Pinpointing vitals
- Points of insertion
- Methods of targeting places to sever
- Pinning applications
- Entrapping methods

Kukishin Ryu, Koden Bujutsu

Another **Ryu** we gain influence from is the **Kukishin Ryu**. Like all the other **Ryu**, we receive many **Waza** from them. For instance, the **Kukishin Ryu** are the main source of most of our **Bojutsu** i.e. **Hanbojutsu, Rokoshakobojutsu, Sojutsu, Naginatajutsu, Jobojutsu**, and a bit of **Tanbojutsu**. Moreover, the **Kukishin Ryu** also gives us:

- Utilization of redirected impact
- How to blend and extend a weapon with attachment to the body
- Our forty-five degree angles in flanking
- Stepping or walking **Tenkan**
- Redirecting force
- Influenced our **Taijutsu** as in treating a body as a staff

Kosen Ryu, Koden Jujutsu

We receive many things from the **Kosen Ryu**. They are one of the largest sources of many of our **Nage Waza** as well as having a small influence on our **Somoho**. Aside from

Waza, we also receive many traits from them.

Among them are:
- Dip, bump, and twist
- Push pull and how it relates to **Kazushi**
- **Happo No Kazushi**
- Twisting and stepping and how it relates to **Kazushi**
- Setting the barrier
- Application of **Suwari Gatame Waza**
- Slipping into **Gatamae**, **Garamae** and **Kansetsu Waza**

Koto Ryu, Koden Koppojutsu

The **Koto Ryu** are our main influence in **Dakentaijutsu**. As well as **Waza**, we also receive a concept of shifting weight and an application of **Tai Ate** and **Koshi Mawari** from them.

- Points of impact
- Application in destruction and breaking of limbs
- Angle of impact
- Generating powerful attacks
- Our **Taijutsu No Kamae**
- Understanding bone breaking and bone attacks
- Understanding of resulting factors within breaking
- Setting up the body of the **Uke** to take as much impact as possible

Fusen Ryu, Koden Jujutsu

Aside from **Waza**, the **Fusen Ryu** influences us with characteristics inside our **Waza**. The largest influence from the **Fusen Ryu** can be seen in our **Suwari Waza**. We also receive the concept of setting barriers for the promotion of throws from the **Fusen Ryu**. The **Fusen Ryu** also inspires us in the attachment (**Tai Atari**) of **tori** and **uke** and how it correlates to the transfer of kinetic energy from **Tori** to **Uke**.

Gyokko Ryu, Koden Koshijutsu
The **Gyokko Ryu** is the source of many of our entanglements. The **Gyokko Ryu** also gives us the idea of wrapping for better connection to the **Uke**. We also receive accents in our **Jutaijutsu** from the **Gyokko Ryu** as well as other characteristics.

Among them are:
- Underhanded gripping
- Transitions
- Our **Taijutsu No Kamae**
- Kicking to get **Kazushi**
- Utilizing connection to apply **Koshi Kudaki**, or **Koshi Mawari** to **Uke**
- Points of impact
- Application in destruction of limbs
- Angle of impact
- Generating powerful attacks
- Understanding muscle, ligament attacks
- Understanding of resulting factors with regard to muscle reactions

Ono Ha Itto Ryu, Koden Kenjutsu
The **Ono Ha Itto Ryu** is a big influence in our **Kenjutsu**. Aside from the **Waza** they give us, we indirectly receive a concept of consistency in application of the sword and how it translates to hand to hand combat.

Yagu Ryu, Koden Kenjutsu

The **Yagu Ryu** is a small indirect influence on our **Irimi Waza**. It has a direct influence on our **Kenjutsu** and **Iaijutsu**. Beyond the techniques they give us we also receive concepts.

Among them are:
- Intercepting angles
- Line of sight
- Feeding the attack/instigating the attack
- Invitation of specific attacks
- Shortening of movements for efficiency

Esshin Ryu, Koden Kenjutsu

The **Esshin Ryu** influences our **Iaijutsu** and our **Tameshigiri**. There are no noticeable influences outside of the **Waza** we have received from them.

Shindo Muso Ryu, Koden Bojutsu

The **Shindo Muso Ryu** has a small influence on our **Jojutsu** but mainly gives us inspirational philosophies.

Shinno Shindo Ryu, Koden Jujutsu

Aside from the **Waza** we receive from them, the **Shinno Shindo Ryu** gives us spiritual inspiration and esoteric concepts.

Nagano Ryu, Gendai Aikijutsu and Gandai Ninjutsu

The **Nagano Ryu** is a large influence on our **Ninjutsu**. They provide us with teachings of obscure **Ninjutsu Waza** derived from the **Akutagawa Ryu, Tenshin Shoden Katori Shinto Ryu** and the **Ugai Koga Ryu**. We also receive concepts.

Among them are:
- Entering with **Taijutsu No Kamae**
- Inspiration on uprooting an enemy's **Hara**
- Utilizing an enemy's weakness
- **Shinobi no mono** *Ninja tactics*
- Some different ideas on the application of **Jujutsu**.
- The importance of **Buyu**

2010 Throwing three men at once during a demonstration on unheard of ability and the power of **Sogobujutsu**. Erin O'Neal, Eric Coberly, And Eric P. Fichter **Sensei** as **Uke**. David C. Falcaro **Sensei** demoing **Sannin Nage**.

This chart is a quick look at the major **Ryu** influences and the direct path which they are transmitted to us.

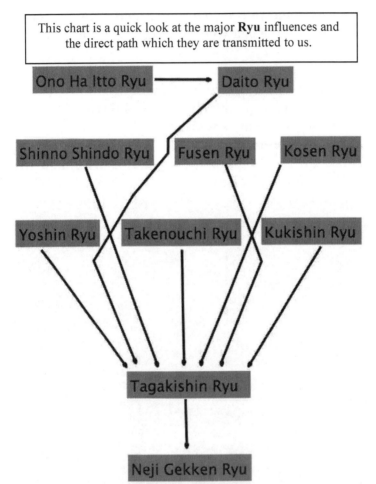

These influences have been passed through to the **Neji Gekken Ryu** directly from three independent and very separate connections. This first chart displays the strongest of the three connections--our lineage to the **Tagakishin Ryu**. This is the most important connection, being the longest, the deepest (where most of our knowledge comes from) and the hardest trained.

<u>Takagishin Ryu</u> Lineage
This is our connection to the **Tagakishin Ryu**

As a Member of the **Neji Gekken Ryu**, you are not a part of the **Takagishin Ryu**, but this is our lineage to the **Takagishin Ryu**. Because we come from a great many **Ryu**, we should not claim to be one of them. In truth, I am the only one of us that can make this claim. This is because since 1995 I have trained directly with my **Sensei** within his **Ryu** the **Takagishin Ryu**. Because the line is so close to the **Neji Gekken Ryu** line, when my **Sensei** and I pass on, as my direct descendents, you could make such a claim. Most likely, no one could dispute such a claim easily. Even the current head of the **Takagishin Ryu** would have to recognize the claim of a member of the **Neji Gekken Ryu**. This section tells the tale of the forceful birth of the **Takagishin Ryu**. It explains how this wealth of knowledge came into the United States of America. I also share all of the research I have done as of 9/29/2011 on the **Takagishin** line and our connection with it.

Katsumi Tanemura 1920-1991

Katsumi Tanemura was born to the name **Okazaki Shuji** in 1920. **Tanemura Sensei** had an affinity for martial arts at a young age. In 1928, at the age of eight, he began studying **Yoshin Ryu** and pre-sport **Judo**. His first **Judo** teacher instructed him in many ground fighting tactics from the **Fusen Ryu**. **Tanemura Sensei** loved all forms of combat. The **Fusen Ryu** was his inspiration in his execution of **Ne Waza** and **Suwari Waza**. In 1939, he started to (not

185

exclusively) use the name he is known by today **Tanemura, Katsumi**. **Tanemura Sensei** also, throughout his adulthood, referred to himself as **Tanemura Kazumi**. As a **budoka**, he is renowned for his mastery and synthesis of many different **Ryu**. His brother in law, **Tanemura Kenji** (perhaps to

impress in **Okazaki**'s sister) took an interest in the young man's passions and introduced him to **Yoshida Kataro Sensei** of the **Daito Ryu**. **Tanemura Kenji** wrote a letter of introduction and traveled with him to meet **Yoshida Sensei**. **Yoshida Kataro Sensei** was his main instructor. He trained exclusively under **Yoshida Sensei** from 1939 to 1948, during some of this time he served as his **Uchideshi**. It was because of his connection to **Kenji Tanemura** and **Kenji**'s clout in Japanese society, that **Shuji Okazaki** took his brother-in-law's name and became known as **Katsumi Tanemura**. He later trained under **Sagawa Yukiyoshi Sensei** of the **Daito Ryu** while staying in **Tokyo**. He last visited his **Sensei**, **Yoshida Kotaro Sensei** in 1953.

After 14 years of direct study, his involvement in the **Daito Ryu** had ended. From 1950 to 1955, he traveled throughout Japan and studied **Shin No Shindo Ryu Jujutsu** among other **Ryu**. His primary focus at this time was **Takenouchi Ryu**. One of two men referred to as "Mr. **Takenouchi**" (we are not sure which one) of the **Takenouchi Ryu**, became another of his instructors. Before long, he met **Tatsuta Yasuichiro Sensei** and began learning from him **Kukishin Ryu, Tenjin Shinyo Ryu**, and **Senshin Ryu**. During his travels, he spent much time visiting with **Masaharu (Masaji) Kimura Sensei** of the **Takagi Yoshin Ryu, Kukishin Ryu, Gikan Ryu, Shinto Tenshin Ryu** (also called **Tenshin Ko Ryu**), **Kito Ryu, Kijin Chosui Ryu** (also known as **Hontai Kijin Chosui Ryu**). We are not sure what their exact relationship was. Whether it was teacher-student, friends, training partners, we can't say. What we do know from the notes kept from **Tanemura Sensei**, is that knowledge was exchanged. I, with the help and support of my **Sensei**, am still doing research into how and from whom he attained knowledge and influences from the **Shin No Shindo Ryu**, **Kosen Ryu**, **Gyokko Ryu**, and the **Shindo Muso Ryu.**

Tanemura Sensei trained for decades in many **Koryu.** To understand how and why this art ever made it into our hands, we must understand a turning point in **Tanemura Sensei**'s life; a time in which he fell in love.

Tanemura Sensei fell in love with a beautiful young woman who deeply loved him back. Their love was forbidden and doomed to fail. The young woman's parents had made plans for her to be married to a member of the **Yakuza** *Japanese mafia*. This was a union that was being forced on her; it was a destiny she could not easily escape.

The **Yakuza** is a perversion of the **Samurai** warrior tradition. Because **Tanemura Sensei** was a noted senior student of **Koryu** *Samurai derived warrior martial arts traditions*, he felt he may be respected and might be able to reason with the husband-to-be. Getting him to be in agreement did not fend easy. **Katsumi** explained the mutual love and dreams to marry that he and his beloved shared if he would only let her free. The **Yakuza** showed amusement at the notion of their love and explained he is not in the business of giving away commodities.

Katsumi Tanemura Sensei had two profitable clothing businesses as well as many business connections. He set up a second meeting with the **Yakuza**; this one was to be all business. **Tanemura** explained that he, too, was a man of business and today he wished to make a transaction. This business deal would be highly profitable for the **Yakuza**. He

188

offered the deed and full ownership of the clothing businesses as well as his contacts in exchange for the release of the hold on the woman. This, **Katsumi** explained, was a deal in the **Yakuza**'s favor; with the businesses being worth

more than her many times over. The **Yakuza** refused. When asked why, he was told, "Because you wish it."

He tried with his heart and then tried a business approach; both were not accepted. In this third meeting, he would use strength. This was something he developed over a lifetime of honed training. This final attempt was accepted. **Tanemura Sensei** sold and got rid of everything he owned. He then found out where the **Yakuza** lived. He went to his home, kicked in his front door, walked in, and as the **Yakuza** came toward him, **Tanemura Sensei** drew and cut him in half with his **Katana**.

On a side note, this was very dangerous and an extremely risky thing to do! Killing a **Yakuza** meant that the rest of the **Yakuza** organization had a mission to find you, at all costs, then kill you and every member of your family. Also, if you kill anyone in Japan, the police were obviously after you. When the police found you, even if they did not kill you in arresting you, you were still not safe. If the cops found you, the **Yakuza** knew where you were and you and your family would be as good as dead.

Tanemura Sensei went straight from the **Yakuza**'s house to do some quick shopping. He bought a plane ticket, a train ticket and a boat ticket for himself. Each of the tickets was set to leave Japan in different directions. He met up with the woman he loved and explained to her that she was free and they could never see each other again. He left, taking the slowest route, the boat.

He traveled a lot, to lose any tailing men. We know that after a while, he ended up in Mexico visiting a friend for several weeks and came into the United States through the Mexican border. He spent some time roaming the Midwest. Finding himself unsettled and missing the city life of **Tokyo**, he thought he might visit her sister city in the U.S., New York City. **Tanemura Sensei** arrived in New York in 1968. He

190

said it reminded him of a much dirtier version of **Tokyo**, but with cultural differences. So, for a time he lived in Chinatown, but was very unhappy with the New York mindset. At the time, a New Yorker would sooner knock you down and step over you than greet you nicely. He had a penpal, a noted **Budoka** of the time, **Yosei Nakai Sensei**. **Tanemura** explained his discomfort to his friend asking him what the nearest neighboring city was. **Yosei** explained that Philadelphia, the "City of Brotherly Love", was one of the closest. **Tanemura Sensei** loved the name of the city and thought it would present a wonderful change from the tough New Yorker mindset. So, he moved and soon found out that he was wrong.

Living out his days in Chinatown of Philadelphia, he made the best of it. He opened a corner grocery store. Then, he opened a dry cleaning shop. In time, he started his own brand of clothing called "Spiderwear". His branded sweatshirt had an embroidered spider logo on the left breast.

Down a tiny alley, behind and under the basement of a building, he ran a small all-Asian **Dojo**. All-Asian, that is, until the day he met a young man that would later become his son, then his successor. **Tanemura Sensei** trained his small group of students hard and displayed extremely advanced, unheard of skills. Such skill was unseen anywhere else in the Western world. Martial artists who were eyewitnesses to his instruction described his movement to me as being remarkable, breathtaking, incredible, and unimaginable.

The genius of **Katsumi Tanemura** is what he was able to accomplish. From his knowledge of all the **Ryu** he mastered, he was able to take the best from each one and integrate

191

them; this made an art that was amazing because it incorporated the strongest ideals from each. He called it **Hokushin Ryu Aikibujutsu**.

Katsumi Tanemura Sensei for a time studied Yu Kwon Sool under Master Choi, Young Sul in Taegu City, Korea. This was something that was not at all common, but **Katsumi** was not a racist. So, if there were a different aspect worth looking at, he would invite the opportunity. The Koreans referred to **Katsumi Tanemura** as "Grandmaster Choi, Jung". They called his method of martial arts movement Jeon Mu Sool. It was known as the "Universal Martial Science".

Tanemura Katsumi believed that no one culture can claim to have developed the martial arts, because since the beginning of time, man has needed to defend himself.

The **Hokushin Ryu**, as it was once called, promoted the use of fast, fluid, and practical **waza** based on the principles of **Aiki In Yo Ho**. It utilizes both **Goho** *hard method* and **Juho** *soft method* techniques. As a **Sensei**, when developing the technical requirements of his art, **Tanemura Sensei** wanted to stress the following:

1) The essence of **Sogo Bujutsu** or integrated martial arts. This is a very old concept, which is now being rediscovered by today's martial artist.
2) The development of **Kihon** that will provide a solid foundation for the study of classical forms of **Jujutsu** and **Aiki Bujutsu**. He wanted the requirements from **Oku iri no mokuroku** to provide a strong set of principles, **Jujutsu/Aiki Jujutsu kata**, and drills so that a student of

his art can be comfortable under any and all training scenarios, whether in a **Judo Dojo**, **Aiki Jujutsu Dojo**, or a street fight.

3) To stress the character and personality of the founder and also of warriors past. He was, first and foremost, a fighter and wanted his art to reflect a warrior's mindset and training habits.

After decades of teaching, he only issued **Densho** to a few students. Edward J. Smith was one of the top students who received **Densho**. **Katsumi Tanemura Sensei** adopted Edward after many years of tireless study. Edward was affectionately known to **Tanemura Sensei** as "**Tanemura Akahisa**" and was his **Uchideshi** for many years. **Katsumi Tanemura Sensei**, shortly before he died, requested the name of the **Ryu** be changed to the **Tanemura Ryu**. A few months before **Katsumi**'s death, **Akahisa** was awarded **Menkyo Kaiden** of the **Tanemura Ryu**. It was **Akahisa**'s belief that his teacher knew he was coming close to his end. He passed away on Febuary 17th 1991.

Akahisa Tanemura 1959-20-

Akahisa Tanemura was born on April 22nd 1959 as Edward J. Smith. He also frequently uses the name Ed Burns; Burns being his mother's maiden name. He began his study of the martial arts at a very young age. He was five years old when he began **Judo**, and at eight years old, he began to study **Jujutsu**. **Nakamura Kenji Sensei** was the name of his first **Jujutsu** teacher or **Kenji Nakamura** when using his name in the Western manner, family name last. He taught at the Rising Sun **Dojo**. Rising Sun was named for its location, Rising Sun Avenue in Philadelphia, not the coincidental

Learning **Nage Waza**,1995 Edward J. Smith
Sensei teaching David C. Falcaro **Sensei**

"rising sun" of Japan. The type of **Jujutsu** that **Nakamura
Sensei** taught was said to be a modern version of **Jujutsu**
with plenty of **Judo** mixed in. "We wore **Keikogi** as worn in
Judo, sometimes **Hakama** for demos," said **Akahisa**. As a
kid, he also studied with a friend of **Nakamura Sensei**, this

194

was the renowned **Sensei, Ishikawa Sensei** of the
Philadelphia **Judo** Club. "**Ishikawa Sensei** was a legend in
Philadelphia **Budo** circles. I spent only twenty to thirty
hours total over the course of a year with him, but he taught a
very clear and precise **Judo** form. I was a kid, though, and
liked to fight." **Akahisa Tanemura Sensei** could
not consider **Ishikawa Sensei** his **Sensei**, but his **Dojo** did
provide much needed attention and details. **Akahisa
Tanemura Sensei** wondered how **Ishikawa Sensei** was; he

Learning **Suwari Waza**, spine-lock, strangulation,
shoulder and elbow lock at the same time. 1996
Edward J. Smith **Sensei** and David C. Falcaro **Sensei**

had heard long ago that he returned to Japan. He had
American students who were much older than **Akahisa**.
Akahisa believes that he has taken his **Sensei**'s place and is
still teaching the art in Philadelphia. After a number of
years, **Akahisa**'s **Jujutsu** teacher, **Nakamura Sensei**, took
him to a demonstration of **Tanemura Katsumi Sensei** and

from that time on he studied under him. "I was introduced to **Tanemura Sensei** because **Nakamura Sensei** had many other priorities and decided to shut down his **Dojo**. **Nakamura Sensei** said that I had a good spirit, but that I was a bit too energetic. I was a wild kid, he was being kind," said **Akahisa**. **Akahisa** was an outsider for a number of years when training with **Katsumi Tanemura Sensei**. He was the

only Caucasian in his class. He remained dedicated to his **Sensei** throughout many years and, in turn for his dedication **Katsumi Tanemura Sensei** adopted him. From that point on, he was trained as if

Edward J. Smith **Sensei** teaching **Kenjutsu** at the **Takeshin Dojo** in 1996 to David C. Falcaro **Sensei**.

he was the son of a **Samurai**. Many would view this type of training as cruel and inhumane, it included many broken bones, being knocked out and being choked until he passed out. **Katsumi Tanemura Sensei** once threw **Akahisa** through a **Shoji** *sliding door made of hard wood and rice paper* then yelled at him for breaking it and made **Akahisa** pay for it to be rebuilt. Throughout **Akahisa**'s high school

196

years, he was attacked many times due to racial differences as he attended a school dominated by African Americans. He embraced these encounters as training and said, "I used this time to apply what I was learning." In 1986, he was able to begin his first **Dojo.** He took the name "**Takeshin Dojo**" in honor of his **Sensei**'s **Bujutsu** philosophies. **Akahisa Tanemura Sensei** then attempted to pass along the vast tradition to various students. Unfortunately, students would come and go constantly, for they did not understand the methods of **Akahisa**'s teachings. This is because he grew up and lived in a world unknown in modern times; as **Katsumi Tanemura Sensei** said, "For other students, there is a life outside of the **Dojo**, family, friends, job, women, dreams. For you, there is only your obsession." His dedication can be seen within his skill; it is unmatched. **Akahisa Tanemura Sensei** received his **Menkyo Kaiden** on January 10, 1991. **Akahisa Tanemura Sensei** changed the name of the then **Tanemura Ryu** back to the **Hokushin Ryu, Aikibujutsu** name. He then changed the name of the **Ryu** again in 2006 to **Shindo Koden Ryu, Aikibudo.** In 2009, he changed the **Shindo Koden Ryu** name again to its current name, **Takagishin Ryu**.

In 2011 **Akahisa Tanemura Sensei** strayed from the Japanese traditions, starting the Islamic Martial Arts Society. At this time he changed his Christian name Edward J. Smith into the Muslim name Salahuddin Muh'min Muhammad to represent Islam. He picked the name Salahuddin to name himself after the greatest Muslim warrior of all time. During the Crusades, Salahuddin drove the Christians out of the Holy Land. Muh'min his second name is a type of Muslim that follows the religion strictly, it also translates as believer. Muhammad, his new last name, is the name of the Islamic prophet, an illiterate businessman, who is said to have written their religious book the Koran. So Edward J. Smith **Sensei**'s new name is best translated as someone who is a very faithful, powerful warrior, a prophet of the Islamic faith.

Learning **Hobokujutsu** at the **Takishin Dojo** 1996 Edward J. Smith **Sensei,** Martin Rivera **Sensei** and David C. Falcaro **Sensei.**

Akahisa Tanemura Sensei now primarily accepts only Muslim students into these practices. He has also greatly changed how he is presenting the martial form. All Japanese terms have been translated into Arabic. All activities involving what Muslims consider shirk *witchcraft* have been removed. **Reiho** *Respectful bowing methods* have been removed from the practices of the art. The **Kamidana** *place of high respect and reflection* as well as the **Kamiza** *Focal point of paying homage and respect to the martial traditions* has been removed. He also removed the ranking structure.

198

He explained because of his new beliefs he has no need for a
Ryu. **Akahisa** dissolved the **Tagakishin Ryu** stating "there
is no **Ryu.**" In his own words he explains that he "maintains
the focus on older martial techniques but with the spiritual
guidance and peaceful teachings of Islam."

⊖-⊙-⊙-⊙-⊙-⊙-⊙-⊙-⊙-⊙-⊙-⊙-⊙-⊙-⊙-⊙-⊙-⊙-⊙-⊙

<u>Yoshiyo Tanemura 1977-20—</u>

I began with my **Sensei** in 1995. I go into more detail in later
pages, so I will keep this brief. The training was typical for
my **Sensei,** but like nothing I had ever experienced in a
previous **Dojo**. For one, I encountered many injuries. My
right knee was displaced, my left elbow back-warded, left hip
pulled out of joint, right wrist displaced, jaw knocked out of
socket, nose broken, left metacarpals broken, and my hair
pulled out in clumps. I was knocked out, choked out, and
beaten up many times. Looking back, it is sometimes hard to
remember the "good old times". To say we trained hard
would not be accurate. We trained with intensity, ferocity
and often a want to hurt each other. **Sensei** set the tone and it
changed often in a split moment. Some nights we beat on
each other with blank or smiling faces and, in the back of our
minds, with a true fear of injury. I would sometimes lie to
myself inside my head, "**Sensei** likes me better than the other
guys. He will make sure nothing really bad happens to me."
Sometimes, I truly wish I could go back in time and save
myself from certain classes.

The reason I stayed was due to what I saw, felt and heard; it
was knowledge and power like I never knew existed. Many
things were familiar: joint-locking, choking, throwing,
striking, and kicking, but many others I had never seen or
heard. How it was being done was hard to understand. It

199

was so powerful and my **Sensei** seemed to put no effort into application. I knew the personal cost did not matter. I had to learn this artform. I had to learn everything--even if it took a lifetime. I set out to do that. Gladly, I am still working on it. It is a wonderful journey; an amazing chain into history I have become a part of. It comes with a responsibility to pass on this tradition as it was passed to me. I always look forward to teaching and helping to develop future links in our chain.

In 2011 **Akahisa Tanemura Sensei**'s Islamic changes

Taken during a class in 2009 at the Northampton **Godaishin Dojo.** Jack Toole, Erin O'Neal as **Uke. Ninin Gatamae** done by David C. Falcaro **Sensei.**

created a strong divide in the practices between him and myself. I consider myself to be a devoted Christian and I don't have any interest in blending religion with warrior arts. I believe it is important to hold true to the traditional aspects of the martial form maintaining the integrity of the traditions. I refuse to remove or change the warrior arts respectful ways. As a **Sensei,** I will not discriminate, because of religious

Learning **Kensetsu Waza** from my **Sensei** in 1995 at the **Takeshin Dojo.** Edward J. Smith **Sensei**, and David C. Falcaro **Sensei.**

views. I reserve the right to teach students no matter what their religious background may be. The **Neji Gekken Ryu** maintains that religion remains a personal choice for each student. It is up to the individuals to find their own personal faith. It is not and will never be maintained or sanctioned by our martial traditions. Religion is not taught at the **Godaishin Dojo**, **Sogobujutsu** is.

The information within this lineage section was compiled from my personal knowledge and experiences and past to me by word of mouth during years of training under the tutelage of my **Sensei.**

Kukishin Ryu Lineage
This is our connection to the Kukishin Ryu

We are not **Kukishin Ryu**, but this is our lineage to the **Kukishin Ryu**. Because we come from a great many **Ryu** we should not claim to be one of them. This section shows all of the research as of 8/1/2010 that we have collected on the **Kukishin** line and our connection with it. The line of **Kukishin Ryu** we are connected to is not the main bloodline; we come from a sect of that line of **Kukishin Ryu** commonly referred to as the **Oouchi** lineage.

YAKUSHIMARU RYUSHIN - 1318

The founder of **Kukishin Ryu** was born with the name **Yakushimaru Ryushin** on January 1, 1318. He was named **Yakushimaru** after the deity **Yakushi Buddha**; his mother had a difficult time with conception and only gave birth after she made a pilgrimage to Mt. **Hiei** where she prayed at the temple **Enryakuji** to **Yakushi Buddha**. **Yakushimaru Ryushin**'s mother was known as **Chiqusa-hime**; his father was **Doyu Shirohogan**. **Yakushimaru Ryushin** was fortunate enough to be born to the **Fujiwara** clan, one of the most influential clans during that time in Japan's history. For generations, they had served as shrine supervisors known as **Betto**. **Yakushimaru Ryushin** learned the warrior arts and sciences of his family from **Shingu-Betto Ariie** and his grandfather **Dojitsu**. **Shinden Fujiwara Muso Ryu** is what he was first taught. Once he had learned mountaineering asceticism, or **shugendo**, from his father, he traveled to **Kyoto** and studied esoteric **Buddhism**. This was taught to

202

Yakushimaru Ryushin at the **Sanmakuin** Temple from Buddhist monk, **Joukai**. **Ryushin Yakushimaru** was also said to be a master of **Kuji-hiho** *the strategies behind the balancing of electric/magnetic power fields* and **Onmyo-do** *the founded way of understanding the esoteric.* When it was time for **Ryushin Yakushirmaru** to commemorate his coming of age in 1335, he joined under **Takauji Ashikaga** of the Northern Court in a war against the Southern Imperial Court. Let it be known that **Chigusa**'s (**Ryushin**'s mother) family belonged to the Southern Imperial Court. One year later, in the month of June, **Yakushimaru Ryushin** led a successful attack on Fort Mt. **Hiei** of the Southern Imperial Court. With the fall of the Mt. **Hiei**, **Godaigo**, Emperor of the Southern Court, and others were captured and held at a palace of a former emperor. It is said that Emperor **Godaigo** received treatment so horrid that **Yakushimaru Ryushin** stated, "It is possible to lose the Emperor from the harsh treatment he receives. I will plot his rescue." **Ryushin** gathered five additional supporters and broke into the palace. They escaped with Emperor **Godaigo** and headed to **Yoshino**. It is also believed that **Ryushin Yakushimaru** had an additional motivation to rescue Emperor **Godaigo**; **Chigusa** was very disheartened that her own son went against her family and it may have been an act to make up for his "mistake." Once the Northern Court was notified of the escape, they sent an army of ten thousand men in search for Emperor **Godaigo**. The six men and the emperor had made it to **Kuragari-Toge**; this is a mountain pass that sits on the border of the **Nara** and **Osaka** prefectures. Each of the six men chose the weapon in which they held the most skill. **Yakushimaru Ryushin** wielded a **Naginata**. As the men were fending off the army, the blade of **Ryushin**'s **naginata** got cut off and he had to use the remains as a staff to knock enemies down and keep them at bay. Once reinforcements arrived from **Yoshino**, the conspirators were able to safely get Emperor **Godaigo** to a small temple in Mt. **Kinpusen**. **Yakushimaru** also managed to regain and store in Mt. **Hiei** the Three Treasures of the Imperial House. Emperor **Godaigo** was so impressed with **Yakushimaru Ryushin** that he questioned him about his techniques. **Ryushin** told the Emperor, "It is a secret technique passed on in my family. It is the secret art of **Kuji**." To which Emperor **Godaigo** replied, "God knows your loyalty. You shall change your surname **Fujiwara** to **Kuki**." **Kuki**, at that period in time, pronounced **ku-kami**, translates as nine great spirits (in modern day it is pronounced **ku-ki**, meaning nine energies). From that day forward, **Fujiwara Yakushimaru Ryushin** was known as **Kuki Yakushimaru Ryushin**. Shortly after the death of his mother, **Kuki Yakushimaru Ryushin** created **Kukishin Bojutsu** in her honor. The techniques of **Kukishin Ryu Bojujtsu** come from what was used by **Ryushin** the day he defended Emperor **Godaigo** from the army of ten thousand.

OOUCHI MINBU YOSHIKANE

OOUCHI GORAOUMARU KATSUHIGE

HATAYAMA SABUROUBEI MASASHIGE

OOKUNI KAWACHINOKAMI YOSHIIE

OOKUNI KIHEI HISAYOSHI

ARIMA DAISUKE TADAAKI

ARIMA KAWACHINOSUKE MASASIGE

KURIYAMA UKON NAGAFUSA

HOSAYA SHINPACHIROU YUKIHISA

KIMURA ITTOUSAI JOSUI

KIMURA GASSUI YOSHINARI

OOSUMI SHIMANOKAMI MASASHIGE

IBA TOYOTAROU

ISHITANI MATSUTARO TADAAKI

TAKAMATSU TOSHITSUGU 1889

Takamatsu Toshitsugu was born in the province, **Hyogo**, within the town of **Akashi** on March 10, 1889. When he was nine, **Takamatsu** was sent to live with his grandfather in **Kobe**. **Shinryuken Masamitsu Toda, Takamatsu**'s grandfather, instantly began training him in **Shinden Fudo Ryu Dakkentaijutsu.**

When **Takamatsu** was thirteen years old, he was awarded **Menkyo Kaiden** *the highest level one can receive in traditional warrior arts* of **Shinden Fudo Ryu** from his grandfather. **Takamatsu** was a very skilled warrior even at a young age; he was once attacked by three people and had no difficulty in defending himself. The next day, those three returned with a gang of sixty at their side; by the time **Takamatsu** had severely injured ten of the gang members, the rest fled the scene. He was arrested and questioned. Police officers demanded to know who helped him, for he could not have done it alone. It was not until **Shinryuken Masamitsu Toda** bailed him out of prison that the officers left him alone. "Thirteen-year-old **Judo** Expert Easily Flung Away Sixty Gangsters" was the headline of the newspaper the very next day. It was not until he was seventeen years old that **Takamatsu** began to learn **Kukishin Ryu Bojutsu,** and it was maybe a stroke of good luck. **Takamatsu**'s father, **Yasaburo**, owned a match factory. **Ishitani Matsutaro** was a famous practitioner of warrior arts in Japan who happened to have distant relatives through ancestors with **Takamatsu**. **Yasaburo** gave **Ishitani** a job at the match factory as a security guard. **Takamatsu Toshitsugu**, along with another man, **Iwami Sakunosuke Nangaku,** began training under **Ishitani**. In 1913 **Ishitani Matsutaro** granted **Takamatsu Toshitsugu Menkyo Kaiden** of **Kukishin Ryu**.

<u>TATSUTA YASUICHIRO 1907-1991</u>

On August 1, 1907, **Tatsuta Yasuichiro Sensei** was born. He began his study of the warrior arts at a young age and through his lifetime, **Tatusta Sensei** had mastered many techniques of many **Ryu**, including **Tenshin Shinyo Ryu,**

Sintou Rikugo Ryu and **Senshin Ryu**. However, he is known for his devoted study of **Kukishin Ryu**. Yasuichiro's first teacher of **Kukishin Ryu**

210

was **Kiba Koshiro**. **Tatsuta Yasuichiro** was the top student of **Kiba Koshiro** and remained loyal to **Kiba** throughout his life. Although little is known about him, it should be mentioned that **Kiba Koshiro** played a main role in uniting the instructors of **Kukishin Ryu** after the bombings of **Hiroshima** and **Nagasaki**. Once **Kiba** had passed on, **Yasuichiro** continued training in **Kukishin Ryu** under **Takamatsu Toshitsugu** and was awarded **Menkyo Kaiden of Kukishin Ryu** on January 17, 1945. He also took over the responsibilities of his first **Sensei, Kiba** in uniting **Kukishin Ryu**. **Tatsuta Yasuichiro** was able to get the **Ryu** through the hardest times after the war. One action he took in order to keep **Kukishin Ryu** alive was a demonstration of staff technique for the United States Army just one year after the war had ended. Later on, **Tatsuta Yasuichiro** passed on his responsibilities to **Fujita Yoshio** and parted from **Kukishin Ryu**. He spent most of his days from that point forward refining the art of **Tanbojutsu** *six to nine inch stick*.

On February 11, 1991, **Tatsuta** passed away; he was eighty-five.

211

Katsumi Tanemura 1920-1991

Katsumi Tanemura was born to the name **Okazaki Shuji** in 1920. He stood 5ft, 5in. **Tanemura Sensei** also, referred to himself as **Tanemura Kazumi**. As a **budoka**, he is renowned for his mastery and synthesis of many different **Ryu**. He studied **Daito Ryu**, Takenouchi Ryu, Tenjin Shinyo Ryu, Shin No Shindo Ryu, Fusen Ryu, Yoshin Ryu, Kosen Ryu, Koto Ryu, Gyokko Ryu, Ono Ha Itto Ryu, Shindo Muso Ryu, and Kukishin Ryu. In **Kukshin Ryu**, he studied under **Tatsuta Yasuichiro Sensei** and received a **Menkyo Kaiden**.

212

AKAHISA TANEMURA 1959 - 20—

Akahisa Tanemura was born on April 22, 1959 as Edward

J. Smith. He also frequently uses the name Ed Burns, Burns being his mother's maiden name. He often was plainly referred to as "Mr. Smith". **Akahisa** became **Katsumi Sensei**'s **Uchideshi** and lived with him as a dedicated disciple for over a decade. **Akahisa Tanemura** received his

Menkyo Kaiden on January 10, 1991 from **Katsumi Tanemura Sensei**. **Bujutsu** was a lifestyle for him; he trained like a **Samurai** and attempted to live his life like one. He tried his art and skills out on thugs and ego- driven **Budoka** who were foolishly trying to make a name for themselves. He once took over 200 challenges in one year. His **Dojo**, where he took on "all comers" frequently, closed and reopened in many different places. Many times he dismissed his students for being too lazy. In his eyes, anyone that was not truly dedicated did not deserve his time and his teaching. His frustration with his students resulted in the breaking of their limbs. He also pitted them against each other in combat. This was done with and without governing rules. Many aspects of training resulted in little support from students and the **Dojo** became a revolving door; as students joined, they were forced to hack it. When they could not hack it, they quit. It was **Akahisa Tanemura Sensei**'s wish that his **Dojo**, the **Takeshin Dojo** be the hardest, strongest, and most painful in its training.

***

YOSHIO TANEMURA 1977-20—

Yoshio Tanemura Sensei (born David C. Falcaro) started training martial arts at the age of seven years old. He bounced from one martial art to the next, giving each about a year before he moved on. David had an utter desire for martial arts coupled with a highly skeptical mindset for it.

At the age of thirteen, he began his study in traditional Japanese warrior arts, beginning with the art of **Ninjutsu** under Stan Triplett **Sensei**. It was in 1995 that **Yoshio** first met **Akahisa Tanemura Sensei**. In the beginning of his

214

training, he was somewhat skeptical of the things he saw. It seemed too good to be true; nothing he had ever seen in the past came close to what **Akahisa Tanemura** was accomplishing. **Yoshio Tanemura** remembers consistently waking up on the side of the mat not knowing what happened to land him there. After a short while, he was persuaded and to this day, he remains a loyal student of **Akahisa Tanemura Sensei**'s teachings. **Yoshio Tanemura** went through many trials as a student and was tested daily. He would have to spend three to fourteen hours each day training, while maintaining a job and attending school. **Yoshio** (David C. Falcaro) showed so much dedication to his **Sensei** that he was also adopted into the **Tanemura** family and given the name **Yoshio** *meaning "righteous one"* **Tanemura**. He also faced many broken limbs and other injuries throughout his

training. In 1999, **Yoshio Tanemura Sensei** opened his first **Dojo**. He named it **Godaishin Dojo** *the universal spirit of the big five elements of creation and destruction martial home* and currently remains the head instructor. By 2005, the **Tanemura Sensei** was awarded two of the seven **Densho** he earned throughout the entirety of his training. With this, he became the **Sodenke**. In 2009, after 14 years of direct study under his **Sensei, Akahisa Tanemura** requested that **Yoshio Tanemura Sensei** become a **Kaiso** *Ryu founder* of his own **Ryu**. After much thought, **Yoshio** decided to call his martial family the **Neji Gekkan Ryu** *family of the spiraling combative edge*; the name was agreed upon.

The information within this lineage chapter was compiled by personal knowledge from David C. Falcaro, which would not be possible if not for Edward J. Smith, and with the helpful work in researching from Edward Philip Hall III, writings from (Wikipedia n.d.), (Koryu n.d.) and (Samurai Archives n.d.).

<u>Daito Ryu</u> Lineage
This is Our Connection to the **Daito Ryu**

We are not **Daito Ryu**, this is our lineage to the **Daito Ryu**.
Because we come from a great many **Ryu**, we should not
claim to be from only one of them. This section shows all of
the reseach as of 7/4/10 that we have collected on the **Daito
Ryu** line and our conection with it. It begins long before the
Daito Ryu does. It is our intention to display the earliest
origins of the **Daito Ryu**. The **Daito Ryu** name may mark
the beginning of the **Daito Ryu** line. This is said to begin
with **Tanomo Saigo Sensei**, while some others state that
Sokaku Takeda Sensei was the beginning.

SENWA TENNO – 850

Senwa (also called **Seiwa** depending on the historical source)
was the fourth son of Emperor **Montoku**. His mother was
Empress **Dowager Fujiwara No Akirakeiko**, also called the
Somedono Empress. **Seiwa**'s mother was the daughter of
Fujiwara No Yoshifusa, who was regent and great minister
of the Council of State.
Before his ascension to the Chrysanthemum Throne, his
personal name (his **imina**) was **Korehito Shinno**. He was
also known as **Mizunoo No Mikado**.

He was the younger half-brother of Imperial Prince,
Koretaka (844-897).

Originally, under the guardianship of his maternal

217

grandfather, **Fujiwara No Yoshifusa**, he displaced Imperial Prince **Koretaka** as Crown Prince. Upon the death of his father, Emperor **Montoku**, in 858, he became Emperor at the age of 8. However, his grandfather, **Yoshifusa**, held the real power.

Ten'an 2 *name of time period*, the 27th day of the 8th month, 858: In the 8th year of **Montoku-tenno**'s reign, the Emperor abdicated and the succession was received by his son. Shortly thereafter, Emperor **Seiwa** is said to have ascended to the throne.

Ten'an 2, the 7th day of the 11th month, 858: The Emperor's official announcement of his enthronement at age 9 was accompanied by the appointment of his grandfather as regent (**Sessho**). This is the first time that this high honor has been accorded to a member of the **Fujiwara** family, and it is also the first example in Japan of the ascension of an heir who is too young to be Emperor. The proclamation of the beginning of **Seiwa**'s reign was made at the **Kotaijingu** at **Ise** Province and at all the tombs of the Imperial family.

Jo Gan 1, in the 1st month, 859: All New Year's festivities were suspended because of the period of national mourning for the death of Emperor **Montoku**.

Jo Gan 1, 859: Construction begins on the **Iwashimizu** Shrine near **Heian Kyo**. This shrine honors **Hachiman**, the **Shinto** war god.

Jo Gan 10, 869: **Yo Zei** was born and he is named **Seiwa**'s heir in the following year.

Jo Gan 17, in the 11th month, 876: In the 18th year of **Seiwa Tenno**'s reign, the Emperor passed his throne to his five-year-old son, which means that the young child received the succession (**Senso**). Shortly thereafter, Emperor **Yo Zei** formally ascended to the throne (**Sokui**).

Gangyo 2, 878: **Seiwa** becomes a Buddhist priest. His new priestly name was **Soshin**.

Gangyo 2, on the 4th day of the 12th month, 878: Former Emperor **Seiwa** died at age 31. At the site of his tomb, he was sometimes referred to as **Mizunoo**.

Tsunemoto Minamoto 894-961

Minamoto No Tsunemoto was a **Samurai** and Imperial prince during Japan's **Heian** Period, the progenitor of the **Seiwa Genji** branch of the **Minamoto** clan. He was the son of **Sadazumi shinno** and grandson of Emperor **Seiwa**.

Tsunemoto took part in a number of campaigns for the Imperial Court,

including those against **Taira No Masakado** in 940 and against **Fujiwara No Sumitomo** the following year.

He held the title of **Chinjufu Shogun**, or Commander-in-Chief of the Defense of the North, and was granted the clan name of **Minamoto** by the Emperor in 961, the year of his death.

Tsunemoto was the father of **Minamoto No Mitsunaka**.

Mitsunaka Minamoto 912-997

He was the son of **Minamoto No Tsunemoto**, a **Samurai** and court official of Japan's **Heian** period. **Mitsunaka** held the title, passed down from his father, of **Chinjufu Shogun**, the Commander-in-Chief of the Defense of the North. **Mitsunaka** is also renowned as being the father of the legendary **Minamoto No Yorimitsu**.

Mitsunaka retired to **Tada** in **Settsu** Province, and is

sometimes known as **Tada Manju**. One of the subfamilies of the **Minamoto** Clan thus came to be known as **Tada** as well.

Mitsunaka appears in the anime **Otogi Zoshi**, along with fictionalized versions of a number of other historical figures.

Yoroimabu Minamoto 968-1084

Yorimasa Minamoto 1106 – 1180

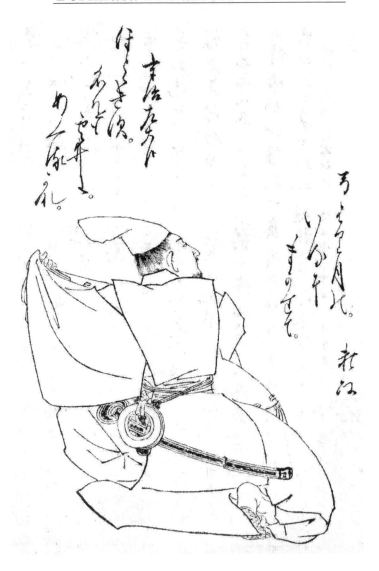

Yorimasa was a prominent Japanese poet whose works

appeared in various anthologies. He served eight different emperors in his long career, holding posts such as **Hyo Go No Kami** *head of the arsenal*. He was also a warrior, leading the **Minamoto** armies at the beginning of the **Genpei** War.

In the clashes between the **Minamoto** and **Taira** clans that had gone on for decades, **Yorimasa** had tried to stay out of politics and avoided taking sides. He did participate in the **Hogen** Rebellion in 1156. For a time, he was even friends with **Taira No Kiyomori**. During the **Heiji** Rebellion of 1160, he leaned just enough in favor of the **Taira** that it allowed them to overthrow the **Minamoto**. However, by the time he officially retired from military service in **Kiyomori**'s army in 1179, **Yorimasa** had changed his mind about opposing his own clan. He entered the Buddhist priesthood. In May of 1180, he sent out an appeal to other **Minamoto** leaders and to temples and monasteries that **Kiyomori** had offended.

The **Genpei** War began with the Battle of **Uji** in 1180. **Yorimasa** led **Minamoto** forces, along with warrior monks from **Mii Dera**, in defending the **Byo Do In**. Despite the monks having torn up the planks of the bridge leading to the temple, the **Taira** managed to break through the defenses and take the temple. Suffering defeat at **Uji**, he committed suicide in the **Byo Do In**. **Minamoto No Yorimasa**'s ritual suicide by **Seppuku** is the earliest recorded instance of a

Samurai's suicide in the face of defeat.

According to legend, his retainer took his head to prevent it from falling into the hands of the **Taira**. He then fastened his master's head to a rock and threw it into the **Uji** River so it could not be found.

Yorimasa's death poem was:

**umoregi no
hanasaku koto mo
nakarishi ni
mi no naru hate zo
kanashikarikeru**

Like an old tree
From which we gather
no flowers
Sad has been my life
Fated no fruit to
produce

224

Yoriyoshi Minamoto 995 – 1082

Minamoto No Yoriyoshi was a head of Japan's **Minamoto** Clan, who is perhaps most notable for having led, along with his son **Minamoto No Yoshiie**, the Imperial forces against rebellious forces in the North. This campaign would be called the **Zenkunen** War and would be followed some years later by the **Gosannen** War.

He held the title, passed down from his father, of **Chinjufu Shogun**, Commander-in-Chief of the Defense of the North. **Yoriyoshi** accompanied his father **Minamoto No Yorinobu** on his own missions to defend the Empire, quelling rebellions and disturbances. Thus, he gained much of his knowledge of tactics and strategy. The **Zenkunen** War in which he fought began in 1051 and lasted, with some brief

breaks, twelve years. In 1073, **Yoriyoshi** founded **Tsurugaoka Hachiman Gu** in **Kamakura**, which was to become, roughly a century later, the primary shrine of the **Minamoto** clan when they began the **Kamakura shogunate.**

226

Shinra Saburu Yoshimitsu Minamoto 1056 - 1127

Shinka Saburo Yashimitsu Minamoto, Soke (1045-1127), a.k.a. **Minamoto No Shinra Saburo Yoshimitsu**, was the last grandson of Emperor **Seiwa**. **Yoshimitsu** was the younger brother of **Minamoto No Hachiman Taro Yoshiie** (1041- 1108), considered the greatest warrior in all of Japanese history.

It is very likely that the earlier combat methods of the **Minamoto** Clan were actually just refined and perfected by General **Yoshimitsu** and his elder brother **Yoshiie**.

Yoshimitsu was a teacher of **Sojutsu** *spear*, **Toho** *sword methods*, and **Taijutsu** *body arts*, as well as archery. He was noted, firstly, for having dissected the cadavers of executed criminals and slain enemy soldiers of the Three Year War (1083).

Through this study of the structure of the human body, he mastered **Gyakute** and **Ichigeki Hissatsu** *techniques of killing with one blow*. Secondly, by watching the silk spider catch its prey, he obtained a hint which led to the discovery of the core of **Aiki**.

Therefore, **Yoshimitsu** is considered to be the one who originally developed the techniques of **Daito Ryu** by adding to the previous secret techniques of the **Minamoto** Clan and passing those techniques down to the **Takeda** family of **Kai** in the 12th century. This merged the techniques of the **Aizu** & **Minamoto** clans into a new style, which he named **Daito Ryu**.

Kyomitsu Takeda 1116 -1159

Nabuyoshi Takeda 1138 - 1186

Nabumune Takeda 1204 – 1267

Nabutoki Takeda 1202 – 1235

Nabumasa Takeda 1171-1256

Nabumitsu Takeda 162 – 1248

Nanutakw Takeda 1239 – 1282

Nabushige Takeda 1349 – 1490

Nabushige Takeda 1382 – 1491

Nabumitsu Takeda 1289 – 1351

Nabuharu Takeda 1291 – 1372

Nabunari Takeda 1244 – 1311

Nabumoei Takeda 1429 – 1527

Nabusigi Takeda 1460 - 1501

Nabusigi Takeda was a **Samurai** of **Japan**'s **Sengoku** Period and the older brother of **Takeda Shingen**. **Takeda Nobushige** held the favor of their father and was meant to inherit the **Takeda** lands, wealth, power, and position as head of the clan. However, **Shingen** rebelled against their father and seized the lands and power for himself. **Nobushige**, nevertheless, fought alongside his brother who relied on him for support. He is well known not only for his strategic insight, but also for his wisdom. He wrote, among other things, **Kyujukyu Kakun**, a set of ninety-nine short rules for **Takeda** Clan members, some of which are erroneously attributed to **Shingen** himself from time to time. He is also known as **Takeda Tenkyu** (**Tenkyu** refers to another rank he held).

231

Nobushige became an important **Takeda** General and led large forces on several occasions. In 1544, **Shingen** had a rebellion on his hands. As part of his punitive effort, he sent **Nobushige** to capture **Fujisawa Yorichika**'s **Kojinyama** castle. He most likely succeeded, though sources differ. **Katsurao** castle, the main castle of **Murakami Yoshikiyo**, fell to **Nobushige** and **Takeda Yoshinobu** in 1553. This drove **Yoshikiyo** to **Uesugi Kenshin** and was really the last significant act before the start of the **Kawanakajima** campaigns.

He died at the fourth battle of **Kawanakajima** in 1561. As he was fighting he was suddenly surrounded by **Samurai** and cut down, but not before he killed his attackers.

Shingen Takeda 1521-1573

Shingen was the eldest son of **Takeda Nobutora** and was known at first as **Harunobu**. Learning of his father's intent to disinherit him in favor of **Nobushige**, **Shingen** gave his support to a "bloodless revolution" (as the affair is sometimes called) that overthrew **Nobutora** and sent him to exile in **Suruga** in 1541. He afterwards began to expand into **Shinano** and had secured that province by 1560. He fought with **Uesugi Kenshin** numerous times and made in-roads in **Hida** and **Kozuke** Provinces. The last few years of his life were taken up fighting **Tokugawa Ieyasu**, who he defeated at **Mikatagahara** in January 1573. His death is often attributed to a sniper's bullet but was most likely due to a respiratory ailment he had been suffering from for some time.

232

In addition to his military endeavors, **Shingen** is well remembered for his sound administration and public works.

<u>Nabutora Takeda</u> 1493 – 1573

Kunitsugo Takeda 1551-1592

Kunitsugo moved to **Aizu** in 1574, where the art of **Oshiki Uchi** was taught to the **Aizu** clan for the next 300

years. **OshiiKiuchi** (also called **Goshikinai**) became the official self defense art at the **Aizu** castle.

The successive lords and their bodyguards practiced it as the secret art of the **Aizu** Clan, and passed it on until the fall of the **Shogunate**. According to history, only the chief **Samurai** with an income of more than 500 **Koku** *unit of rice used to determine one's wealth*, the pageboys, the court ladies, and those who served directly under the **Shogun** were allowed to learn the art.

It was at this point that the fighting system developed by the **Minamoto** Clan merged with the martial art of the **Aizu Gumi** to become what we now call **Daito Ryu.**

234

Katsuyori Takeda 1534-1582

Katsuyori was a **Japanese Samurai** of the **Sengoku** Period, who was famed as the head of the **Takeda Gumi** and a successor to the legendary warlord **Takeda Shingen**.

Kunisigi Takeda 1546-1582

Masayoshi Matsudaira

Yoshizumi Matsudaira

Yoshichika Matsudaira

Yoshitaka Matsudaira

Yoshiyasu Matsudaira

Katamori Matsudaira

Katamori Matsudaira was a **Samurai** who lived in the last days of the Edo Period and the early to mid **Meiji** period. He was the 9th **Daimyo** of the **Aizu Han** and the military commissioner of **Kyoto** during the **Bakumatsu** Period. During the **Boshin** War, **Katamori** and the **Aizu Han** fought against the **Meiji** Government armies, but were severely defeated. **Katamori**'s life was spared, and he later became the chief of the **Toshogu** Shrine.

236

Hoshina Chikanori

Soemon Takeda 1758-1853

Takeda Soemon, Soke taught a system known as **Aiki In Yo Ho** *the aiki of ying & yang* and is the first to use the term "**Aiki**" in recorded Japanese martial arts history. He can be rightly called the true "Father of **Aiki**".

He was the grandfather of **Sokaku Takeda** and the instructor for **Tanomo Saigo**, both of whom were involved in the governmental uprising to prevent the Emperor from assuming control over all the provinces and territories in Japan.

Tanomo Saigo 1829 - 1905

During the early 1800s, there arose in Japan an ideology that rallied around deposing the **Tokugawa Shogunate** and replacing the Emperor to the throne. Clans were the political parties of the time and the **Aizu** Clan was in favor of the Shogun. The **Aizu** leader Katamori **Matsudaira** had served the **Shogunate** for many years and thus the loyalty of the **Aizu** lay with the **Shogun**. The **Aizu** fought many battles in an attempt to keep the Emperor and his forces from the throne. They were pivotal in the **Bakumatsu** wars. Now, the **Choshu** and **Satsuma** Clans, who were in support of the Emperor, threatened their political lifestyle. As a result of their opposing ideologies, the **Aizu Samurai** under the leadership of **Saigo Tanomo** (1830 - 1905), clashed against the forces of **Choshu** and **Satsuma** at **Shirakawaguchi**.

Saigo Tanomo Sensei was an **Aikijujutsu** and **Kenjutsu** student under **Takeda Soemon** (1758 - 1853). **Saigo** had studied for years with the **Takeda** schools and was a famous warrior even though he was defeated by the **Choshu** and **Satsuma** clans. Because of this loss, however, the family of **Saigo Tanomo Soke**, 21 in all, committed suicide thinking that **Tanomo** had been killed. Unknown to his family, **Saigo Tanomo** survived the battle of **Shirakawaguchi**. Now that his family was gone, **Tanomo** returned to **Aizu** and became a teacher of **Mizoguchi Ha Itto Ryu** and **Koshu Ryu Gungaku Kenjutsu**.

Soke Saigo Tanomo was also known as "**Chikanori Genzo**" and "**Hoshina Genshin**". He was sixth generation of the Emperor **Seiwa**, although he still called the system **Oshiiki Uchi**, he was the second generation to use the term **Aiki**. He was born into the **Kikuchi** family based in **Kyushu**.

His father, **Saigo Chakamoto**, was a prominent **Samurai** of the **Aizu** Clan (the **Saigo-Hoshina** family were retainers of the **Matsudaira** Clan).

He was a believer in a sentient deity or spirit world (one **kami** or god), which was a unique belief in the **Shinto** world of his day. He reportedly preached this in his **Nikko Toshugo** shrine in later years, causing much friction with the mainstream Shintoists of his day.

His religious and political views made him many enemies. On several occasions, assassins were sent to kill him, but he was never hurt. One story recounts how he was a paid assassin caught him alone, but because he showed no fear, although unarmed, the assassin was psychologically unable to kill him. After guards captured this assassin and asked him why he didn't kill **Tanomo**, he said, "How can you kill a man who is already dead?"

This is something that the Western mind may have a hard time fully comprehending. It is based on the **Shinto** prefix that without freedom, one is never really alive. And to

Tanomo and many other like him, the **Meijii** Restoration Period meant the end of freedom for the **Samurai**, so to them, they were already dead.

He had training in **Misoguchi Ryu** swordsmanship and **Koshu Ryu**, and his resistance of the **Meijii** government, led to the ritual suicide of his mother, wife, five daughters and 14 other members of his family who thought he had been killed by the government.

He then served as a **Shinto** priest and adopted **Shiro Saigo** as his son, hoping he would take over the **Daito Ryu** system, but **Saigo Shiro** joined the fledging art founded by **Jigoro Kano**, which became known as **Kodokan Judo**. This led to **Saigo Tanomo** asking a young fighter by the name of **Sokaku Takeda** to become the next inheritor of this art.

During the early 1800's, there arose in Japan an ideology that rallied around deposing the **Tokugawa Shogunate** and replacing the Emperor to the throne. Clans were the political parties of the time and the **Aizu Gumi** *Aizu clan* was in favor of the Shogun.

The **Aizu** leader, **Katamori Matsudaira**, had served the **Shogunate** for many years and, thus, the loyalty of the **Aizu** lay with the **Shogun**. The **Aizu** fought many battles in an attempt to keep the Emperor and his forces from the throne. They were pivotal in the **Bakumatsu** wars.

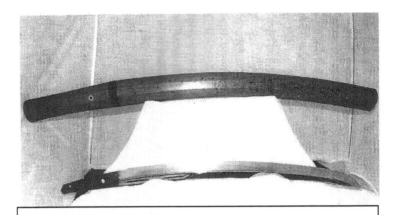

Tanomo Saigo's Katana. It is proudly displayed at the **Daito Ryu Hombu Dojo** under the possession and care of **Katsuyuki Kando Soke** (current head of **Daito Ryu Aikijujutsu**)

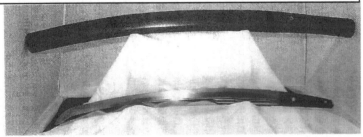

Now, their political lifestyle was threatened by the **Choshu** and **Satsuma** clans, who were in support of the Emperor. As a result of their opposing ideologies, the **Aizu Samurai**, under the leadership of **Saigo Tanomo** (1830 - 1905), clashed against the forces of **Choshu** and **Satsuma** at

242

Shirakawaguchi.

For almost 20 years, **Tekada Sokaku** wandered from **Dojo** to **Dojo** challenging almost every known martial arts master, and he was never defeated. Many of these bouts were to the death, which greatly enhanced the reputation of **Tanomo Saigo** and **Daito Ryu**.

Soke Shiro Nashiyama (1846 – 1932), a student of **Tanamo Saigo,** founded the **Kaze Arashi Ryu** system. This is sometimes considered a branch, or version, of **Daito Ryu** or **Aiki**. **Nishiyama** was first trained by the priests of the **Shugendo Shinto** sect at **Dewa** Shrine located at Mt. **Haguro** before he trained under **Tanamo Saigo** at the **Nik ko Toshugo** Shrine. Although not pure **Daito Ryu**, **Kaze Arashi Ryu** was influenced greatly by the techniques taught by **Tanomo Saigo**, which is why we list it here.

We realize that **Kaza Arashi Ryu** is not **Daito Ryu**, and can be argued that it is not even true **Aiki**, but it has techniques in it that are identifiable to those of **Daito Ryu Aikijujutsu,** and so it is related to **Daito Ryu**.

Sokaku Takeda 1858 - 1942

In 1876, **Tanomo** received a new student into his tradition named **Takeda Sokaku**. **Sokaku**, the grandson of **Takeda Soemon**, was born in **Aizu** on October 10, 1860. He studied **Aikijujutsu** from his grandfather and other arts from his

244

father. By the time he was sixteen, he had studied **Jikishinkage Ryu Kenjutsu** from **Sakakibara Kenkichi** and received his **Menkyo Kaiden** in **Ono Ha Itto Ryu** from **Toma Shibuya** of **Tokyo**. **Tanomo** remembered **Sokaku's** grandfather well, as he had also been taught by him. For

many years, **Sokaku Takeda Sensei** studied **Daito Ryu** with **Saigo** and mastered many arts such as **Aikijujutsu**, **Battojutsu**, **Yarijutsu** and **Kenjutsu**. Finally, in 1880 at the **Nikko Toshogu** Shrine, **Tanomo** passed on all his knowledge, including the secret teachings, to **Sokaku**. From that day forward, **Takeda Sokaku** would be headmaster of **Daito Ryu**. He took time traveling to instruct others, often staying with the student for a period of time before moving on. He intelligently concentrated on government officials and military leaders as well as local police departments for his student body. In this manner, his reputation spread quickly. He was the second son of **Sokichi Takeda** (1819-1906) and **Tomi**, his mother. He was a direct descendant of the **Minamoto** lineage.

His main teacher was **Tanomo Saigo**, a **Jodai Karo** *minister or chief councilor* of the **Aizu Gumi** *Aizu clan*. His skills as a martial artist are the subject of popular oral traditions describing extraordinary feats of strategy and technique, but his relevance in **Daito Ryu** history is the fact that it was he who first taught **Daito Ryu** openly to individuals who were not related to the **Aizu Gumi** *Aizu clan*. His students number in the thousands, including some foreigners such as the 26th President of the United States, Theodore Roosevelt, according to the surviving records. Many of those students head the majority of the lineages of **Daito Ryu** who teach openly today. It is undeniable that without **Sokaku**'s efforts, **Daito Ryu** would have died, or at most survived only as an obscure art taught to only a few like so many other styles of **Koryu Bujutsu**.

Sokaku Masayoshi Minamoto Takeda, Soke (1858-1942), the grandson of **Takeda Soemon** (1758-1853), inherited the

246

system from **Tanomo Saigo** after mastering several other martial arts systems, including **Ona Ha Itto Ryu Kenjutsu**, and **Hozoin Sojutsu**. Also, he trained with the renowned **Sakakibara Kenkichi** of the **Jikishin Kage Ryu**.

Sokaku was instructed by **Takeda Soemon** and his father before studying under **Tanomo Saigo** in preparation to teach this art to the general population. **Sokaku** traveled throughout Japan for the remainder of his life, giving seminars to the descendants of **Samurai** and the upper classes of society. He kept written records of everyone he

taught, which was well over 30,000 people, although he was illiterate.

Sokaku Takeda usually used the term "**Daito Ryu**" *great Eastern style* to describe his version of **Aikibujutsu**.

The last true **Samurai, Sokaku**, killed dozens of men with the sword or spear and was known as the "little demon" because of his constant duels with both the live sword and other weapons.

At the end of the 1800s, the **Samurai** were politically disbanded and many **Jujutsu** or **Kenjutsu** schools died out. **Jujutsu** schools came in from the countryside to the city, and by doing so were exposed to other **Ryu**.

There were many contests between **Jujutsu** schools at the time, each trying to prove they were the best. Many **Jujutsu** styles were defeated and discredited, some unjustly. Nevertheless, they were forced out of existence, or the practitioners simply joined other **Ryu**. It was also a time of bullying on the part of the **Jujutsuka** *Jujutsu practitioner*.

248

Many of the younger students found enjoyment in trying the techniques out on unsuspecting city folk. Also, many bar brawls were started in order to practice their techniques. **Jujutsu** itself fell into ill repute and many of its practitioners were seen as troublemakers. Because of this view, the practice of **Jujutsu** was restricted to a very few traditional schools.

Sokaku Takeda first introduced **Daito Ryu** to the world, after the **Meiji** Era. Since before that time, details were hardly known and it wasn't shown to the public. It was a secret art of the **Aizu Gumi**.

The "**Aiki**" technique that **Sokaku** had mastered was strongly influenced by traditional **Jujutsu**, as evidenced by

249

photos published in a book by **Takuma Hisa**, which shows **Sokaku** twisting his opponents by force using **Kansetsu Waza**.

In 1882 things began to change. It was then that **Kano Jigoro** founded a new type of **Jujutsu** that he called **Judo**. **Kano** was a **Jujutsu** teacher who had studied under **Sensei, Teinosuke Yagi** and **Hachinosuke Fukada** of the **Tenshin Shin Yo Ryu** for two years. Later, he also studied under the tutelage of **Tsunetoshi Iikubu** of the **Kito Ryu** for another two years. He studied with the **Sekiguchi Ryu** for about one and a half years. This was a total of less than six years, which is why no established **Jujutsu** school masters at the turn of the century considered him to be a **Jujutsu** master, rather, they thought he was genuinely interested in preserving the traditional **Jujutsu** systems. This is why they taught him some of their techniques and took photos with him.

<u>Yoshida Kotaro 1883 – 1966</u>

Yoshida was a 19th to 20th Century Japanese martial artist and member of the **Amur** River Society (also known as the Black Dragon Society), an ultra-nationalist organization of disenfranchised ex-**Samurai**. They promulgated "pan-Asiatic ascendancy" in line with the rise of **Japanese** imperialism. While by all accounts a prolific martial artist and teacher, there is little surviving documentation of **Yoshida**'s life that has been translated into English. Because he was known to have lived an extremely ascetic lifestyle, and possibly as a result of his political activities and connections, most information on **Yoshida** today has been passed down through oral transmission by primary sources.

When I met **Katsuyuki Kando Sensei** at the **Daito Ryu Hombu Dojo** and showed him an this book he maintained that this was not a photo of **Yoshida**. Others from the **Yanagi Ryu** maintain it is.

In relating a speech given by one of **Yoshida**'s   top students, it is noted that **Yoshida** came from a family that had held **Samurai** rank during the Pre-Restoration Period of Feudal **Japan**. At a young age, **Yoshida** apprenticed himself to **Takeda Sokaku**, head of the **Daito Ryu Aikijujutsu** School, which would soon become popular throughout **Japan** as part of the public revitalization of the martial arts. **Yoshida** would become **Sokaku**'s top student, and there is some disagreement as to whether mastery of the art was passed down to

Yoshida himself   or another **Sokaku** pupil. What is known is **Yoshida**'s status as a top student of **Sokaku**'s is undisputed and he is, in fact, credited with introducing **Morihei Ueshiba**, founder of **Aikido**, to **Sokaku Takeda**.

A rare photo of **Yoshida Sensei** my **Sensei** gave me.

<u>Sagawa Yukiyoshi 1902 - 1998</u>

Sagawa Yukiyoshi Sensei was once considered to be the successor to **Takeda Sokaku**, should **Tokimune** not survive World War II. **Sagawa**, an extremely conservative teacher, ran only a single **Dojo** and taught a relatively small number of students. **Sagawa** began studying **Daito Ryu** under **Takeda Sokaku** in 1914, after first learning the art from his father, **Sagawa Nenokichi** (1867–1950) who was also a student of **Sokaku** and a holder of a **Kyoju Dairi** *teaching license* in the system. Although considered by many to be one of the most accomplished students of **Sokaku**, **Yukiyoshi** received the **Kyoju Dairi** in 1932, but did not receive the **Menkyo Kaiden** *certificate of mastery of the system's secrets*. **Sagawa** often served as a teaching assistant

253

to **Sokaku** and traveled with him to various locations in

Japan, teaching **Daito Ryu.** He is said to have remained very powerful in the art until very late in life and was featured in a series of articles in the **Aiki** news magazines prior to his death in 1998.

Katsumi Tanemura 1920-1991

Tanemura, Katsumi was one of the most knowledgable and skilled teachers of **Jujutsu** and **Aikijujutsu** of this century. He was known for his unlimited mastery of thousands of techniques and their direct application to realistic combat. Examining his years of study and the path that he walked will help one to appreciate his rich martial legacy.

He was born **Okazaki, Shuji** in 1920 and began the study of

Yoshin Ryu Jujutsu and pre-sport **Judo** in 1928. In 1939, he changed his name to **Tanemura, Katsumi** and began to study **Daito Ryu Aikijujutsu** under the renowned **Sensei, Kotaro Yoshida**. He remained with **Yoshida Sensei** from 1939 until 1948, and even served as his **Uchideshi** for some time.

He also studied for some time with **Sagawa, Yukiyoshi Sensei** in **Tokyo**.

From 1950 until 1955, he traveled throughout Japan studying **Takenouchi Ryu, Tenjin Shinyo Ryu**, and **Shin No Shindo Ryu Jujutsu**. His primary focus at this time was **Takenouchi Ryu**. He also learned many groundfighting tactics of the **Fusen Ryu** from his original **Judo** teacher. He advocated the use of **Ne Waza** long before the current grappling craze. This included chokes, locks, neck cranks, and many leg-locking techniques. Much of this material came from the **Fusen Ryu**, the school that badly defeated the **Kodokan** by using groundfighting skills. After this, he continued to be influnced by many other **Koryu**.

In 1955, he founded the art of **Hokushin Aikibujutsu** as an integrated study of various schools of **Jujutsu** and **Aikijujutsu**. This includes the **Hiden Mokuroku, Aiki No jutsu, Hiden Ogi**, and **Goshin Yo No Te** of **Daito Ryu**, 70 **Kata** and **Waza** of **Yoshin Ryu** in the form of his **Yoshin No Kata**, and all of the 65 throws of **Judo**. The art also includes an in-depth study of **Takenouchi Ryu Kata** and the study of 18 traditional weapons. This is a unique art that bridges the gap between the old **Koryu** combat arts and our modern age.

Tanemura, Katsumi passed away February 17, 1991.

Tanemura Sensei had trained under both **Yoshida Kotaro** and **Sagawa Yukiyoshi** who were both trained under **Sokaku Takeda**, which is why they are mentioned above.

256

After decades of teaching, he only issued **Densho** to a few students. Edward J. Smith was one of the top students who received **Densho**.

Katsumi Tanemura Sensei adopted Edward after many years of tireless study. Edward was affectionately known to **Tanemura Sensei** as "**Tanemura Akahisa**", and was his **Uchideshi** for many years.

Tanemura Sensei last visited **Yoshida, Kotaro** in 1953, and his total involvement in the **Daito Ryu** lasted 14 years of direct study. This, combined with his varied experience in other **Ryu** of **Jujutsu** and **Aikijujutsu**, made for a solid technical base from which to draw upon.

Katsumi Tanemura Sensei, shortly before he died, requested the name of the **Ryu** be changed to the **Tanemura Ryu**.

A few months before **Katsumi**'s death, **Akahisa** was awarded **Menkyo Kaiden** of the **Tanemura Ryu**. It was **Akahisa**'s belief that his teacher knew he was coming close to his end.

<u>Akahisa Tanemura 1959-20--</u>

Akahisa Tanemura (Edward J. Smith) began **Budo** at age 5 in **Judo** when his mother placed him in a **Judo** club in Philadelphia.

Taken 1995 Teaching **Aikijujutsu** at the **Takeshin Dojo.**

When he was eight years old, he began **Jujutsu**. His **Sensei** was not fond of him because he spent so much time in the **Dojo**. He would try to stay after the **Dojo** closed, to ask

Taken 2009 Teaching
Aikijujutsu at the
Northampton
Godaishin Dojo

more questions and to train longer. This first **Jujutsu Sensei**, after trying for years to get rid of Edward came up with a foolproof plan. **Tanemura Katsumi Sensei** was doing a small demonstration of superior martial arts. He knew that as soon as he made the introduction, he would be rid of this pesky kid for good--he was right.

259

He never considered these to be his beginnings in martial arts. When asked, **Akahisa** replies, "All of that was to get

me ready to begin **Budo** and I began when I met **Tanemura Sensei**."

Akahisa began, and remained for many years, an outsider in

Taken 1995 at the
Takishin Dojo

Taken in 2008 at the
Northampton **Godaishin Dojo**

his own **Dojo**. **Tanemura Katsumi Sensei** only taught
people of Asian descent and **Akahisa** was of Italian-
American descent. He was not well liked by his peers or
beloved by his **Sensei**. Edward was raised and adopted by
Katsumi and taught as a son, but put under what the modern
world would consider cruel, inhumane training practices.
ometimes, being **Katsumi**'s **Deshi** was torturous. Edward
incurred injuries of all sorts, such as broken bones and being
knocked or choked out. **Katsumi** broke Edward's arm for
watching the television show *Three's Company*
consecutively once a week for three weeks. **Katsumi**
remarked afterward, "You're too lazy!" This was done even
though Edward had completed the chores and training asked
of him by his **Sensei**. These were not just physically, but
mentally, strenuous practices commonplace within the
training. **Katsumi**, while training Edward, threw him
through a **Shoji** *opening and closing ricepaper screened wall*

262

and yelled at him for breaking it then forced him to pay for the wall's reconstruction.

Edward grew up in a primarily African American school district. As a result of racial prejudice, he often found himself attacked before, after and during school hours. This conflict was avoided for years. Yet, many times Edward was forcibly engaged in fighting with multiple people attacking him. By the last years of high school, Edward's mindset was coerced, altered, flipped and he began to invite it.

When asked about this time in his life, he said, "I used this time to apply what I was learning." Because of the common conflict, **Katsumi Sensei** sent Edward to Larry Holmes Boxing Gym; not to train boxing, but to learn applicatio n against it. These lessons he would later pass on in a similar way to his **Deshi**.

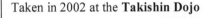
Taken in 2002 at the **Takishin Dojo**

As a young adult, Edward was fond of walking around shady parts of Philadelphia flashing and pretending to count twenty dollar bills. This invite to potential thieves was "practice" as he put it.

Many times throughout his training, **Akahisa** would accompany **Katsumi Tanemura Sensei** back and forth to Japan.

In 1986, **Akahisa** founded the **Takeshin Dojo** and taught, non-commercially, in the Allentown area. The **Dojo** moved from location to location. It proved difficult to get funding to maintain any of the locations. People were always coming and leaving; most students did not stay very long, a few months to a year at most. During this time, a single enthusiast sometimes solely funded the **Takeshin Dojo**. This did not last long. While open in the late 1980s and the 1990s, **Akahisa Tanemura Sensei** took on all comers, breaking and beating anyone with a dissimilar view of what **Budo** was. Over the years, hundreds challenged **Akahisa**'s skill and they fell prey to his mastery of the arts. Unlike the defensive martial arts of the time period, **Akahisa** was quick to attack. He hit fast and hard, tossing people and breaking

Taken 1996 at the **Takishin Dojo** while learning **Juttejutsu.**

264

their bones. The people who stuck around after the beatings to become students did not stay very long. This was undoubtedly the result of **Akahisa**'s strict brutal training regiment.

Edward J. Smith grew up in the 1960s and 1970s but lived much of his life in a different world. **Katsumi Tanemura** used to tell him, "For the other students, there is a life outside

Taken 2010 at the
Godaishin Dojo
in Northampton
while learning
Aiki No Jutsu.

of the **Dojo**, family, friends, job, women, dreams. For you, there is only your obsession."

He founded the **Koden Bugei Kyokai**, the **Nihon Budo Hokushin Kai**, and the International Society of **Jujutsu**ins.

He is also an instructor of **Kodokan Judo** and was a member of the United States **Judo** Association. He is highly ranked in **Judo** and teaches a specialized submission grappling course for advanced **Judoka** United States **Judo** Association rank # 326923.

In the early to mid 1980s, **Akahisa Tanemura Sensei** toured the tristate area giving seminars on **Jujutsu** and **Hapkido** *Korean Jujutsu*.

Taken 1996 at the **Takishin Dojo** while learning **Chushin Gatamae.**

A great many times in his life, he has experienced true combat. He has been stabbed by knives and shot by firearms. He was fond of dangerous work, hiring himself out for security, personal security, and bail enforcement.

Akahisa Tanemura a.k.a. Edward J. Smith, received the **Kaiden No Koto** and **Menkyo Kaiden** from **Katsumi Tanemura Sensei** on Jan 10th, 1991.

Yoshio Tanemura 1977-20--

Yoshio Tanemura Sensei has spent his life doing martial arts, the last 20 of which were spent training in **Koryu**-based Japanese Warrior Arts.

In 2005, **Yoshio** was awarded two of the seven **Densho** earned throughout his training. **Yoshio** became a **Sodenke** at this time. He would have been awarded more if it had not been for monetary restrictions.

Aside from the **Densho**, he holds many titles, ranks, and positions in the martial arts. In 1999, **Yoshio Tanemura Sensei** opened the **Godaishin Dojo** and to date remains the head instructor. **Yoshio** is the Head of the **Neji Gekken Ryu**. In 2009, **Yoshio** was asked by his **Sensei**, **Akahisa**, to officially become **Kaiso** of his own **Ryu**. The name "**Neji Gekken Ryu**", meaning *The Martial Family of the Spiraling Combative Edge*, was agreed upon.

In 2002, **Yoshio** co-founded the **Jihi Bujutsu Kai** with long-time friend and colleague Jamie Ellerbe, **Soke** of the **Nagano Ryu** and the **Mikeba Ryu** traditions. In 2004, **Yoshio Tanemura** assumed the position of **Kaicho** *Organization head* of the **Jihi Bujutsu Kai.**

The information within this lineage chapter was compiled by personal knowledge from David C. Falcaro which would not be possible if not for Edward J. Smith, also with the helpful work in researching from Erin S. Oneill, writings from the (Aiki News / Aikido Journal n.d.), (Wikipedia n.d.), (George Sansom 1958), (Aikibujutsu n.d.), (Kando n.d.), (Koryu n.d.).

<u>Takenouchi Ryu</u> Lineage
This is our connection to the **Takenouchi Ryu**

We are not the **Takenouchi Ryu**, however, this is our lineage to the **Takenouchi Ryu**. Because we come from a great many **Ryu**, we should not claim to be just one of them. This section shows all of the research as of 9/20/2010 that we have collected on the **Takenouchi** line and our connection with it.

Takenouchi Nakatsukasa Dayu Hisamori, Lord of **Ichinose** of **Haga** (a castle in the province of **Mimasaka**, present day **Okayama**) created this **Ryu**. This was done during the **Sengoku** Era, when armed confrontations took place every day.

In recent times, the department of **Okayama** has classified the surroundings of central **Dojo** as an important historical site, because it is the birthplace of **Takenouchi Ryu**. The art form is passed from generation to generation in the **Takenouchi** family until the present day. The line of **Takenouchi Ryu** we are connected to is one of the main bloodlines. As our new **Ryu** has developed over the past decade, the **Neji Gekken Ryu** pulls **Koshi Mawari**, **Tai Saigo**, striking vitals, points of insertion and severing points with the **Tanto**, entrapping and entangling, and many aspects of our **Jutaijutsu**.

Hisamori Nakatsukasadaiyu Takenouchi

In 1532, **Takenouchi Hisamori** retreated to the mountains near the **Sannomiya** shrine to train his martial arts. It was on the sixth night that he was awoken by a **Yamabushi** *mountain warrior priest*. **Hisamori** felt threatened by the **Yamabushi**'s appearance and attacked him. He was quickly thrown to the ground over and over and was defeated quite easily. The stranger then took his **bokken** and broke it in half. He told the traveler, "Such long weapons are useless in combat and there is no need for them." He gave them back and explained how two short swords work much better. The **Yamabushi** told him to put them in his belt and call them **Kogusoku** and taught him how to use them in grappling and close combat. Using vines from a tree, he also taught **Takenouchi** how to bind and tie his enemies. These teachings became known as **Hojojutsu**. After this day of training, the **Yamabushi** seemingly disappeared back into the mountain terrain. Some records say this was reality, others say it was all in a dream.

This story seems a little far-fetched to base an entire art around the one day of training described, but it is what the present day **Takenouchi Ryu** believes. Its unarmed **Jujutsu** techniques include **Tehodoki** , **Ukemi Waza**, **Nage Waza**, **Kansetsu Waza**, **Shime Waza**, **Ne Waza**, **Hojojutsu**, and **Ate Waza**. **Ate Waza** is the form of striking, their hits were not like what is seen today but rather to strike **Kyusho** *vital organ striking* to either unbalance the enemy, to set up for a joint lock or throw or to completely disable. Vital organ striking was also very important to them. The **Ukemi Waza**, or art of receiving the ground, went hand in hand with the

269

Nage Waza. Many of the **Ryuha**'s throws were designed to drive even the most experienced warriors into the ground.

Aside from these traditional **Koryu** art forms, the **Ryu** also, of course, focuses on the usage of the two short swords given to **Hisamori**, known as **Koshi No Mawari**. Very few weapons are used, but those in their arsenal are the **Katana**, **Nagenata**, **Hojo**, **Jutte** and **Rokushakubo**. The **Rokushakubo** is where most of the form is drawn from. Rope restraints are another important adjunct to the arresting arts of **Torinawa**. The techniques of tying up opponents, **Hojojutsu** or **Hoboku**, are taught using the **Haya Nawa**, which is a two **Shaku**, which is about a foot in length, traditionally of a purple color.

Hisakatsu Hitachinosuke Takenouchi

Hitachinosuke Hisakatsu was the son of the founder. He was responsible for establishing a **Dojo** that gathers more than 500 movements of **Koshinomawari Kogusoku**, **Kenpo Taijutsu**, **Kenjutsu**, **Bojutsu**, **Hobakujutsu**, etc.

Hisayoshi Kaganosuke Takenouchi

Kaganosuke Hisayoshi also helped in establishing a **Dojo** that gathers more than 500 movements with his father **Hitachinosuke Hisakatsu**.

Hisatsugu Toichiro Takenouchi

The **Betchu-den Takenouchi Ryu** developed back when the fourth generation had split and **Takeuchi Seidaiyu Masatsuga** moved to the **Bitchu** Province. Despite hundreds of miles and many years of separation, the **Bitchu-den**, still to this day, stay very strong to their roots. So strong, that from the time they started to now, they will not teach anyone outside of the **Takenouchi** family. They have, in fact, recently compared themselves to the original lines and proved how close they still are. It seems the only thing that has changed is the name, instead of **Takenouchi Ryu**, they refer to it as the **Takeuchi Ryu**.

Hisamasa Toichiro Takenouchi

Hisashige Toichiro Takenouchi

Hisataka Toichiro Takenouchi

The **Takenouchi Ryu** has been a major influence to **Ryuha** around the world, and also has three branches of its own. They are the **Soke** line, **Sodenke** line, and the **Bitchu-den**. After the 8th headmaster, **Takenouchi Toichiro**

271

Hisataka, the lineage was split between two brothers. This was done to ensure that the bloodline and tradition would be preserved. The first headmaster of the **Soke** lineage was **Ikeuchi Gamonta**, whose name was changed to **Takenouchi Gamonta Hisayori** when he was adopted into the **Takenouchi** family. The **Sodenke** lineage began with **Takenouchi Tojuro Hisatane**.

Jigoro Kano (**Judo** founder) had the help of four high ranking **Takenouchi Ryu** practitioners to develop modern **Judo**. Some other **Ryu** that draw from them are the **Rikishin Ryu**, **Fusen Ryu**, **Sosuishitsu Ryu**, and the branches of the **Takagi Ryu**.

Takenouchi Gamonta Hisayori	**Takenouchi Tojuro Hisatane**
Takenouchi Toichiro Hisao	**Takenouchi Tojuro Hisamori**
Takenouchi Toichiro Hisanori	**Takenouchi Tojuro Hisamitsu**

Tanemura Katsumi

In the years 1950 to 1955, **Tanemura Katsumi Sensei** trained under a "Mr. **Takenouchi**", as he referred to him. We are not sure which of the two lines he trained under. Although, we do know it would have to have been one of the eleventh generation instructors, **Toichiro Hisatsugu** or **Tojuro Hisahiro**. These two **Ryu** train one right below the other on the side of a mountain in the same area. We have contacted some the descendents of the **Takenouchi Ryu** who live in the U.S. and they were confident that there were records kept of his training. Thus far, we have no way of accessing these records. These records remain strictly guarded by the family.

Tanemura Sensei continued to train what he had learned and added this knowledge to his teachings.

Tanemura Akahisa

Akahisa Tanemura Sensei adored the **Tantojutsu No Waza** that was derived from this tradition. He trained the **Jujutsu No Waza** and when it was expressed and taught to his students, it had a defined **Daito Ryu** influence. This was somewhat unavoidable because of the principle movement stressed in his training.

Tanemura Yoshio

As I learned from my **Sensei**, the teachings that were once derived from the **Takenouchi Ryu** now exist within our

273

Ryu. It should be noted that many of these teachings no longer have the strictest form of the **Takenouchi Ryu** as we train and perform them. Principle-based movement, first and foremost, governs the art form of **Sogobujutsu** as taught by the **Godaishin Dojo**. These principles were derived from a great many **Ryu**, the **Takenouchi Ryu** being one of them.

The information within this lineage section was compiled from research done by Nevin Moyer, Jr. and by personal knowledge from David C. Falcaro, which would not be possible if not for Edward J. Smith, writings from the (Takenouchi Ryu n.d.), (Koryu n.d.) as well as phone conversations and email correspondence between current members of the **Takenouchi Ryu** and Nevin Moyer, Jr.

Phoenix **Ninpo Ryu** Lineage
This is our connection to the Phoenix **Ninpo Ryu**

All things being equal, in truth, we have little influence from this line that still exists within our **Kyoka**. Most all of our collective knowledge stems from other places, these places are documented within the other lineages found in this chapter of the book. This book is about our history and I wish to honor all of it, no matter how much or how little was taken from each experience. Although only a small amount was filtered out and passed on from this source, there is realized a true quality to the acquired material. Having stated that, we are better off as a **Ryu** having had this influence.

Stan Triplett

Stan Triplett spent many years training in different martial arts. Stan started his martial journey with Southern Shoalin Kung-fu, but discontinued after a year from lack of interest. His first main direct study was in Pentjak Silat. After years of training, he gained great proficiency in this style. Stan had a true love for Silat and hoped to one day open a school. This proved impossible because his Guru (teacher) was traditional and quite strict; he stated, "There are few islands, one Guru per island. There are only two ways you can become a Guru--your Guru dies and you take his place or you kill him and take his place." After some time, Stan's Guru moved away to start a school somewhere else and Stan was left with his acquired skills, desire to teach and no certification. At that

275

time in the 1970s, it was quite apparent that a black belt would earn him the accreditation needed to teach. For him to be properly recognized, he would need to start over and climb through the belt ranks. This was the original reason he began an American blend of **Isshin Ryu Karatedo** and "Ninga" (not **Ninja**). As a side note, Ninga came out of New Jersey, USA. I have had some difficulty finding Ninga origins. Grandmaster of the Ninga system was Fredric Godfree. His teacher was Grandmaster Bose. The story goes that Bose brought it from Japan. I know how strange Ninga sounds; it was a name created to mean the "American version of **Ninja**". I got the information decades ago verbally from Stan Triplett **Sensei**. GM Godfree taught Ninga to Grandmaster Versocki.

This blend was named Ninga-**Isshin Ryu** by its founder, actor/martial arts Grandmaster, Joseph Versocki. Under the instruction of Versocki **Sensei,** Stan flew through the ranks. With his versatile, effective Silat skills, he was known to make short work of many higher ranks during **Karate** sparring sessions. This is what earned him the nickname "The Phoenix". When he seemed to be beaten, under the use of his **Karate** skills, he would "rise from the ashes" of possible defeat with his Silat skills and win. Stan Triplett, to date, holds a steadfast connection to his **Karate Sensei**, GM Versocki, who now recognizes Stan as a 9th Degree Black Belt under him.

In the mid 1980s, the martial arts craze of the day was **Ninja** and **Ninjutsu**. Having a developed interest in the **Ninja**, Stan started his informal training in the **Ninjutsu** Seminar circuit. He attended a great deal of them. Some of the instructors were Charles Daniels, Bud Mounstrum, **Shoto**

276

Tanemura and others. He sought out every seminar he could, recorded them and traded copies of recorded seminars with others. He also bought the books Steven Hays wrote, the videos that Robert Bussey made and did his best to acquire any knowledge he could from the **Ninjutsu** world. This went on for years and when the opportunity came about to join the then new **Ninjutsu/Ninpo** organization, the **Genbukan**, he took it.

As a member of the **Genbukan**, he had access to many other training materials, such as books and videos that only members and training partners in the U.S. could get. Training in the **Genbukan** is unlike other training because your **Sensei** resides in **Japan** and you cannot make class on a regular basis. For instance, if one were to brag about going

to **Japan** to train with their **Sensei**, what they are really saying is they never train with their **Sensei**. In the U.S., if someone said they trained five times last year with their **Sensei**, anyone hearing it would laugh as if it were a joke and yet, five times would be a whole lot compared to most everyone in the **Genbukan**. To compensate for not having their **Sensei** around, the instructors hold events in which they share their own experiences while visiting with **Shoto Tanemura**

Stan Triplett **Sensei** with his instructor Dan McEaddy **Sensei** taken after an event 2000

Sensei (the one or two times they did). There was not day in and day out training. Because of this, it must have felt, at times, like the blind leading the blind (although no one was at fault because everyone was in the same boat). It was difficult to learn this way after having the normal training experience with present **Sensei** in a nearby **Dojo**. Because of this, and a general lack of support in learning, Stan left the organization. He had the **Genbukan** curriculum in books and videos and continued to train it by himself and with his students.

He learned and studied much about **Isshin Ryu Kenjutsu**. I am not sure where he obtained this information.

Triplett acquired and studied many video recordings of **Masaaki Hatsumi**, founder of the **Bujinkan**. He attempted to join the American **Bujinkan** at one point, but left because of feeling unimpressed with the quality of instruction. Years later, he studied more of the **Bujinkan** under Bruce Snyder.

In the mid 1990s, Stan Triplett began his development under Grandmaster Dan McEaddy, founder of the Angelic **Ninjutsu** System. GM McEaddy recognizes him as a 10th degree Black Belt. McEaddy's **Ninjutsu** came from the world famous **Koga Ryu Ninjutsu** Grandmaster, Ron Duncan, Sr.

Stan Triplett founded the Phoenix **Ninpo Ryu**. The Phoenix **Ninpo Ryu** is an American **Ninjutsu**-based curriculum that includes traditional and non-traditional techniques.

Stan Triplett is also a member of the Circle of Masters. He is a certified instructor of the Pyramid School of the Masters and the Spiritual Training of the Circle of Masters.

David C. Falcaro

In late1990, I began my study under Stan Triplett. **Ninjutsu**, for me, was amazing and powerful. I remember, as a young teen, being quite obsessed. In my teenage mind, Triplett **Sensei** was one of the greatest martial artists in the U.S. He was quite better than most all **Ninjutsu Sensei--** that was easy to see.

His movement was sharper and better refined than all the rest of the sloppy **Ninjutsu** that was out there. I had unfair expectations of him, his knowledge, his ability and also the art of **Ninjutsu** as a whole.

After I met Edward J. Smith **Sensei** in 1995, and after seeing what little he showed me, I formally asked Triplett **Sensei** for permission to begin training with Smith **Sensei**. Triplett, confident in the training he impressed, responded, "Sure, if you want to. It won't take long for you to see that the grass only looks greener on the other side." The statement Stan Triplett **Sensei** had made that day would have been true with almost any other martial artist. Truly, if it were anyone else, but not in this case. The experience of beginning training with Smith **Sensei** destroyed my internal image of who I thought Triplett **Sensei** was. I had built him up so much that

279

it was a true, but necessary, blow to my ego. This was mostly because I had wanted to be just like him. Smith **Sensei** displayed a world of knowledge that appeared endless and his ability and power were unmatched. It was something I had never seen. To date, no one comes close. When I saw all that Triplett **Sensei** did not know, although not aware of it then, it was the beginning of the end of my training under Stan Triplett. For over two more years, I tried to train in both **Dojo**. In 1997, after over seven years, I left my old teacher. Nearly everything I had learned from Triplett **Sensei** was forcibly ripped apart, altered, remolded or thrown out. I was changed into what I am today by Smith **Sensei**. I sometimes look back on those days with the understanding that what I took from the experience was good basics. At that time (I have no way of knowing if they still practice this way), Triplett **Sensei** taught more precisely than most all **Sensei** in **Ninjutsu**. His movement was entrained and crisp. He began my study of many aspects of **Bujutsu**. Under his study, I attained my first black belt and I earned it. His curriculum was vast compared to that of the **Genbukan**. He was a fine teacher--holding true to his standard. He sculpted his **Kyu,** making sure that each and every one of them continued to learn at all times. Much of my beginning teaching style, the first four years before I came into my own fully, I owe to him. I knew Stan Triplett **Sensei** as a man of moral integrity. As a teen, he was an easy man to look up to. My one regret is that ties were severed. That was never my intent.

The information discussed in this section came directly from the personal experience and study of David C. Falcaro as well as a bit of research gathered from (Triplett n.d.), and (Tanemura n.d.)

<u>Nagano Ryu</u> Lineage
This is our connection to the **Nagano Ryu**

Nagano Ryu was created from **Asayama Ichiden Ryu, Gyokushin Ryu Koppojutsu, Tenshin Shoden Katori Shinto Ryu, Ugai Koga Ryu Ninjutsu, Daito Ryu Aikijujutsu**, and **Akutagawa Ryu Jutaijutsu**. The **Nagano Ryu** history is being researched. It is currently believed that **Nagano Shigazato Soke**'s father founded the **Ryu**.

<u>Nagano Shigazato Iyo</u>

<u>Jamie Ellerbe</u>

Jamie Ellerbe **Sensei** began his martial arts training in August, 1980. He has spent his life since then studying the martial arts and, over the years, has received several honors. In 1997, Ellerbe **Sensei** was honored with a **Menkyo Kaiden** license from **Nagano Shigazato Iyo**. It was at that time that Ellerbe **Sensei** began teaching and working with the public. He began to teach **Jujutsu** seminars, rape prevention workshops, and defensive tactics courses for law enforcement. Ellerbe **Sensei** began his Capoeira journey in 1996 while he was a student at North Carolina A&T State University. At the university, he met Dr. William Martin, who was at the time, a student of Mestre Nego Gato. Dr. Martin founded the first and only student martial arts organization on campus for Capoeira and **Jujutsu**. It was under Dr. Martin's training that Ellerbe **Sensei** studied Mestre Nego Gato. Therefore, he asked him if he could join his group. In 1998, Ellerbe **Sensei** was honored to meet the founder of Mestre Nego Gato, Mestre Nego Gato himself. He also met Contra-Mestre Jo who, in 2002, accepted him as her student. After many years of training, Ellerbe **Sensei** now teaches and trains students in Capoeira Regional and Angola as an Estagiario in Equipe Jo Capoeira at the **Kazoku Dojo**.

ᅵ

David C. Falcaro

After many years training in the **Samurai** arts, I felt my training was lacking in the area of **Shinobi No Mono**. I wished to rectify this by finding a teacher of **Ninjutsu** by searching the Internet. I was very unimpressed with mainstream **Ninjutsu** for many reasons. The largest being a general sloppiness in execution of their art, as well as a lack of knowledge combined with a large amount of ego indulgence. It seemed to be, in a very real way, a common thread among those organizations. It left a bad taste in my mouth and I continued my search for years. It was a result of this search that I came into contact with many of my **Buyu** *warrior brothers*. I closely examined the material that everyone was presenting about their history and their art forms. Jamie's history stood out. In 2001, he had a website that was quite in-depth, explaining a rich warrior art deeply rooted in Japanese martial history. This was right up my alley; I contacted him. Many emails and phone conversations later, we agreed to meet. In 2002, I rented a 15 passenger van and loaded up my **Kyu** for a trip to North Carolina. From our first meeting, a kinship was formed. Ellerbe opened the books to me, allowing me to see and study his **Ryu**. He quickly awarded me a **Godan** within his **Ryu**. The teachings from his **Ryu** were an easy thing for me to pick up. Ellerbe **Sensei** visited my home in Pennsylvania

and we trained his curriculum. I truly enjoyed our first sessions; knowledge came flying out as fast as I could take it in. Most all were movements I had trained before, for many years prior, but there was an element of **Ninpo** that I truly missed, one that stemmed from **Ryu** I had never trained in before. After years of an established friendship, Ellerbe **Sensei** asked me to return the favor and show him aspects of the **Neji Gekken Ryu**. We have shared many things with each other. Over the years, our families have become very close. We look forward to our visits not just for the training, but also as fathers. It is fun for us to get the kids together and catch up. I am honored to call Jamie my close friend and brother in the arts. I know that both of us look forward to the future and all that we will learn from one another.

The information discussed in this section came directly from the personal experience and study of David C. Falcaro as well as some writing given to me by Jamie Ellerbe, and (Ellerbe n.d.).

Chapter 6

The Nine Principles of our **Ryu**

Fuhengenri No Neji Gekken Ryu
Universal Principles of the Spiraling Combative
Edge Martial Family

Preamble to the nine principles

The nine principles are examples of warrior ways of conduct. They are an outline by which the **Neji Gekken Ryu** conducts itself. Also, they each go over **Sanshin** *the three hearts*: the heart of Mental, the heart of Physical, and the heart of the Spiritual. These cover the aspects of war and life. One does not need to bother with these ideals if one is merely interested in fighting. To understand this, one must understand the difference between warring and fighting. A **Bugei** will never fight, yet he will when he must, wage war. The warring that the **Bugei** take part in is an impartial, impersonal hunt in order to take down or take out the enemy. There is no conflict in this practice. Fighting is a personal conflict between two or more people. In all cases, no matter what the cost, a **Bugei** will not fight.

When reading these principles, remember again this is a way of living one's life. Do not spend time thinking about how to debate these points so that you can get away with not fulfilling your honor. Instead, focus on understanding what is written. This is what is expected of you. Your **Giri** *duty* is owning up to your commitments to yourself, **Ryu**, **Sensei** and **Dojo**. One does this by living out the Nine Principles.

2010, Taken at an **Aiki No Jutsu** Seminar while displaying the **Aiki** concept of **Toin**. David C. Falcaro **Sensei** demonstrating with **Uke** Anthony Rodriquez. Wayne Mancuso in the background. Seminar held with Edward J. Smith **Sensei** at the Northampton **Godaishin Dojo**.

Furthermore, a warrior works to grow and strengthen himself. You cannot pick and choose which principles to follow and which principles to ignore. The eventual recourse for the continual unfulfillment of one's **Giri** is expulsion. Only in a rare and severe case, a **Hamon** may be issued.

The lower the rank you hold, the less we will expect of you. So white belts need not worry! It is all brand new, and we know this. The higher the rank, the more we will expect of you. With being a **Kyu** comes leniency, with being a **Dan** comes none. As you read, know that the principles are equally important and were not put in any order of importance.

Aiirenai
The principle of Conflict

Introduction
This refers to the concept of only dealing with what is and being in conflict with nothing that is. When something "is" it means that this instant has already occurred and there can be no action taken upon it to prevent its occurrence. This does

2007, Teaching two-man throwing with Erin O'Neill and Eric P. Fichter **Sensei**.

287

not mean one cannot have a reaction to this incident. In fact, one should have a reaction. This is what is meant by "dealing with what is".

Section 1. Mental aspects of the Conflict Principle

When someone is angry with you, deal with it; don't be in conflict with it. Remember what it is like to be angry, relate to their opposing view. When they cast aspersions toward you, understand where they are coming from; don't argue and don't take it personal. Never allow anyone to hurt your feelings; stand strong and emotionally unaffected. Agree whenever possible and offer your support in coming to a mutual understanding. Be content with disagreeing, there is no problem unless you allow there to be one. Look for logic in their argument; it can act as a key in ending the dispute. If one is irate, they are emotionally strained. When this happens, most times this person will become increasingly angered if you seem unaffected by their attempts at putting you down or making you angry. Attempt to calm them; speak to them as if you respect them. Soothe them with your voice, be genuine and nice. Never engage in conflict.

Section 2. Physical aspects of the Conflict Principle

When applying martial techniques in a combative form, go with what comes. Many martial artists make a claim to use the enemy's energy or force against them. This principle puts that claim into practice. When the enemy is fighting a technique you wish to apply on him, don't fight back (a **Bugei** does not fight). Use the force behind his fight to take you into your next technique. If something doesn't work, don't force it, try to fix it and as soon as you realize that you can't fix it, move on.

Section 3. Spiritual aspects of the Conflict Principle

If a bad situation comes up in your life, hit it head on and deal only with what is. Once something "is", it already exists; wishing that it never was or thinking about if things went differently is not a good use of time and energy. When one is in conflict with anything that "is" they are invariably in conflict with everything that "is". This, in turn, means that one is in conflict with the entire universe. If it feels like sometimes the world is crashing down around you, that is because it "is". Come to the realization that if something "is", the only way to change it is to affect it in the present. Putting it off to the future or dealing with it later is not effective. Looking to the past can only give a perspective on the inevitable, unchangeable (from this time perspective) acts that came together for this to occur. Live in the now; enact change now. Do not give time to worrying about it or wanting it to have never happened. Set your attention and focus to your intention and desires in life. Don't view things as obstacles or barriers, view them as wet clay. Start molding what you already have into what you want before asking for more. View life in this way. The universe has already given you the tools of the trade, just learn your trade. If things are pushing you in a direction, then flow in that direction. Do not stand in conflict.

Arinomama
Truth, Devotion to the truth

Section 1. Mental aspects of the Truth Principle

One must devote one's self to a truthful life. Lying, like anything, can become an addiction; it can consume one's entire life. A warrior must never lie to himself, his **Ryu**, family, or close friends. Lies break the bonds of closeness in relationships; they promote distancing. It is the warrior's duty to uphold the bonds of brotherhood, friendship, loyalty, love and family the best way they can. It has been said that truth is love and love is truth. If a warrior finds this to be true, then one must live inside of love as one lives inside of truth.

1992 Taken during a **Tantojutsu** demo, I was a **Hachi Kyu** at the time.

A strong concept of reality is imperative to the warrior's lifestyle. What we take as truth shapes our world. Things must be kept real on all levels or the art itself will degrade and fall apart. Since we are striving for truth, as we find it,

2004 Taken during a class on **Ninin Gata**. Northampton **Godaishin Dojo,** David C. Falcaro **Sensei** teaches with Liz Hamilton and a young Eric Fichter.

we must not allow it to be tainted or added to. The truth must be refined and stripped of all falsehood. If one has a skew on the truth, then they have a skew on living. He must devote himself to understanding and upholding the truth. Without truth, any action taken is foolish and wrong. With

291

truth comes right action. With pure truth comes spontaneous right action.

Section 2. Physical aspects of the Truth Principle

Be true to your art. Know that this art form has everything needed for combat. There is no reason to step outside of the art to incorporate movements from other arts. See truth in what you are doing. There have been good, capable marital artists who have entered physical confrontations and who have dropped everything they knew about body movement and technique. They became street fighters. They were quickly taken down. It is not because the art failed, it is because the practitioner failed to see the truth in their art. This art has been battlefield tested for hundreds of years. Thousands of men died in the perfection of this art. So, the truth is, the art works. Understand what it is that you are doing and you will have no need for trust. Trust is a wonderful thing, but only if it leads one to truth. Trust alone, as strong as it might be, is prone to attack. Truth stands, whereas trust can be weakened. Do trust in yourself and in the art, but only long enough to find the truth of it. You are training in a warrior art, training to perfect your movement, to live the art, to one day pass on the art, and to use the art. One must be willing and ready to hurt, injure, and maybe maim people. This is the truth about the art. This is the truth about life. You have to look at it in this way, so that you are more than ready to use the art. Understand application, train for real, and be truthful with yourself. Know which techniques you can pull off in the street and which techniques you wouldn't dare try. Throw away the flash and get to what is real. So, what is real? The movements that you have been working on all along are your basics. That is what will save you in combat and that is what will keep you alive.

292

Section 3. Spiritual aspects of the Truth Principle

The concept of **Inyoho** has a lot to say about truth. After understanding this duality, many people get the feeling that there is no point in believing in, or caring about, what is true or not true. This is because in this world, all things seem neither white nor black, but rather different shades of gray. That much is true. However, one must see the duality in that statement as well; for we are not merely physical beings. A part of us is bound by this "gray" universe, another part is not. While the physical lives out its whole life in the "gray", the spiritual is not bound by these confines. That unbound part of us must be realized. Then it must be tapped into and relied on in matters of truth. It is there where we will find truth and it is here where we must use it.

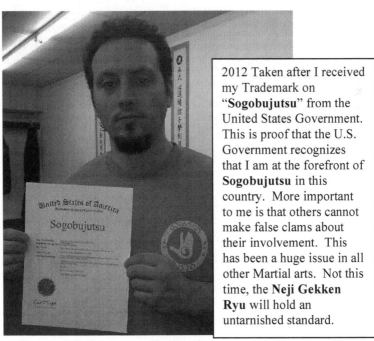

2012 Taken after I received my Trademark on **"Sogobujutsu"** from the United States Government. This is proof that the U.S. Government recognizes that I am at the forefront of **Sogobujutsu** in this country. More important to me is that others cannot make false clams about their involvement. This has been a huge issue in all other Martial arts. Not this time, the **Neji Gekken Ryu** will hold an untarnished standard.

Baransu
Balance, Maintain Balance, Control the center

Section 1. Mental Aspects of the Balance Principle

This is the same teaching as the warrior concept of **Wa**. **Wa** is the concept of "Harmony". It is a teaching of the warrior concept of **Inyoho**. The warrior must see and be able to recognize the **Wa** in all things. It is seemingly easy for most of us to see harmony in forests, streams, ponds and wildlife, but the warrior pushes his understanding further to see the harmony in anything--even war. A warrior could look at two warring enemies and not see two conflicting sides. Rather, he would see the war as one harmonious action with both sides, spending their time, energy and lives getting ready to play out their part in a combined effort to create harmonious destruction. In this way, one accepts that their own enemy is not a foe. One sees their enemy as their partner, both working hard together toward an end result. Harmony is valued for the freedoms it allows. After the warrior comes to this understanding, he no longer has a use for resentment, hatred, upsetment or distain. He is no longer holding on to any thoughts or feelings of ill will. This freed up energy can now be put toward the campaign.

2007 Taken during a class on **Hanbojutsu** Eric Fichter **Sensei** was my **Uchideshi** at the time.

2009 Taken
during a demo
Eric P. Fichter
Sensei and I show
walking throws.

Section 2. Physical Aspects of the Balance Principle

Through the understanding of **Tai Atari** *attaching one's self
to the enemy*, we understand that you and the enemy become
one being with one combined center of balance. We must
become in control of that center. We accomplish this
through the knowledge of **Chushin Dori** *the physical
occupying of the center of the enemy's balance points*,
through the application of **Happo No Kazushi** *the methods*

of eight directional off-balancing and **Hando No Kazushi**
the methods of tricking the enemy into off balancing himself.
We do this while maintaining our own **Taisaigo** *proper body
posturing and alignment.* This must be stressed throughout
all **Waza** *techniques.* The result will be that the enemy's
balance will rely on ours. As we withdraw our presence, the
enemy has such a lack of balance that he cannot stay on his
feet and will fall down. Without balance, the enemy is weak
and extremely prone to attack. When in control of balance,
we are strong and capable.

1992 Demo on **Jutaijutsu**

Section 3. Spiritual Aspects of the Balance Principle

This principle is firstly about the understanding of balance, which is **Inyoho**. After reaching this understanding one must maintain this balance in every interaction. This means that one should never treat the people they care for poorly. Always put on your best face to your loved ones. Shower them with love, attention and care; give of yourself unto them. The contrary is true as well and that is where we find the balance. There is a saying to "never be nice to your enemies". This means don't spend too much time giving them compliments, your feelings or your ideas. Not only will the enemies (people who don't like you) not appreciate it, but they will also have no use for it. A similar saying is, "Don't cast your pearls among swine."

The second part of this principle is about controlling the center. The center is who you truly are; neither end of the spectrum. By always being wonderful to those close to you, it is only natural for them to believe that you are the perfect friend, lover, or brother. They may, in time, put you up on a pedestal. You must lead them to believe otherwise by maintaining that you are only human. Humility is so important to the warrior's life. This type of idealizing could prove to be extremely detrimental to their overall view of you. All you would have to do is screw up once and do something "human" and they may hate you for it. This would happen because you were unable to live up to the perfect image they had of you. A warrior must strive to be that of an angel, but never to be seen as anything but a man. The opposite is also important; you don't want your enemies thinking that you are a demon or such a bad guy. This is the maintenance of maintaining balance.

Bonsatsu
Temple, The Body is the Temple

Section 1. Mental Aspects of the Temple Principle

This is keeping the doors open and keeping "one's cup empty". It is always being ready to accept new knowledge and looking to greater empower one's mind. This also envelops mental fortitude and the ability to stay morally straight in the face of temptation.

2008 **Koshi Garuma** done during a private demonstration for the students on the power of **Sogobujutsu.** Erin O'Neal throwing Eric Coberly. Taken at the Bethlehem **Godaishin Hombu Dojo.**

Many sages have quoted, "Try to toss a stone into the pond without making any ripples." The idea is that every action has its effects on the whole. Mentally, we must be a temple and we must stand strong with a foundation in deep-rooted moral ethics. The walls of our temple consist of the concepts of the warrior code. This binds us, holds us up, teaches us and guides us. What we are holding up with our strong foundation and protecting with our reinforced walls is our insides. We are laden with ideals of bringing about more selflessness, self expression, introspection, self motivation, internal change, self worth, and self love into our own lives. In truth, we are the stone that hits the water. By living out this principle, the ripples that we create in our lives will be about love, understanding, forgiveness, compassion, and caring. They will ripple out and touch our families, our loved ones and our fellow man.

2009 Stopping quick to pose for a pic on a family training day, Liam, Jody, David Falcaro. Taken at the old Hellertown **Godaishin Dojo.**

Section 2. Physical Aspects of the Temple Principle

The warrior's body is maintained as a sacred place of dwelling, a true temple. Great physical maintenance is kept up on the proper feeding, clothing, healing, exercising, and strengthening of the body. Also, no one can be permitted to physically harm the temple. This, of course, refers to outside influences such as an angered person, an enemy, etc. Also, this includes refraining from Sadomasochism of any form. Certain acts, such as attempting suicide, may be a cry for help from a broken person, nevertheless, the act itself is considered forbidden. Selfmutilation, such as cutting wrists and arms, scarring, or piercing, are marked as forbidden behavior as well. In our history, pertaining to this principle, you will find that tattooing was refrained from and reserved for criminals alone. One must refrain from the use of any and all addictive drug use, including any and all narcotics, marijuana, cigarettes, or cigars. There is no such thing as recreational drug use for those caring to follow the warrior code. Even alcohol must be given up should it become addictive to the individual. Drug dependency is looked down upon and is to be ended and stopped whenever possible. Caffeine, if "needed", should also be given up.

These values do not translate well in today's society. No matter, they must be upheld in the face of adversity. We have all heard the misguided rants about how it's no big deal, but we must fight those types of thoughts, hold our own, and remain on the right path. Understand that there will always be people who feel that this is the way to go in life, but it is not for us and it is not our way.

As for experimenting with drugs, all the experimentation with drugs we could ever do was overdone in the 1960s.

There is no such thing anymore as experimentation with drugs, there is only drug abuse.

Section 3. Spiritual Aspects of the Temple Principle

This is a constant work on refining the spirit, searching the self for inner change, and striving for greater awareness of the self. The goal is **Satori** *enlightenment*. The path to it is the warrior concept of **Seishin Teki Kyoho**. This is also referred to as **Seishin Tanren**. **Seishin Teki Kyoho** is the concept of forging of one's spirit. For some, the only purpose of the spirit is for use in the afterlife. There is a focus on where the spirit goes when we die. This is where Religion comes into play. **Seishin Teki Kyoho** is not religious. It is about what we are doing with this gift of life and how we use our spirit to move through it. A warrior sees the body as a vehicle, the mind as a map, the spirit is the driver and life is the road we are driving down. The vehicle (the body) alone would be a useless instrument. A vehicle without the use of a map (the mind) would be driving without a clue as to where it is going. Therefore, the mind is an important instrument as well. The other instrument is the driver (the spirit). You can know where you are going and have a fast car, but without a competent driver you'll crash into a lot of things. Each of the three instruments must be fine tuned in order to make life a nicer trip. **Seishin Tanren** is about the great importance of the spirit in this life and how it must be forged into a more useful tool, a better driver. Just as one forges iron into a sword, so does the warrior forge the spirit.

One must commit themself to the forging process. Learn the concepts of the Warrior Code, the Nine Principles and their **Oyo** *application.*

<u>Chuugi</u>
Loyalty, Loyalty to the **Ryu**

This principle is about fulfilling all of the **Giri** *duties* expected of you no matter what your rank, your title or the position you hold in the **Dojo** or in the **Ryu**. It entails:

Taken in 2007 during a class on **Toamijutsu.** Jack Toole at the Northampton **Godaishin Dojo**.

303

Dedication to the nine principles
Being there for the members of the **Ryu** whether in times of
need or not
Never selling out the **Dojo** or the **Ryu**
Appreciating and upholding one's position and rank
Extending the hand of brotherhood mentally, physically and
spiritually
Learning and living the art

Anyone who attends classes could claim to be a part of a
Ryu, this principle asks one to prove it.

2010 **Zempo Nage** done by Jacob B. Fouts **Sensei** Training in a field with his student.

To become truly loyal as a **Kyu**, one must understand first
the inner workings of the **Dojo** and **Ryu**. In this chapter, I
have outlined some of the most important terms. As I define
these terms, I go into detail on what our individual (as a **Ryu**)
approach is. Most will be found to be customs seen in most
Dojo, yet some are sure to be very different.

To get us started with this principle, let us define "**Ryu**" further and talk about the brotherhood aspect and how it comes about.

Ryu (Literal translation "martial arts family")
The **Giri** *duty* for a **Ryu** is to grow in numbers and personal growth, to get stronger through training and interpersonal relationships, and to maintain a brotherhood that loves, protects, and cares for each other.

When you train in martial arts, you put your trust in your **Sensei**'s hands. This trust includes lending your body for instructional purposes. In skilled hands, when you are joint locked, choked, thrown, punched and kicked, you immediately become comfortable having witnessed firsthand what could have happened to you and how the skill of your instructor prevented your injury. When training with classmates, this comfort and trust usually takes a bit longer to attain. The beginner is not quick to trust the other students just because they have been training longer. The more accomplished student is certainly not quick to lend his body to the toiling of a novice. This process is not just about getting to know each other's movements. You eventually share a great deal of yourself with your classmates. They learn your hangups, fears, and frustrations. They share your desires, drive, and passion for martial study. They are there to lend new perspective, pushing you to go further faster, and share firsthand in your successes. You learn to draw off of each other's strengths and support each other through forging out weakness. Culture, race, sex-- these things fall by the wayside. What you find is brotherhood.

Brotherhood is something that happens as a result of each individual's dedication to attaining proficiency in the art. The dedication is seen in making class so that you may learn and grow. A more selfless side quickly evolves as you find yourself also making classes so that your training partner

has you to train with. We see this in the drive to earn rank to represent our growth. Added is a sense of responsibility to help your training partners to attain rank and to display a return on a successful investment for the efforts put forth by those who worked in helping learn the material.

Taken in 2006 while demonstrating **Sogobujutsu** at the Bladez Demonstration. Showing a powerful hands-free spine-lock while explaining aspects of **Aiki** to the crowd. An event put on for all of the martial arts schools in the Lehigh Valley PA, USA.

Section 1. Mental Aspects of the Loyalty Principle

This refers to being loyal to the teachings of our **Ryu** and to appreciating the **Dojo** or **Ryu**, our history and where we are going in the future. Our goal is to make sure that our future is a bright one and to never speak out against its ideals. It's about living life by the code and principles set forth by the **Neji Gekken Ryu**.

White belts, specifically, may want to ask themselves: Is this right for you? This may not be the right place for you depending on what you are looking for in the martial arts. Our school holds classes in Japanese **Bujutsu** *the warrior arts of ancient Japan*. We hold other classes also (kids class, self defense, healing), but **Bujutsu** is our main focus. This art that we share was developed over a time span of about 2,000 years. The art is huge. The knowledge it brings is vast, spanning across the globe, delving into every study of self development imaginable. The art is designed to help a person to grow physically, mentally and spiritually. It is brought to you as a lifestyle; something to help you through everyday life and something for you to bring to life through your training. It is not something to fall back on; rather, it is something you become. It is extremely empowering. For these reasons, it will not be dumbed-down, and it is certainly not something to throw a price tag on. I hope that you find what you are looking for in the martial arts. If you are looking for a lot less in an art, please ask **Sensei**. If we cannot accommodate you, we can refer you to many other different artists in the area.

2010 Ed Hall III showing **Ura Osai** from **Kata Kaiten** on **Uke** Kyle Keys during the Hellertown **Godaishin Dojo** Grand opening demonstration.

Beginning Promises Made by a **Kyu**

When a student begins training, he promises the following:
1. To be a friend of the **Ryu**
2. Loyalty
3. Time

4. His physical self
5. Class dues
6. Honesty
7. Willingness to learn

If the **Kyu** does not fulfill these promises, his **Sensei** is not required by the code to teach him. Also, if anyone breaks the warrior code, no one else is honor-bound by it with regard to that person.

Another promise that is expected, but not required these days, is to learn the Warrior Code and to live it.

Our Focus in the Beginning of our Training
At our **Dojo,** we focus on the **Ryu**. The members are most important. The goal of the **Ryu** is to keep members learning and growing--prospering through the extent of their lives. A plain martial arts school does not offer all of the interesting and informative things that a true **Dojo** can. We are, in reality, much, much more. We are a group of people who come together periodically to learn about ourselves and to grow with the knowledge of the self. Yes, and to train, but to do so in a realistic way while gaining an understanding of culture, awareness, flow, and balance. All the while, we are experiencing life by having fun, making memories, and sharing in the teachings of mountain sages--true Masters. These teachings are centuries old and proven to work by the life experiences of countless thousands. What are these teachings about? They are about improving the quality of life. How? By taking away the fear of an attack, whether verbal or physical and by strengthening the body's flexibility, agility, tone and mind.

What We Focus on Later in Our Training

Sogobujutsu *everything.*

Problems:
When problems arise, bring them to the attention of those in charge of caring for you. Don't complain or ever make bad comments about the **Ryu** or its members to outsiders. The **Ryu** and its members must never be given a poor image. Don't keep things inside, share with the **Ryu**. Through this sharing, the **Ryu** will grow strong. Be loyal to your **Ryu** and help to better explain any contrary view. Have the patience and fortitude to help create change for the betterment of the whole. We must come together and heal any internal strife. If you feel that somehow there is a problem and something might be unjust, do not remain silent. If a problem arises that becomes too large for us to handle, instead of informing outsiders, the **Sensei** will first gain council with a group of **Ryu**.

Negative Circulation:
The circulation of lies, deception, dark secrets, back talking, cursing, hidden motives, insults, backstabbing, mean tricks, bullying, yelling, complaining, and mistreatment of any kind in the **Dojo**, or involving any of the **Ryu**, is forbidden. It is the witnessing of these forbidden acts that gives a **Kyu** the opportunity to prove himself. It remains the **Giri** of each **Kyu** to look after their **Ryu**. This is done by the **Kyu** swiftly putting an end to the witnessed act and reporting all findings. **Kyu** are not permitted to mount conflicting sides. No one is allowed to ask you to take sides against another. No one is to be singled out. Every member is a part of the **Ryu** and we stand together. There is only one side and that is the **Ryu**. The idea is that if someone is messing with one of our members, they are messing with all of us.

310

Drama:

Never force involvement into personal discussions. Accept the fact that not everything includes you. Know that you are cared about and that you are cared for. Do not force members to prove it to you. The use of guilt, pity, drama, and staged outbreaks of emotion for the purpose of manipulation is looked down upon here. Holding someone emotionally

2010 Eric Fichter **Sensei** during testing for his **Shodan**. Taken at the Northampton **Godaishin Dojo**. He was given a bath towel to demonstrate **Nandemo Buki Ni Nareru.**

hostage is a twisted way to extort energy from them. Extortion is not allowed. These attention-getters are unbecoming of a **Kyu**. This behavior is to be reported and ignored by the **Ryu**. We must not reward this outcry for attention; it would merely add to the problem. Instead, it will be dealt with by a support team under **Sensei**'s supervision.

Guidelines of Humility:
Never boast about self, family, bloodline, **Dojo**, **Ryu**, etc. You may, of course, speak well of others with regard to these things. Truth stands, yet don't offer the truth. Offer the humble version, plain facts with no emotion. The understanding of humility begins with the understanding that even that which seems perfect is not perfect 90% of the time. Even our understanding of perfection is tainted by the confines of our reality. Know your limitations as well as your abilities, yet state neither (unless if asked by a higher up in your **Ryu**). Teach and talk about what is possible, not what you can do. The experienced man knows that he has no experience. When learning, no matter how much one believes he knows, begin each class with a clean slate and learn it again.

Ryugi:
Ryugi is the warrior concept of wearing the moral and ethical values of your **Ryu** like a **Gi** *uniform*. One does this daily whether they wish to or not. It is an important part of being a member of a **Ryu**. For a **Kyu**, this is sometimes a struggle. For a **Dan**, it is as easy as breathing. For a **Dan**, this is a good way of looking at it for they must maintain **Ryugi** as they must breathe. Everyone feels like they are being choked once in a while, and it may seem hard for the young **Kyu**, at first, to deal with an oncoming attack. In time, they will

312

learn and it will become natural. They may not agree with
the moral values, but that is not important. They may not
understand the ethics, it does not matter. What is needed is
for the **Kyu** to maintain their own **Ryugi** in every instance
throughout their life.

Reporting:
It is the **Kyu**'s own **Giri** to report all wrongdoings. This is
not "ratting" or "narking", it is loyalty. Many people like to
take the comfortable standpoint of "It's none of my business
what that person does with his life." Although this may be
acceptable thinking for some people outside of the **Dojo**, as a
member inside of the **Dojo**, you are asked to be more
responsible. If a person's actions affect the **Dojo** or reflect
on the **Dojo**, it is everyone's business; it is **Dojo** business.

One starts with themselves, and then cares for others. To not
report wrongdoings is a dishonorable act. This could result
in the tearing apart of the **Ryu**. One reports directly to
Sensei whenever possible. The **Dohai** should be informed
and they will pass on this knowledge. Never assume **Sensei**
knows already, make sure. When something dishonorable
takes place, **Sensei** will sit on the problem for days,
sometimes weeks, without stating a word. This is done to
test the **Kyu**, to see if they have the respect enough to fess up
to what they have done.

Dating:
Dating between **Kyu**, as a rule, in many **Dojo** is not allowed.
In the **Godaishin Dojo**, it is permitted as long as it remains
constructive. An adult **Kyu** is not allowed to date a child or a
teenager. A teenage **Kyu** is not allowed to date a child. This
is not up for debate. The rule of thumb is if they are not in

your class, you are not permitted to date them. **Kyu** involved in dating are expected to conduct themselves in a kind and respectful manner. Physical affection, no matter what the relationship, has no place and does not exist on the **Tatame Dojo** *floor* and will never be expressed during class. Should the relationship become destructive, it will end. Continued inappropriate behavior will result in punishments and steps will be taken to make certain it does not continue.

Honor:
One's main goal is to attain great honor. One does this through dedication to learning the nine principles and then a dedication to living them out as an honorable warrior. Without honor, a warrior is merely a skilled fighter. Without honor, a man is nothing. Throughout the 2,000 years this art has been around, the greatest importance was placed on the strong sense of honor. Warriors killed for it. Warriors died for it. Its importance cannot be measured, for it is more important than life.

2007 Jack Toole showing **Mute Kensetsu Waza** during a demonstration at the Hope Festival. Eric Greis as **Uke.**

Honor Bound:
This means to be bound, or tied to, by the honor shared between two warriors or warrior pages *students*. This is the same honor felt and shared between all of the honorable members of the **Ryu**.

Dojo Log:
The **Dojo** log is a written text consisting of the great contributions set forth by contributors to the **Ryu**. This book contains the accounts of who, what, when, where, why, and how these events took place. This book is maintained by only an elite few members of the **Ryu**. Only these few have access to the log.

Kubi Hinari, Zempo Otoshi

2010 **Koshi Harai** done by Jacob B. Fouts **Sensei.**

Also included in this log, is a written account of all **Kyu** (hopefully never **Dan**) who have dishonored themselves and the **Ryu** and have not made amends. Accountability for one's actions is an extremely important trait of a **Budoka**.

This trait must and will be cultivated. If the offense is amended, the names, dates, times, and events will not be recorded at all (or if already recorded, the recorded entry will be erased from the log for good).

Section 2. Physical Aspects of the Loyalty Principle

Genchi:

Genchi means to physically take care of the **Dojo** and the **Ryu**. It is living up to one's **Genchi** *commitment* financially (class dues or otherwise) and living up to one's physical **Genchi** (getting to class on a regular basis and training).

Gake Ken, Irimi Nage done by Jacob B. Fouts **Sensei.**

Fuku:

Dojo Fuku *member of the martial home* is sometimes called **Fukushu** *to be an active part of the whole.* To become a **Fuku,** one works hard toward mutual trust, respect and honor.

316

Traitors:
If you are a member of the **Godaishin Dojo**, you either remain a member or leave. It is wrong to jump back and forth between two or more **Dojo**, or **Sensei**, and it is not allowed. In the old days, the **Ryu** you were "born into" was the **Ryu** you died in. Little has changed as far as we are concerned. This was loyalty.

Also, anyone below the **Outai** *rank* of **Shodan** is not permitted to show, demonstrate, or teach outsiders of our **Ryu** techniques without the strict permission of **Sensei**. Anyone who does so is considered a traitor.

After the attainment of the rank of **Shodan**, it is much easier to get this permission to show outsiders martial material, but one must continue to do so only with spoken and (sometimes for the **Dan** ranks) written permission.

Speaking to other **Sensei, Dojo** or **Ryu**:
Sometimes you can't help but speak with people from other arts and **Dojo**. If it is an informal conversation, then it is no big deal; it is proper just to inform **Sensei** of its occurrence. For a staged meeting, or a formal meeting with another martial artist, it is proper to get spoken permission from **Sensei** first.

Writing to other **Sensei, Dojo** or **Ryu**:
Whether writing a quick email or sending a formal letter, one must let **Sensei** know first. This is done so that you don't make the **Ryu** look bad accidentally. Some important things to note when addressing the letter: First, put their name followed by their title (**Sensei, Shidoshi, Renshi** or whatever it might be). Never put the title first. Even if they do it, it is

317

improper and it means that their title is more important than their family name and their Christian name. Second, the first line in the letter should read your name (short), then your rank and then the full name of your **Sensei**. It is also proper to then put the name of your **Sensei**'s **Sensei**. It is inappropriate and may be considered boastful to date yourself back more than three generations in an introductory letter (and you should not do so anyway unless asked). Unless you are doing it to show a shared link in our lineage with the person you are writing, then it is acceptable. Thirdly, write what you have to say. In the old days, it was considered wrong to ask any questions before the fifth letter. So, if they are of the old mindset, don't ask them anything. If they are not **Koryu** or **Koryu**-based, you can consider it safe to write them questions in your second letter to them. The body of the first letter should consist strictly of an introduction and compliments about them. Refrain from writing about yourself and your thoughts, they are not considered important enough to go in the first letter. You can start to add that information in the fourth letter. Stating things about your self too soon is considered self-centered and egotistical. Fourthly, (in closing) write your *full* name (unlike at the opening of the letter), your rank, and then any title you might hold. After the title (if you have one and even if you don't) you write "...of the **Godaishin Dojo**". If you are sending the letter through the mail, it would then be proper to stamp your **Hanko** next to your name should you have one. You can ask **Sensei** to stamp the letter with the **Dojo**'s **Hanko** and the **Dojo**'s seal. As a side note, it is extremely improper to have a **Hanko** made with any rank or title displayed on it.

Visiting other **Sensei**, **Dojo** or **Ryu**:
You are permitted to train in other **Dojo** and with other **Ryu**

only when accommpanied by your **Sensei** and never without **Sensei**. In rare instances, when formally asked, **Sensei** may grant permission for a **Kyu** to go off and train alone with outsiders. Permission must be granted in two forms: spoken and written. The written document granting permission must accompany the visiting **Kyu** (in **Sensei**'s stead or in place of **Sensei**) to the host **Dojo**. The signed, stamped (with **Sensei** personalized **Hanko** and official **Hanko** of the **Godaishin Dojo**) and sealed (with the **Godaishin Dojo**'s personalized seal) document must be presented to the host **Sensei** directly. This document must be given before the training begins and before entering the training area. Included in this document will be the guidelines agreed upon and set forth by **Sensei** and the hosting **Sensei**. It is sure to include the date or dates of the event, start time to finishing time, and the place or places allotted for training. It may or may not include a list of agreed upon techniques or lectures.

It is not a rarity for a **Dan** to be granted this; in fact, for a **Dan** it may become a common occurrence.

Buyu:

The making of new **Buyu** *warrior brothers* is an important part of coming up through the arts. One can always use a good friend. Make many! Reach out and befriend all like-minded and like-spirited warriors.

Bachi:

Bachi *punishment* is looked at very differently in a **Dojo** setting. One may be punished for forgetting a task or overlooking a social norm, basically some type of mistake. **Bachi** can be anything from having to complete a physical exercise to getting cracked for absentmindedness. Sometimes, in rare cases, demotion in rank, or position, is used to make a more public display of **Bachi** to the **Ryu**. This public display of punishing a **Kyu** is only done when **Sensei** fears other **Kyu** may think about following the wrong lead. This is done in the hopes that it will teach multiple lessons. **Bachi** is only used for small infractions. It is the **Kyu's Giri** in all cases to learn from the mistake and then to brush themselves off and keep going, while never dwelling on the infringement. After the **Bachi** is administered, the debt is paid. No one is to speak poorly about the incident again. The punishment for a repeat offender will not become increasingly worse, instead the **Bachi** will change until the point gets across and the offending **Kyu** learns from his actions. All events are to be treated with loving compassion and are to help the individual grow. Punishment is never meant to hurt, put down or shame anyone.

Dealing with the loss of honor:
Any large infringement is considered dishonorable. This is only prevalent when the **Kyu** knows the right path to take, yet they choose another. The willful decision to turn one's back on that which is honorable will result in the loss of it.

Dealing with the loss of honor is not the handing out of a punishment. We (the **Kyu**) are made up of young adults and adults. When you know what you have done is wrong and continue to do it, punishment is pointless. Punishment is only used to teach the right way. If you knew the right way and failed to do the honorable thing, punishment does not apply.

When one dishonors themselves, they have dishonored the **Ryu** as well. This is seen through the ideals of the warrior concept of **Ryugi**.

320

To regain lost honor:
One must make it right. They must first make their apologies
to the **Ryu** they have shamed. Secondly, they must make it
up to the **Ryu**. After the apologies are done, the **Sempai** will
offer the **Kyu** the chance to redeem himself. This is done
through some given physical gesture meant to re-strengthen
the **Kyu**'s bonds to their **Ryu**. This act is also meant to give
energy and time in order to strengthen the **Ryu** itself.

The gesture given to redeem one's self should never be
referred to as a punishment, nor looked at as a punishment.
If it is thought of as a punishment, then the offending **Kyu** is
missing the importance of the action and it becomes
pointless. If the **Kyu** does not understand the meaning of this
offer, even after the completion of the physical tasks, the
Kyu will have not regained their honor; they will have failed.

It takes more than just a "physical pay-off"; throughout this
process, the **Kyu** must learn anew that the taking part in the
wrongful action was a mistake. They must learn to forgive
themselves and learn the importance of not making the same
decision twice. Once this is done and the action is
completed, honor is restored. No one is to hold grudges, all
is forgiven.

Complete the given task:
As long as there exists **Kime** *focused intention* inside of the
Kyu to regain their lost honor and put things right, the **Sensei**
is honor bound and will continue to present the opportunity
to do so.

Hinin *dishonored person*:

Any failure to regain the lost honor and the unwillingness to care is noted. This information is dated, explained and recorded in written form along with one's rank and position at the time. This information is logged in the **Dojo** record. This dishonor is held over the **Kyu**'s head. The first refusal will result in no second offer of repeal. Until the first dishonor is dealt with and repaid, any later dishonorable acts will accumulate and be logged. This also changes the status of a **Kyu** depending on how great the dishonor. For one, the **Ryu** is no longer honor bound to this person. This means the dishonored **Kyu** is allowed to be uncared for and ignored. Secondly, they are not looked at as a real member, for they turned their back on their **Ryu**. Worse than that, they had the chance to make it up and did not. Without maintaining your honor, you are not on the warrior's path. The accumulation of dishonorable acts will gain one expulsion.

Hamon:

To receive a **Hamon** is to receive the greatest dishonor. It is the worst punishment given. A **Hamon** is second only to being put to death (which is not done anymore). Many of the old warriors felt that it was worse than death because a **Hamon** meant living out the rest of your life without honor, living out the rest of your life in shame.

When a person receives a **Hamon**, it will be delivered in person (whenever possible) in written and spoken form. A recipient of a **Hamon** will, from that day forth, no longer be welcome in any **Dojo**. They will be blacklisted. The whole **Ryu**, all **Buyu**, every **Kai**, and friend or affiliated **Ryu** will be informed. Everyone will follow suit in making it as if they never existed. Even outsiders will be told of their disgrace. Everyone will know. Everywhere they go, they will find closed doors. We will make every attempt to get the authorities (police or state-governing agencies) involved. If we can, we will prosecute, stand witness, or do anything it takes to put them in jail. It is the worst of the worst. No one is allowed to help them in any way, talk to them, or be near them. Everyone is to turn their backs to them. They are not a member, they never were, and they never will be. They no longer exist in the hearts, minds and memories of the **Ryu**.

Should the person find admittance into another **Dojo**, that **Dojo** and its members will be contacted and ordered to comply with the given **Hamon**.

Although the giving out of a **Hamon** is always at the **Sensei**'s discretion, the reasons for giving out this punishment are always the worst crimes possible against the **Ryu**, crimes such as rape, murder, molestation, the selling of drugs, the wrongful harsh beating of someone, spousal abuse, child abuse, and other things along these lines.

It must become extremely difficult (next to impossible) for any **Kyu** to get this bad. It is up to each and every one of us to set a good example and lead by that example. It is up to each member to see that no harm is done. Only when one strays away from the warrior path do things get out of hand and **Hamon** are issued. Do not stray from the path, do not let others stray.

Quitting the **Ryu** or leaving the **Sensei** and **Dojo**:
The proper protocol for leaving an instructor is as follows: Firstly, the request for leaving should be made in person to the **Sensei**. Secondly, you must put all reasons for leaving in some written form, i.e. letter or email. In some cases, a

323

phone call may be acceptable. After this is done, time should be allotted to the **Sensei** for him to look over and think through the reasons. Thirdly, a sit down discussion with the **Sensei** about the reasons one is leaving should be arranged. This process is not a quick and get-it-over-with ordeal. There should be at least a one week time period from the first step to the last.

Transferring to another **Dojo**:
There should never be a reason to transfer to another **Dojo**. It is said that "the **Ryu** you're born into is the **Ryu** you'll die in". Often times, people who attain **Shodan** make a selfish move to better themselves. However, any transfer should be done for the sake of your **Ryu**--never oneself. The idea is to respectfully venture out to acquire more knowledge and bring it back to share it with your **Ryu**. Your number of instructors may vary, but you can have only one **Sensei**. Through having one **Sensei**, you build strength, loyalty and backing.

Reasons to train with other **Ryu**:
Acceptable reasons for training with other **Ryu** are if, for some reason, your **Sensei** has become incapacitated or has died. Once you receive **Shodan**, no selfish move should be made; therefore, any transfer should be done for the sake of the **Ryu**. This should never be a reason to leave your **Ryu**. **Sensei**'s personality is no reason to leave your **Ryu**.

Reasons for leaving the **Ryu**:
It is acceptable to leave the **Ryu** if someone who outranks you has broken the warrior code and if this (breaking of the code) personally affects you and honor could not be regained (even by **Sensei**). You would no longer be honor-bound to this person if no action is taken by the **Ryu** to remedy the

situation or if no one is doing anything to take care of the offending member. Only when the **Ryu** has personally failed

2006 Taken during a demo on **Aikijutsu.**

you would you no longer be honor-bound by the **Ryu**. At this time, you could leave honorably at your convenience. This must be done in open view for many reasons. One reason is so that everyone who is able gets the chance to make it right (if it is within their power to do so). Another reason is so there is no dispute as to what happened and why.

Note: If the offender is a lower rank than you, they are your responsibility; therefore, you must fix the problem. You remain honor-bound and cannot run from the problem.

If someone breaks the warrior code, they are nothing because their word is everything. Without it, what else can they be?

If there is any possible way of regaining honor, it would become the warrior's mission in life.

Ronin:
In modern times, this term has been adopted to mean the loss of one's **Sensei**, **Dojo**, and **Ryu**. Many take it on as a term for self description. **Ronin** means "wandering homeless warrior". This is because you could not drop one family and pick up another. Presently, it is rarely considered dishonorable to leave one **Ryu** to join another. However, this is modern self-centered thinking.

Zokusei *attribution*:
No matter what accrues between you and the **Ryu**, it is very important to attribute information to those to whom it belongs. Even if it illustrates your loss of face (**Hamon**), you must give proper credit. **Zokusei** is an act of humility, honor, and lineage. Though lineage is not something most Americans appreciate, it was very important to the Japanese mindset that spawned **Bushido**, and its importance can be felt.

Outai *rank*/Obi Outai *belt rank*:
Because the **Kyu** represent all of the **Kyu Outai** *student ranks*, one should understand the purpose of rank. The reason for rank is to show one's progression in training. It

326

aids in understanding a progressive order to accomplishing understanding and knowledge in the warrior arts. The purpose in the physical display of ranked colored belts is often overlooked and misunderstood. It is never for boasting. It is not to hold anyone above anyone else. It is for knowing who to go to for help. One can always come to the **Sensei**, but oftentimes, when having trouble, it is helpful to go to someone that just made it past the level you are struggling with. **Outai** *rank* is so that you know who to listen to and who to listen to more. The reason for written forms of documented **Outai** is so that no one can dispute your true claim of **Outai**. The most important reason for **Outai** always has been to represent one's **Sensei**, one's **Dojo**, and one's **Ryu**. Achieving a higher rank is the method of displaying to your **Sensei** and to onlookers that you have listened, worked at, learned and appreciated all that your **Sensei** has taught you. The passing of **Outai** from teacher to student is the method for the teacher to reciprocate the honor felt by his student's achievements. The acceptance of rank is a promise to honor it.

Section 3. Spiritual Aspects of the Loyalty Principle

This pertains to one's own self growing spiritually and also to having the commitment and patience to help others do the same. In matters of the heart, it is important to remember what is important. There is a good saying my father uses, "It is more important to be loving than it is to be right." Express yourself to another, but do it in a supportive manner. Drama must be avoided and **Ryugi** embraced. Internal distress over an emotional relationship with another member of the **Ryu** can rip a **Ryu** in half, forcing its members to take sides. Interpersonal relationships are almost never easy, but one must remain loyal to the unity of the **Ryu**. Asking members

327

to take sides against another member of the **Ryu** is disgraceful. This is why dating with **Fuku** should be avoided whenever possible.

2011 Jack Toole Teaching **Kusari-fundojutsu** with Nevin Moyer Jr.

<u>Guuzen</u>
Chance, Leave nothing to chance

Section 1. Mental Aspects of the Chance Principle
This is the mental preparation for combating any situation.
When engaged in a struggle, leave nothing to chance. Think
out the scenario as follows: the enemy already knows about
all of your tricks, weaknesses, and strengths. He has already
made his plan to defeat you. Put it in your mind that the man
you are facing is stronger, faster, smarter, and can take
anything you throw at him and reverse it. There is an old
warrior saying, "Only when you are ready to be beaten are
you ready for victory." Know how he might come at you.
Know how he could win, then don't let him!

Section 2. Physical Aspects of the Chance Principle
We all work on our advanced two-man throws and three-man
entanglements. Just know that when it comes down to street
combat, and three men are on you, leave nothing to chance--
just "go for the jugular". Use the techniques that are easiest
to pull off and best suited for the situation, and if you have
the shot, take it because it may be your only chance. All of
those advanced techniques should be saved for confronting
skilled fighters or other marital artists. When it's time to war,
make war with your full potential. Apply all techniques for
real; if a joint restraint isn't put on for real, the person will be
able to retaliate. Never allow retaliation. Think of him as the
greatest fighter alive. In this way, nothing you do will be
chanced; you will hit as hard and as fast as you can, jointlock and throw as hard and as accurate as you can, and you'll
never leave an opening. It will also be hard for you to be
caught off guard. Also, never meet a man on his strength.
Always attack their weakest side. Never play by the rules of

2011 Teaching **Juttejutsu** with Jacob B. Fouts **Sensei**.

their game. There is such a thing as a fair fight, but a **Ninja** does not fight. If they force a confrontation, make them meet you on the battlefield.

Section 3. Spiritual Aspects of the Chance Principle

Some religions warn to never "sell your soul". This is the same concept. Never take yourself down a path in life that doesn't feel right. Until it feels right in our **Hara**, it is wrong. A warrior takes no chances with his soul.

2006 Eric P. Fichter **Sensei** doing **Fu No Mesoho** *the mediation method of attuning with the wind.*

<u>Kakureru</u>
Disappear, Do not be seen

Section 1. Mental Aspects of the Disappear Principle

This deals with many aspects, one being manipulation. We manipulate people every day with our actions and the things we say, but the principle deals mainly with the manipulation of one's enemy. It is the truth that must be hidden from the enemy so that when he mounts an offensive, it will be based on false assumptions and fake information. **Kyojutsu** *the art of integrating truth and falsehood* is used to hide motives and truth. It is used to mislead and misdirect the enemy. This is taught and must be used, but never unjustly. **Saiminjutsu** *the hypnotic art, mesmerism, the power of mind directing* is also used to remain invisible to one's enemies and to disappear.

Section 2. Physical Aspects of the Disappear Principle

When in combat, stay out of the vision of the enemy. One can do this through attacking with blinding strikes or through the understanding of lineasight. Lineasight refers to the line of sight; this is the line that no one can see beyond. It is where one is unable to see either because of obstruction or because of finite sight. Finite sight could be described as the horizon. Whether one is using the lay of the land to hide or joint locking the enemy while moving outside of his vision, lineasight is an important tool in understanding the enemy's visual capability. Utilizing shadows, mist, smoke, fog, blinding strikes, pain compliance, **Metsubushi** *blinding powders*, jointlocks and anything and everything at our disposal to move outside of an enemy's sight. This involves the teachings from the Ninja arts of **Hensojutsu** *disguise and impersonation*, **Kakurejutsu** *the art of stealth*, **Onshinjutsu** *the art of invisibility* and even **Tonpo** *escaping techniques*.

Section 3. Spiritual Aspects of the Disappear Principle

In life, this is the spiritual attempt to not be seen by **Karma**. The way one does this is to disappear out of **Karma**'s

1992 Demon-strating **Kenjutsu**.

watchful eyes. Just as in the physical, one must know what is looked for and what is not seen. **Karma** is the law of cause and effect; it is the teacher so as long as one has something to learn they will "be seen". Here is an example of how a **Ninja** would make moves without being seen: when taking out an enemy, a person does not use the techniques of martial arts on the enemy, for that would be wrong no matter how right the scenario may seem. Instead, when the time is right, the person transforms into his warrior self and commits the act as a **Ninja**. This transformation does not take place easily. It takes much study and practice. The warrior practitioner is

332

taught to separate all emotion from physical action; he is taught to develop, and when need be, to reach a different state of consciousness. This state of being is called "warrior consciousness". Through this method, the **Ninja** disappears out of the view of **Karma**. Just as a lion takes down a zebra, a snake kills a mouse, a bird eats berries, and a tree grows tall, so does a **Ninja** enact change. A hunter may kill many deer and not worry about **Karma** at all, for that is what hunters do. But a person that feels justified in doing so, or gets some type of sick pleasure in doing so, will be subject to Karmic retribution. A **Ninja** is mindful of what he finds pleasure in; he gives up the want for justification.

Demonstrating the use of **Aiki** within the application of **Teppojutsu No Gyaku Waza** with Nevin Moyer Jr. 2011

<u>Kankyou</u>
Environment, Utilize the environment or the circumstance

No matter where you are, you are fine; you are surrounded by things that will help you enact your will.

Section 1. Mental Aspects of the Environment Principle

When an enemy is quick to anger, feed into that anger and make them irate and emotionally flustered. If an enemy's actions are unjust, expose them and look to gain support from

2008 Taken during a public showing at local fair. Eric Gries and I display effortless throwing from **Ni Waza**.

righteous people. If an enemy is righteous, dig up dirt on them to burst their ego. The idea behind this principle is to see things for what they are and to accept them; to learn the enemy's attack and to use his attack to defeat him. If he comes with "fire", feed the fire until he burns himself out. Also, use anything and anyone around in your support.

2011 Taken during a black belt class while I was teaching no handed leg locks from **Suwari Waza**.

Section 2. Physical Aspects of the Environment Principle

In times of war, any and all things are weapons. One reason why we train so many different types of weapons is so that when we encounter an object, the chances are that we will be able to quickly translate that object in our minds into a weapon that we have been training with for years. We will know exactly how to utilize its form. Another aspect of this principle is the understanding of proper **Maii**. This is knowing where any walls are in relation to you, any objects, any other people and where the enemy is. This includes the reach of his weapons, whether fist, legs, **Rokushakubo**, **Shuriken**, or **Teppo**. How and where can you work your craft? **Inton**: where to hide and conceal. **Nobori Gata**: what can you climb up? **Shoten No Jutsu**: what obstruction can you run up or down to distance the enemy from you? **Gotonpo**: which of the five elements are around you and how can you use them? These are the teachings of **Katon**, **Chiton**, **Suiton**, **Futon**, and **Kuton**. **Chimon**: knowing the lay of the land and using it to your advantage. A common **Ninja** practice is to go into any new room or area and shut one's eyes, then to state how many items they could use as weapons and how they could be used. One works at this until they can get at least ten right away. If some of your **Ryu** is with you, utilize them to formulate a stronger attack or defense.

2006 Taken during a public demonstration for the martial artists of the Lehigh Valley, Pennsylvania. While showing **Aiki Waza**, this is a no handed three-man spine lock.

Section 3. Spiritual Aspects of the Environment Principle

There is no time like the present; if you have a friend, teacher or fellow student around you, utilize your environment. Bring out what is bothering you. Ask for help, answers, and guidance. Any and all times you are among your **Ryu**, draw on them and ask them. Learn and grow from the examples that are right in front of you and from those that naturally occur around you in your life.

Yunifai
Unification; Unify body, mind and spirit

Through **Toitsu**, the warrior concept of unification of the mind, body and spirit become one. They enact change all moving at the same time on the same frequency toward the same goal. Once one has reached **Toitsu**, there is no more time for honing, they have become the finished blade. They are the most focused of intention, they are the mental intention, they have tapped into the spiritual plenum of intention, and they have become the embodiment of intention. They can move so swiftly with the clarity and strength of a polished diamond. This is one step closer to **Satori**, one step closer into **Kensho**. It is said by some that "God intended for all three of his gifts to be used and experienced all of the time, but often we take one at a time."

2012 Taken during a class while I was teaching **Hobokujutsu No Waza**.

This is what is meant by being *one*. Once someone is *one* with themselves then they can see that they are one with everything. No longer "the three winds" blowing in all directions. No more **Sanshin**. Now, only **Shin**!

It is said that when one reaches this point, they will be able to turn it on and off much like a switch. We are turning it on for use in life, turning it off to break it back down into the three components once again.

The first glance of success if often found in the most simplistic, refined action, such as a punch, a kick or picking up a drinking glass. Once touched on, one merely exercises the "new muscle".

Sections 1, 2, and 3

Learn to do this with everything mental. Use your physical and your spiritual strengths to overcome any mental problems. Learn to do this with everything physical. Use your spiritual and your mental strengths to overcome any physical problems. Learn to do this with everything spiritual. Use your mental and your physical strengths to overcome any spiritual problems.

2009 Overseeing training with my **Sensei.** His "normal expression" to someone delivering the proper pain.

Closing Statement

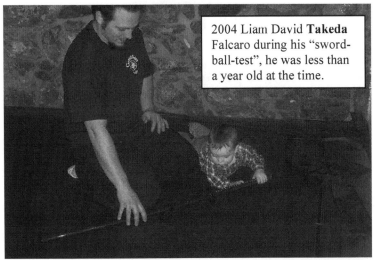

2004 Liam David **Takeda** Falcaro during his "sword-ball-test", he was less than a year old at the time.

Parts of this book may have been a hard read. It is, in truth, more of a reference book compiled to teach and help teach, to inspire and govern our **Ryu.** Hopefully, it is the first of many written. Let this be a stepping stone toward a bigger and better future. I have done what I can and continue to do what I can to solidify this **Ryu.** We are one of the first American **Ryu**, and we are the first and only to date **Ryu** of **Sogobujutsu** in the USA. We have much to be proud of and thankful for; a strong heritage to share in. Remember and take care of this. A **Ryu** cannot exist without the bonds of brotherhood. If we fail, crumble, and die, this will be why. Always continue the journey of self-improvement and self-discovery while making time to build up those that surround you.

Yours in the spirit of **Budo** and **Buyu**,
David C. Falcaro **Kaicho**, **Sensei** of the **Godaishin Dojo**, **Neji Gekken Ryu**, **Sogobujustu**

Glossary

Don't get lost in jargon!

This glossary is to benefit you, not to trap you. One could easily spend way too much time on this, attempting to learn every term. Please remember why you wanted to learn the warrior arts; it was to learn warrior arts, not to become a walking dictionary. So, balance your time, make sure you are physically training.

A

> **Abumi:** stirrup; used in **Bajutsu**
> **Adake bune:** Largest ships in general use by the 16th Century; these ships were powered by up to 80 oarsmen; used in both trade and war, generally acting as flagships in the latter endeavors.
> **Age joro:** The name for a courtesan in old times
> **Age ken** also called **age zuki** and called **age tsuki:** Rising punch
> **Age tsuke:** rising punch
> **Age uke:** Rising reception. Also known as a high or upper reception.
> **Age uke gyaku ashi:** upper reception (reverse foot)
> **Agemaki:** Ornamental **Samurai** bow; commonly done while wearing armor.
> **Ago:** "chin"
> **Ai:** "harmony," this term is associated with **aikijujutsu, aikijutsu, aikibudo, aikibujutsu,**

aikido, where one combines their energy with their opponents.

➢ **Ai hanmi:** A ready position where both opponents have the same leg forward

➢ **Ai hanmi katate dori:** A cross grip on the opponent's wrist in **ai hanmi**

➢ **Ai uchi:** Simultaneous striking, mutual kill. (Used now as a sport term for simultaneous techniques by both contestants. Used in **Judo, kendo, sumo…**)

➢ **Ainu:** Indigenous Japanese; Caucasian people; now confined to **Hokkaido.**

➢ **Aiki:** "Harmony meeting." When one combines an opponent's energy with their own.

➢ **Aiki nage:** Any **aiki** throw

➢ **Aiki otoshi:** Any **aiki** dropping throw

➢ **Aikibudo: Budo** based on the **Aiki** principle, sometimes thought of as the earlier name for **aikido**, but really a predecessor.

➢ **Aikido: Aikido** (eye-kee'doh) "spirit way". Unarmed method of self-defense founded in **Tokyo** in 1942 by **Morihei Uyeshiba.**

➢ **Aikidoka:** practitioners of **Aikido** their art form attempts to involve their partner in turning around their own center axis.

➢ **Aikijutsu:** "Martial art form of harmonious spirit." A branch of ancient **jujutsu** from which **aikido** was developed. All forms are commonly attributed to have been derived from the **Daito Ryu.**

➢ **Aisha: Ninja** method of manipulating soft hearted people

➢ **Aite:** "Opponent" or "partner." An adversary in a contest.

➢ **Aizujutsu** also called **Angojutsu:** The **Ninja** martial art of signaling and writing.

- ➤ **Ame no ukihashi:** A floating bridge to heaven, symbolizing the connection between earthly and heavenly realms of existence.
- ➤ **American Karate:** hybrid form of traditional **karatedo** founded in the United States which adopts techniques from anywhere and attempts to develop them to meet the indigenous needs of the American practitioner.
- ➤ **Aiuchi:** "Mutual striking down or simultaneous point." A simultaneous score by both competitors in the sport aspects of Japanese sport martial arts such as **Kendo**, **Karatedo**, **Judo, Sumo**.
- ➤ **Aka obi:** Red belt
- ➤ **Akindo**: Merchants/Traders; Men of commerce, they were the lowest of the four major classes.
- ➤ **Ako gishi:** The name given to the incident of the "47 **Ronin**" (of the **Edo** Period)
- ➤ **Akuryoku**: Gripping Training
- ➤ **Akuso:** Rowdy Monks; the old term given to warrior monks later they became known as **Sohei**.
- ➤ **Akuto:** Outlaw bands prevalent in the **Kamakura** period; during 1301 to 1333 the **Hojo** weakened but they could not completely destroy the **Akuto**.
- ➤ **Amado:** lower neck
- ➤ **Amaterasu:** "Great Divinity Illuminating Heaven"; (revered in **Shinto**); this was the sun goddess from whom the Japanese imperial family claimed descent.
- ➤ **Amegasa**: Sedge Hat
- ➤ **Amigasa:** a wicker straw hat for hiding the face and hiding messages
- ➤ **Anatoshi:** trapping used in **Sekkojutsu** (the martial art of scouting)

- **Ankoku toshinjutsu:** The **Ninja** martial art for seeing in the darkness
- **Antei:** "Balance," "stability," or "equilibrium."
- **Ao obi:** Blue belt
- **Arare:** Caltrops a kind of **Tetsubushi**
- **Arashi:** storm
- **Aruki Kata:** The proper form of walking.
- **Ashi:** Leg or foot.
- **Ashi ate:** "Foot strikes" or "leg strikes."
- **Ashi barai** also called **ashi harai:** Leg sweep.
- **Ashi gatami:** Leg lock.
- **Ashi guruma:** Leg wheel.
- **Ashi gyaku:** "leg overturn"
- **Ashi hishigi:** Leg crush.
- **Ashi kubi:** Ankle.
- **Ashi kubi hishigi:** Ankle crush.
- **Ashi no ura:** Sole of the foot.
- **Ashi sabaki:** "Foot work" or "foot movement."
- **Ashi waza:** Foot techniques including kicks and throws in which the pivot point is the leg or foot.
- **Ashibo kake uke:** leg hooking reception
- **Ashigaru:** Light feet infantry; Developed in response to the **Onin** War, the **Ashigaru;** became the backbone of all **daimyo** armies in the 16th Century, especially after the widespread adoption of the matchlock rifle. Until the 1590s, an **ashigaru** was normally a peasant who worked in his home village when not on his lord's campaigns.
- **Ashiguru:** foot soldiers; the lowest level of **Samurai** (the lightly armored ones)
- **Ashikaga:** The military house whose **shogun**s "ruled" (maintained some control) of Japan in the name of the emperor for more than 200 years, from

1336 to 1573, during the time of constant civil strife (during the warring states)

➢ **Ashikubi kake uke:** Ankle hooking reception
➢ **Ashiko:** Spikes worn on the feet
➢ **Ashikubi hishigi:** Ankle crush
➢ **Ashikubi kake uke:** Ankle hooking reception
➢ **Ashinami Jukka Jo:** The ten ways of walking prescribed in the **Ninpo** book **Shoninki** (we don't just do these).
➢ **Ashiyubi:** Toes
➢ **Ashura:** A deity of 3 heads 6 arms, 4th level of existence, Protector of the Buddhist realm
➢ **Asuka** period: From 592 until 710.
➢ **Atama:** Head, or more specifically, top of the head.
➢ **Ate:** Striking. To strike.
➢ **Ate waza:** striking techniques; striking the vital points
➢ **Atemi:** Striking. To strike another word for **Ate**.
➢ **Atemi no tanren:** hitting/striking practice
➢ **Atemi no tanren, ten:** striking the air to improve accuracy in motion
➢ **Atemi no tanren, chi:** striking solid objects to condition the weapons
➢ **Atemi no tanren, jin:** striking bodies to gain affect from the target
➢ **Ato geiko:** After-training training, this is when the higher belts throw the lower belts to give them more **ukemi** practice after the regular class is over.
➢ **Ato ni kai:** Two more times
➢ **Ato san kai:** Three more times
➢ **Atsu:** to press
➢ **Atsumori:** Particularly popular No drama depicting an important event in the **Gempei** War, the death of

344

young **Taira Atsumori** during the Battle of **Ichi no Tani**.

- **Au:** To encounter an opponent in any Japanese martial arts contest.
- **Awase:** The act of clashing weapons or coming to grips with an opponent
- **Ayumi ashi:** "Natural stepping" footwork in which leg passes on each step from the movement of the **Hara.**
- **Azuchi:** Castle in **Omi** completed by **Oda Nobunaga's** request in 1578. Designed by **Niwa Nagahide; Azuchi** was the greatest castle of Japan in it's day. It was lavishly decorated. **Nobunaga** went to great lengths to attract merchants to **Azuchi**'s castle town. After **Nobunaga** died in 1582, **Azuchi** was pillaged by **Akechi Mitsuhide**'s troops then burned- either by looters or maybe from the orders of **Niwa Nagahide** himself. Also the term **Azuchi** is occasionally used to describe the period of **Oda Nobunaga**'s ascendancy (1573-1582).
- **Azuma kagami:** A historical work completed in the early 14th Century, dealing from the years 1180 to 1266. The **Azuma kagami**'s day-by-day treatment of the **Kamakura Bakufu** makes it an invaluable tool for historians of that era.

B

- **Bachi:** punishment; it was not unheard of to be buried up to one's neck in the earth and, given very little to eat, left there for weeks. If found to be a **ninja** one would have their back and legs sliced open and seared shut with molten lead, then later killed.

- **Bajo:** Cavalry.
- **Bakemonojutsu: Ninja** ghost martial arts
- **Bakufu:** Military of **japan,** "Tent government"; military government (AKA the **shogunate**); originally the field headquarters of a general
- **Bakufu buke-zukuri:** A more modern method of sword mounting with a cross taped handle.
- **Bakuhatsugama: Kusarigama** with container for explosives
- **Bakumatsu:** Fall of a military regime
- **Bajutsu:** Martial arts of horsemanship
- **Banpen fugyo:** The sprit of never being surprised or afraid.
- **Bansenshukai:** 17th century book of the history of the techniques and methods of **Iga** and **Koga Ninja**
- **Bansho:** Captain; found sometimes in 16th Century records (especially relating to the **Hojo** clan).
- **Barai** also called **harai:** Sweep; a sweeping motion
- **Barai uchi:** Sweeping strike
- **Basho:** Grand **sumo** tournaments scheduled six times each year in Japan.
- **Bassai:** Breaking down the fortress
- **Batto:** Flowing motion of sword drawing and cutting
- **Battojutsu:** Defensive sword martial art
- **Benzaiten:** Goddess of music, fine arts and eloquence and literature
- **Betto:** A device common in the early **Heian** Period normally used to signify the owner of an important office.
- **Bikenjutsu** also called **Benkai:** Martial arts of the bladed weaponry
- **Bisento:** Huge heavy battlefield halberd; a variety

naginata

- **Bishamon:** God of War and Defense, one of Seven Deities of Good Luck.
- **Bishamonten:** A guardian of the Heavens/ God of warriors, treasure and war (see **Tamonten**)
- **Bo:** staff
- **Bo shuriken:** straight throwing blades, knives, spikes
- **Bogu:** Term **kendo** uses for **Keiko yori** full practice armor that consists of: **Men**: Helmet, **Do**: Trunk protector, **Kote**: Hand and forearm protector, **Tare**: Hip protector
- **Bojutsu:** Martial arts of staff fighting
- **Bokken** also called **bokuto:** wooden practice sword
- **Boryaku:** Battle strategy
- **Bosatsu: bodhisattva**
- **Bosen:** A defensive battle; to fight the defense.
- **Boshi:** Tip of the blade
- **Boshi ken:** Thumb drive fist
- **Bu:** Military/ war arts/ war/ battle/ fight
- **Bodhisattva:** One who has attained enlightenment but rather then move on to **Nirvana** waits to aid others in their quest to get there.
- **Budo:** Martial arts/ martial ways/ a reflection of human perfection, according to **Shinto**
- **Budoka:** Martial artist; one who studies the martial way
- **Bufu:** the warrior's wind; A code of conduct.
- **Bufu Ikkan:** The inspiration of the warrior code of conduct.
- **Bugei** also called **bushi** and called **musha:** Warrior
- **Bugeisha:** Warriors
- **Bugi Juhappan:** 18 general categories of martial art techniques

- ➤ **Bugo:** Martial (warrior) name
- ➤ **Bugu:** Collection of martial training weapons
- ➤ **Bugukake:** Weapons rack.
- ➤ **Bugyonin:** Lower-level versions of a chief, especially in the **Kamakura** Period.
- ➤ **Bujin:** Warrior spirit
- ➤ **Bujinden:** Transmitting the warrior spirit to one's **Deshi Bunji:** A noble; a member of the imperial court.
- ➤ **Bujutsu** Warrior martial arts
- ➤ **Buke:** Military house; family whose duties include always being armed. This most often applied to those warrior clans prior to and during the **Gempei** War (1180-85) but in use into and beyond the **Momoyama** Period. **Buke** is sometimes and misleadingly translated as 'equestrians'.
- ➤ **Buke hatoo** also called **buke shohatto**: "Laws for Military Households"; laws instated in 1615 that specified the obligation of the **daimyo** to the **shogun** and were the legal basis for control of the **daimyo.**
- ➤ **Buki:** Weapons and warrior tools
- ➤ **Buki waza:** Weapon techniques
- ➤ **Bukijutsu:** The martial art of weaponry. **Bukijutsu** is sometimes called **Kobojutsu**. The term **Kobojutsu** is an old term which originally referred to the older **Koryu** arts. At that time it was called **Kobujutsu**. This term encompassed unarmed and armed combative form. Only in recent days do some people refer to the weaponry arts as **Kobojutsu**. This idea supposedly came from the island of **Okinawa**. In older times weaponry arts fell under the heading **Bukijutsu**. Recently some **Ryu** use this term to refer to the secret weapon arts.

348

- **Bumon:** Warrior gate
- **Bunbu ichi:** Term referring to the old **samurai** debate over the relative importance of letters and learning versus martial skill, is the pen mightier than the sword?
- **Bunei:** The first Mongol Invasion (1274).
- **Bunkai:** Interpretation of application of movement or technique
- **Bunkoku:** Provinces that in the **Heian** Period were governed by court nobles; in the **Sengoku** Period, **Bunkoku** was also used to refer to the territory of a **daimyo**.
- **Bunmon:** The learning and understanding of warrior culture.
- **Bunraku** also called **joruri:** Popular puppet theatre
- **Buppo:** The theory of a Buddhist.
- **Burakumin:** "village people"; outcasts
- **Bushajustu** also called **Kyujutsu:** Martial art of archery.
- **Bushi no-ichi gon:** "the word of a warrior"; the **samurai** is obliged to speak the truth it is his **Giri**, and all **Samurai** that hear are obliged to believe what the **samurai** says.
- **Bushido:** Way of the warrior, their code of conduct
- **Bushin:** Highest level of spiritual communion
- **Butoku:** Warrior virtue or spirit
- **Butoku Iko:** The shining virtue of the warrior arts.
- **Butsudo:** way of Buddha; Buddhism.
- **Butsumetsu:** The secret weak point in the chest.
- **Buyu:** martial brothers/ friends
- **Byobu:** folding screens

C

- > **Cha:** Tea
- > **Cha no Yu:** Tea ceremony; an effort refined in the later 15th Century and popular among the **samurai** and court nobles. Considered in many ways difficult art form.
- > **Cha obi:** Brown belt
- > **Chado** also known as **Sado:** The Way of Tea; the art and practice of the tea ceremony.
- > **Chambara:** a realistically <u>staged</u> (like a play or a movie) display of fighting or warring
- > **Chanoyu:** Hot water for tea ceremony
- > **Chasengami:** Style of top knot named after its resemblance to a tea wisk.
- > **Chi:** Earth
- > **Chi no kata:** Earth form
- > **Chi ryaku:** Earth strategy
- > **Chiburi:** "Removing blood from the blade." In **iaijustu** (martial art of fast sword drawing), a sharp downward stroke of the sword done in such a way as to shake off the blood accumulated from previous cutting actions.
- > **Chichi:** Father
- > **Chigawa:** Leather loops on either side of the **Keiko yoroi**
- > **Chika ma:** Close quarter distance
- > **Chikuto: Shinai**
- > **Chimon:** Earthly forces, geography, physiographic
- > **Chimpan:** The referee of a match. Also known as "**shimban**," "**sinban** (the term we mostly use)," or

"**shimpan.**"

- **Chinjufu shogun:** Rank of the General of the northern pacification command, a rank held by **Ashikaga Takauji** during the **Kemmu** Restoration from (1333-1336).
- **Chinzei:** Medieval term for **Kyushu** (a place in **Japan**).
- **Chiren:** Knowledge attained through training
- **Chitsumishi** enemy citizen collaborating with a **ninja** network
- **Cho:** Unit of land measure that was equivalent to 2.94 acres until 1594, when it was reduced, now equaling 2.45 acres.
- **Cho wa:** Harmonious mental and physical reaction while at practice.
- **Choho:** Espionage
- **Chokkatsuchi:** A lord's personal territory; his personal land.
- **Choku:** Straight
- **Choku tsuki** also called **Choku zuki:** Straight punch.
- **Chokuritsu rei:** Any standing bow
- **Chokuzuki:** Direct thrust
- **Chonin:** A class term for the merchants and artisans, who were figured in below the peasants and above outcasts on the social scale; city people
- **Chori:** outcast class; those who did not belong to any of the four castes/classes and who were isolated in ghetto-like communities; for example, tanners, morticians, grave-diggers, sandal-makers, gardeners; see also **hinin.**
- **Chosen:** Korea.
- **Chu:** Middle
- **Chubu:** Central Japan

- **Chudan:** Middle level
- **Chudan soto uke:** Middle outside reception
- **Chudan tsuki:** Front gut punch
- **Chudan uchi uke:** Middle inside reception
- **Chudan uke:** Middle level reception
- **Chugi bara:** Suicide out of loyalty; performed by a **Samurai** in order to admonish or follow his master in death.
- **Chui:** "Warning." Admonition by a referee in a match, short of actual penalty.
- **Chuken:** The middle of the five players on a **kendo** team. **Chunin:** "Middle person." The second of three **ninja** military ranks designating the leader of a group of **ninja** on assignment. Those led by **chunin** (master level) were the **genin** (expert level); those who obtained the assignment were the **jonin** (grandmaster level).
- **Chusei:** Scholarly term broadly describing the medieval (warring states) period in Japanese history; the time between the late **Heian** Period and the **Momoyama** Period.
- **Chusei Period:** The middle ages 14th century until the 16th century.

D

- **Dachi:** Stance.
- **Dai** big
- **Dai Kissaki:** Enlarged, thick point on a Japanese sword, a style more commonly found on swords from the 1700's.
- **Daijo Daijin:** Great Minister of State. The highest

appointment awarded by the imperial court. This rank was held by such figures as **Taira Kiyomori**, **Oda Nobunaga**, and **Toyotomi Hideyoshi**.

➢ **Daikan** – Deputy intendant, manager. It could refer to the official tax collector for a **daimyo**.

➢ **Daikokuten:** god of earth, wealth, prosperity and farmers

➢ **Daikomyosai:** The great light event, a martial arts party

➢ **Daikongo in:** sign to increase one's energy and direct it, **kyo / pyo (mikkyo)**

➢ **Daiku:** Carpenter

➢ **Daimon:** a **kyusho** point (called big gate), middle of shoulder joint

➢ **Daimyo:** "big name" Feudal Lords, leader of warriors

➢ **Dairai:** Imperial Palace.

➢ **Dairyo:** District magistrate

➢ **Daisan:** The completed drawing phase of **kyujutsu** (martial art of archery).

➢ **Daisensei:** Title of great respect, meaning great teacher, given only to a teacher of high rank.

➢ **Daisharin:** wheel and axle assembly

➢ **Daisho:** "Big and small." The matched pair of long and medium-length swords; **Katana** and **Wakizashi**. These only the **samurai** class could legally wear.

➢ **Daito:** long sword, anywhere from 2.5 feet to over 3 feet; type of **katana** can be called a **tachi**.

➢ **Dajo Tenno:** Honorific title for an abdicated emperor

➢ **Dakentaijutsu:** Martial art of striking

➢ **Dame:** wrong, bad

➢ **Dan:** The rank of first-degree black belt and beyond.

➢ **Dan tsuki** also called **Dan zuki:** consecutive punches

➢ **Danjun** also called **tanden:** Part of the body just

below the navel which is believed to be the source of
ki.

- ➢ **De:** Advance forward
- ➢ **De ashi harai:** Advancing foot sweep
- ➢ **Deai:** Initiatory action in combat
- ➢ **Deai osae uke:** Pressing block stepping in
- ➢ **Debana waza:** techniques used in **Kenjutsu** to strike
  opponent
  just prior to their attack.
- ➢ **Den:** Transmission, legend, tradition
- ➢ **Dengaku:** Country music, rustic music; music
  popular with the common people, often including
  dance routines as part of a performance.
- ➢ **Densho:** transmission documents issued by a classical
  ryu
- ➢ **Deru pon:** The winning of a **judo** contest in the
  opening seconds before a contestant has had time to
  adjust him or herself, or even grasped the opponent's
  jacket.
- ➢ **Deshi:** "Disciple" or "student."
- ➢ **Deus: Samurai** name for Jesus Christ
- ➢ **Dim mak:** (a Chinese term but should be learned
  because of it's common usage) death touch, a delayed
  action strike aimed at an acupuncture meridian, able
  to cause death to a victim within hours or days of it's
  delivery.
- ➢ **Do:** "Way" or "path." When this term is used as a
  suffix to a particular style of the Japanese martial arts,
  it is indicative of more than just a means of combat.
  Do indicates a discipline and philosophy with moral
  and spiritual connotations, with the ultimate aim
  being enlightenment.
- ➢ **Do in:** self massage tradition

- **Do jime:** Choke applied to the opponent's trunk of the body
- **Dogi** also called **Keikogi:** A martial arts uniform.
- **Dogo:** Village leader, headman, especially one whose wealth and assets allow him a certain amount of political and/or military clout locally.
- **Dogu:** Tools, equipment, or instruments used in martial arts. Another meaning for **Dogu** and in this case also called **Bogu** or called **Keiko yoroi:** practice armor protectors (**men**, **kote**, **do**, **tare**)
- **Dohyo:** A circular ring, fifteen feet in diameter, for sumo contests to be conducted.
- **Dohyo iri:** The ceremonial entry of the **sumo** champions into the arena.
- **Dojo** "The place of the way." Martial arts home; A training hall or gymnasium where Japanese martial arts are practiced.
- **Dojo cho:** Official branch of a **dojo**
- **Dojo Kun:** The **dojo** creed
- **Doka:** A poem about the way, Pocket warmer
- **Dokko in:** Sign of physical and mental strength (**mudra**), **rin** (**mikkyo**)
- **Dokkotsu:** A **kyusho** point (called the single bone), Adam's apple
- **Doko:** Place of power, angry tiger
- **Dokubari:** Poison needles in plant fiber, caltrops
- **Dokuenjutsu:** Poisonous smoke
- **Domaru** also called **haramaki:** lightweight, wraparound iron body armor that fastened on the side or back, worn by **samurai** infantrymen
- **Dome:** To stop; arrest
- **Domo:** Much
- **Donohi:** Medical substance

- **Donjon:** Castle keeps, popular in the later 16th Century. The first castle keep was built by **Matsunaga Hisahide** in 1567 at **Tamon. Donjon** were ultimately designed as much for appearance as defensive capability.
- **Dontonjutsu:** The martial art of earth concealment
- **Dori:** Seizure, dance, it can be the spelling of **tori** when following another word
- **Dosa:** Action, movement
- **Doshi:** The title of Master originally came from the Chinese, later adopted by the **Ninja** until the **Kamakura** Period
- **Doshin:** (**Tokugawa** period and **Edo** Period) law enforcement official held their place under the **Yoriki**
- **Doshu:** "Master" or "master of the way." Way leader, head of a **budo**
- **Doso:** (Muromachi Period) Pawnbroker, moneylender
- **Dotatsu** also called **Ate** and called **Atemi:** strike
- **Doton:** using earth and stone
- **Dokyo:** Teachings from China
- **Doza:** The copper guild.
- **Dozukiri:** Placement in **kyujutsu** in which the archer sets his body into a firm stance.

E

- **Ebi:** lobster, shrimp, prawn
- **Ebi jime:** lobster choke
- **Ebisu:** god of fishermen, good fortune, commerce, honest labor
- **Eboshi:** Cap, usually black and often fastened to the head with a silk cord, worn by the **samurai** in all

formal circumstances.

> **Edo:** Castle in **Musashi** and capital of the **Tokugawa Bakufu**. Built in 1456 by **Ota Dokan**, **Edo** came under the **Hojo** clan's control in 1524. When the **Hojo** were defeated in 1590, **Tokugawa Ieyasu** made **Edo** his home castle at **Hideyoshi**'s suggestion. It remained the capital of the **Tokugawa** until 1867; in 1868 the Emperor **Meiji** moved the Imperial Court to **Edo** and renamed it **Tokyo**.

> **Edo** Period: 1600-1867

> **Egoshu:** Council, especially one composed of civilian community elders-often applied to the governing merchant body of **Sakai**.

> **Ekkyo:** Divination

> **Embujo:** A place of exhibition or athletic performances where martial arts events are often held

> **Emishi:** Derogative term for the **Ainu**.

> **Emma:** God of Hell.

> **En sho:** round heel

> **Enbu sen:** Center of the **Tatame** (mat, **Dojo** floor) Demonstration line

> **Enryakuji:** Temple complex on Mt. **Hiei** (**Omi** province) founded by the monk **Saicho Dengyo Daishi**) in 788. The spiritual capital of **Tendai Buddhism**, the **Enryakuji** maintained a virtual army of warrior monks and played an active (also at times destructive) role in **Kyoto** politics until 1571. In that year, **Oda Nobunaga**, whom the **Enryakuji** had defied, destroyed the **Enryakuji** and killed thousands of its monks. It was later rebuilt though almost no buildings predate 1571.

> **Emakimono:** scroll meant to be unrolled horizontally

> **Embukai:** A public demonstration

357

- **Empi:** elbow
- **Empi uchi** more properly called **Shuki ken** or **Shuki uchi:** elbow strike Embu Pre arranged two person training technique
- **Empi uke:** Elbow reception
- **Enbu:** Demonstration, lecture
- **Encho:** Continuation, extension; overtime period of a match (sport martial arts).
- **Endokuken:** Poisonous smoke assembly attached to **shuriken**
- **Enteki:** Long-distance archery technique.
- **Eri:** Lapel, collar.
- **Eri dori:** Collar grab
- **Eri katsu:** The lapel method of resuscitation used in **judo**.
- **Eta:** A descriptive term for people who handled tasks considered exceptionally distasteful; such as executioners, butchers, undertakers, midwives, and tomb attendants; generally any job which required the handling of the dead or the remains of the dead. Even the makers of leather armor could be considered **Eta**. The term is possibly derived from **Etori** (butcher). **Eta** were considered practically subhuman, especially in the **Edo** Period, and to have **Eta** roots remained a stigma into the 20th Century. These people are currently known as **Buraku min**. This term **Eta** was also used as an impolite word for **burakumin fudai** the many **daimyo** who supported **Tokugawa Ieyasu** prior to the Battle of **Sekigahara** in 1600, which earned them (and their descendants) positions of trust in the **shogunate**; also known as Hereditary Vassals.

F

- **Fu:** negation, wind
- **Fu antei:** Instability, lack of balance.
- **Fuchi:** The metal sleeve located at the base of the handle next to the guard of a **katana**.
- **Fudai:** The inner lords; these were hereditary vassal; retainers of long standing. In the **Edo** Period, this came to mean those lords who had supported **Tokugawa Ieyasu** in the **Sekigahara** Campaign (1600).
- **Fudo:** immobility
- **Fudo dachi:** A rooted position, solid stance
- **Fudo kanashibari no jutsu:** the art form of making an opponent hesitate by immobilizing any living thing with the power of the mind
- **Fudo ken**: Clenched fist position with fingers bent at all of the knuckles
- **Fudo Myo** also known as **Achala:** Deity of Fire; attendant to **Dainichi**, depicted with a sword in one hand and a rope in the other.
- **Fudo Shichi Baku In:** A strategy used to immobilize the enemy.
- **Fudochi:** The immovable wise heart.
- **Fudomyo O:** Guardian of the heavens.
- **Fudoshin:** Immovable mind
- **Fugen:** Bodhisattva depicted sitting on an elephant.
- **Fukai:** To hold strongly.
- **Fukibari:** Spitting needles from within the mouth with the use of a blowpipe
- **Fukidake** also called **fukiya**: Blowgun

- **Fuku**: Member
- **Fukume: Ninja** veil, cover found on the end of a **shinobizue**
  fu no kata wind form
- **Fukumibari:** small needles blown at the eyes from the mouth
- **Fukuro shinai**: training sword made of split, slivers of bamboo encased in leather; Invented by the **Yagu Ryu**
- **Fukurokuju:** godliness of wisdom, longevity, virility and fertility
- **Fukushidoin:** assisting instructor, a title used for an **aikido** teacher, 2-3 **dan**
- **Fumi:** step on; tread on
- **Fumi waza:** Stomping techniques
- **Fumie:** Device used to search out Christians after that religion became prohibited (starting to an extent in 1587). Normally an image of Jesus, the **Fumie** was dropped on the ground and individuals made to step upon it, in the belief that a true Christian would not commit such a sacrilege.
- **Fumikiri:** cutting kick, kick with the edge of the foot to the opponent's knee
- **Fumikomi:** stomping kick
- **Funakogi undo** also called **torifune:** rowing exercise
- **Fundoshi:** Loincloth, "the big dipper looking thing".
- **Funsen:** A brave battle; to engage an enemy bravely.
- **Funshi** also called **munen-bara:** Suicide out of righteous indignation
- **Furi:** to spin or twirl
- **Furi tama:** "Shaking down the spirit", cleanse and polish the soul, exercise to still one's **ki**
- **Furi zuki:** Swing crazy roundhouse punch

- **Furibo:** Heavy training club used in **Jikishinkage ryu** to develop proper technique and stamina
- **Furikaburi:** Lifting the sword above the head when practicing **Iaijutsu**
- **Furisode:** Long-sleeved **kimono** worn by young unmarried women
- **Furinkazan:** wind, forest, fire, mountain (A motto used by **Takeda Shingen**)
- **Furoteppo:** The early bronze pistols
- **Furui:** old
- **Furusato:** one's home village
- **Furyu:** A group dance making use of crazy costumes to tell an often energetic and occasionally bawdy tale; it started out as a ritual of exorcism, **Furyu** was quite popular by the 16th Century, especially among commoners.
- **Fusuma:** sliding doors
- **Futari Jinba**: Two man jumping technique used to launch a **Ninja** over a wall
- **Futaridori** also called **futarigake**: two attackers

G

- **Gagaku**: "Elegant music"; the ceremonial music of the imperial court.
- **Gai wan:** Outer arm strike
- **Gaijin:** "outside person"; foreigner
- **Gake:** Hooking action used in throws; can itself be a throw.
- **Gakko:** School.
- **Gakure:** to hide, disappear

- **Gakushi:** Musician or Strolling Player
- **Gakushu:** Scholarly monks
- **Gando:** Specialized Lantern
- **Ganmen** also called **Kao:** Face
- **Ganseki:** boulder
- **Ganseki dome:** stopping the boulder throw
- **Ganseki geri:** kick the big rock throw
- **Ganseki goshi:** bringing the huge rock over one's hip throw
- **Ganseki makikomi:** Scrolling lay on top of the boulder throw
- **Ganseki nage:** big rock throw
- **Ganseki ori:** breaking the big rock throw
- **Ganseki oshi:** big rock press
- **Ganseki otoshi:** "dropping the boulder" Heels over head drop
- **Garami** also called **karami:** entangle
- **Gari:** to reap
- **Gassho:** peaceful gesture; hands together in greeting or prayer, palms flat together, **mudra** of greeting, respect, submission and veneration
- **Gasshuku** training camp, lodging together
- **Gata:** form, pattern of movement
- **Gatame:** Locking or holding someone in a locked position.
- **Gawa:** River, side of the body
- **Geashi** also called **Keashi:** spin, spinning, can imply reverse; as in spinning a throw done on you to create a new throw done on them
- **Gebakuken in:** sensing intention (**mudra**), kai (**mikkyo**)
- **Gedan:** Lower level, low area of the body; from the waist downwards

- **Gedan barai uke:** Downward Sweeping reception
- **Gedan gaeshi:** Circular movement with the **Jo** aimed at the lower part of the opponent's body.
- **Gedan gake uke:** Downward Hooking reception
- **Gedan uke:** Downward reception strike
- **Gedan uke nagashi:** low level receiving flow
- **Geiko:** Training
- **Geisha:** "accomplished person"; traditional female entertainer.
- **Gekisai:** Destroy & demolish, attack & smash
- **Gekken:** A term meaning "live" blade or real sword combat, often used during the **Meiji** era (1868 - 912), especially by the military of that time.
- **Gekokujo:** "overthrow by underlings"; The low overcome the high; when a younger belt beats an older belt in **rendori**. The term came from the **Muromachi** Period that described someone of high standing being unseated by an inferior. Often applied to the frequent political upsets of the **Sengoku** Period. **Gekokujo** can mean armed rebellion; the reason for many of the laws and regulations of the **Shogunate** government.
- **Gempei** War: The conflict between 1180 and 1185. This was the defeat of the **Taira** (**Heike**, **Heishi**) and the rise to power of the **Minamoto** (**Genji**) led by the warlord **Minamoto Yoritomo**.
- **Gendai:** "modern"
- **Gendai budo:** "modern martial arts"
- **Gendai geki**: modern drama (stories during the **Meiji** restoration)
- **Gendai ryu:** "modern martial family"
- **Genin:** Foot Soldiers, **Ninja** of the lowest rank, experts who were often responsible for carrying out

dangerous assignments.

- ➢ **Genjutsu:** Martial art of magical illusions
- ➢ **Genko:** Mongol Invasions (1274 and 1281)
- ➢ **Gennin:** Attendants to **samurai**, whose responsibilities included horse care, equipment and maintenance.
- ➢ **Genpuku** also called **genbuku:** Coming of age ceremony generally celebrated on a boy's 14th or 15th birthday.
- ➢ **Genzen Okusezu:** An air of dignity.
- ➢ **Genzoku:** The act of a monk returning to lay life. Most **sengoku daimyo** had rules regulating the return of monks to secular life, presumably because many defeated **samurai** were spared execution if they took up a monk's habit and no one wanted **ronin**.
- ➢ **Geri:** Kick.
- ➢ **Gesu:** Estate manager, administrator (**Heian** Period).
- ➢ **Geta:** Wooden sandals with projecting slats
- ➢ **Gi:** martial arts uniform.
- ➢ **Gikan:** having regards for justice
- ➢ **Ginza:** Silver guild (**Edo** Period).
- ➢ **Giri:** Duty or obligation arising from personal honor. It can also mean to cut/stab and in this case can also be called **Kiri**
- ➢ **Go:** five and an ancient board game with an emphasis on careful strategy, popular throughout **samurai** history. It can also be an affix denoting "Later". For example: **Go-Daigo** The Later **Daigo**. As **Go** is also 5 in Japanese, the same affix sometimes indicated five of something.
- ➢ **Go no sen** also called **machi no sen:** responsive initiative
- ➢ **Godai:** "five big" the five universal elements of

creation and destruction
- **Godai kokyuho:** five elemental breathing techniques
- **Godaishin:** "five big spirits" the spirit or intention behind the five universal elements of creation and destruction (a term made by **Sodenke,** David C. Falcaro **Sensei**)
- **Godaishin Dojo:** "five big spirits martial home" the spirit or intention behind the five universal elements of creation and destruction martial arts home. This is the exclusive name for the **Dojo** of the **Neji Gekken Ryu**.
- **Godan:** fifth degree black belt
- **Gofu:** Talisman, good-luck charm
- **Gogyo:** five transformations (**mikkyo**)
- **Gogyo setsu:** The theory of the five elements
- **Gojo gyoku:** principle of five feelings and desires
- **Gokamon:** Used by the **Tokugawa Bakufu** to refer to members of the **Matsudaira** families.
- **Gokenin:** A retainer/vassal family of the **Kamakura Bakufu**, especially those who had served under **Minamoto Yoritomo**; generally having a certain amount of influence.
- **Gokui:** hidden or secret understanding
- **Gokuhi waza:** Special techniques; these are taught by the Grand Master to his most gifted students having the highest ranks and most understanding; these are often described as hidden techniques, or secret techniques
- **Gokui no uta:** a poem or phrase given to a **deshi** as a hint toward his quest for mastery
- **Gokuraku:** paradise; heaven
- **Gokyu:** fifth degree student
- **Goho:** Hard method

- ➢ **Goju:** Hard/soft
- ➢ **Gorei:** Word of command
- ➢ **Gorin no sho:** Book of Five Rings, by **Miyamoto Musashi**
- ➢ **Gorinso:** Work on the principles of sword fighting composed by **Miyamoto Musashi** in the early to mid-16th Century.
- ➢ **Goroshi** to kill; destroy
- ➢ **Goshi** also called **Koshi:** Midsection or Hip. Used classically as a term for farmer warriors; **bushi** who held and worked land
- ➢ **Goshi waza:** Throwing techniques in which the hip is used as the pivot point.
- ➢ **Goshin waza:** Survival techniques
- ➢ **Goshinjutsu:** Martial art of survival
- ➢ **Goson:** Village; self-governing village important in the later 16th Century and **Edo** Period.
- ➢ **Gotai** hard body, static training
- ➢ **Goton santon no ho:** The 30 methods of disappearing
- ➢ **Gotonpo:** The high order of five element concealing and escaping methods
- ➢ **Goyoshokunin:** Performers or artisans kept on a retainer by the **daimyo** and allowed special privileges.
- ➢ **Gumin:** "Stupid commoners"; **Edo** Period **samurai** derogatory phrase for peasants and townspeople.
- ➢ **Gun:** Country, military, army or it can mean administrative division of a province.
- ➢ **Gun sen:** Folding war fan often made out of metal.
- ➢ **Gun yaku:** A tax, military service or a levy
- ➢ **Gun yakushu:** Taxpayers in the 16th century who gave military service or provided soldiers in return for

an exemption on rice/money taxation.

> **Gun yuukakkyo:** A rivalry of dangerous powerful warlords.
> **Gunbai:** A rigid iron or wooden fan carried by generals in battle and used today by **sumo** referees as a symbol of authority.
> **Gunbaisha:** practitioner of battlefield divination
> **Gunkimono:** War tale; type of written work that dealt primarily with warriors and their deeds.
> **Guruma** also called **Kuruma:** to wheel
> **Gunryaku heiho** military combative strategy
> **Gyaku:** overturning, or classically known as Climbing feat in which the **Ninja** lies at full length, upside-down, on the ceiling
> **Gyaku ashi:** Reverse Foot
> **Gyaku hanmi:** a ready position in which opponents have opposite feet forward as you do.
> **Gyaku juji gatame:** Palms up overturning strangle
> **Gyaku nage:** Reverse throw
> **Gyaku mawashi geri:** Overturning Round Kick
> **Gyaku tsuke** also called **Sei ken:** Reverse Punch
> **Gyakute:** A way of holding a sword or blade underhanded
> **Gyakute waza:** Overturning the hand techniques
> **Gyobusho:** Ministry or Minister of Justice; court ranked office established as part of the **Taiho** Code (702) and later a ceremonial title.
> **Gyoja:** Mountain priest
> **Gyoji:** The referee at a **sumo** match.
> **Gyoku:** A gem, jewel, testicles
> **Gyorin:** "Fish scale" battle formation. Supposedly thought up by some **daimyo** in the 16th Century, the **gyorin** was intended to make an army appear as if it

were preparing to retreat and thereby tricking an enemy into attacking.

H

- ➤ **Ha:** edge of the blade
- ➤ **Habaki**: the sleeve or collar that fits over the blade of a sword at its juncture with the **tsuba** *gard* just before the **seppa** *washer*
- ➤ **Hachi:** Eight
- ➤ **Hachidan:** An 8th degree Black Belt, **Hachi** means Eight. In Japanese Martial Arts the title denotes a professor of the art.
- ➤ **Hachikyu / hakkyu:** orange belt rank eight (8th **Kyu**)
- ➤ **Hachimaki:** "Head wrapping." A light cotton towel, also known as a **tengui**, wrapped around the forehead to restrict perspiration from running into the eyes and face. Also the binding was/is a physical representation of an emotional commitment to the training.
- ➤ **Hadaka jime:** naked strangle
- ➤ **Hagakure:** Hiding in the leaves, classic **samurai** book from the early 18th century compiled by **Tashiro Tsuramoto** from the recollections and precepts of **Yamamoto Tsunetomo**. Considered one of the foremost works of **samurai** thought.
- ➤ **Hai wan:** back arm strike
- ➤ **Hai wan negashi uke:** back arm sweeping deflection
- ➤ **Haibu yori:** from behind
- ➤ **Haiku** used to be called **Haikai:** a popular form of Japanese lyric poetry consisting of three unrhymed

lines of 5,7, and 5 syllables each, with the subject matter originally confined to nature but later expanded to include all other subjects

> **Haishoku** also called **Sokugyaku:** instep
> **Haishu ken:** backhand strike done with the knuckles
> **Haito ken:** ridge-hand strike
> **Hajutsu:** the martial art of escaping out of techniques
> **Hajutsu kuho:** nine releasing methods
> **Hakama:** "Divided skirt." The skirt-like trousers or culottes primarily worn in the **koryu kendo, aikido, iaido,** and sometimes the upper ranks of **judo.** The most common style worn are called **joba hakama** and were derived from the undergarments of the **Samurai yoroi** *armor*.
> **Haku yakuso:** offensive **kiai**
> **Hakuda waza:** close combat techniques
> **Hamon:** the blades temper line, formal expulsion from the **Ryu**
> **Han:** half, A **Daimyo**'s domain in the **Edo** Period
> **Hanbo** also called **sanshakubo:** A three foot staff, said to be the walking stick of the **ninja.**
> **Hanbojutsu** also called **sanshakubojutsu:** the martial art of the three foot staff
> **Hane goshi:** A springing hip throw
> **Hane makikomi:** Springing winding throw
> **Hanka waza:** variation technique
> **Hanmi:** half front of the body facing the enemy
> **Hano no kiai:** reacting shout
> **Hanshi:** Master of an unspoken title; A respected master of martial disciplines, who is of eight to tenth degree black belt rank.
> **Hantachi:** a modern term for **Za no kamae**
> **Hanzei:** A tax or obligation that called for one half of

the income of a particular holding to be rendered to the **Daimyo**.

➢ **Haori:** a type of jacket worn over the **kimono**
➢ **Happa ken:** eight leaves fist, palms of both hands strike
➢ **Happo:** eight directions, eight sides
➢ **Happo geri:** assisted kick, eight ways of kicking (practice only)
➢ **Happo biken shihan:** master of infinite ways of weapons
➢ **Happo kirigakure:** scattering mist hiding
➢ **Happo undo:** exercising drills in all eight directions
➢ **Hara:** "Abdomen." Center of gravity and mass in the human body, traditionally considered in Eastern thought to be the seat of the soul and center of **ki**. For our art, it is where all movement begins and ends. The place from which true power is derived; one of the **Sanki** *three power bases*.
➢ **Hara ate:** strike to the lower abdomen, Traditional armor type normally reserved for the lower classes that protected only the front of the torso.
➢ **Hara kiri:** Ritual Japanese suicide by disembowelment with a knife, practiced by the **samurai**. This phrase is the informal word for **seppuku**.
➢ **Haragei:** intuitive thought, The art of concentrating **ki** in the abdomen; disciplines focusing on developing the **tanden** for combat/ for life.
➢ **Harai:** "Sweep" or "sweeping."
➢ **Haramaki do:** Style of armor developed during the 14th Century that was more easily fitting than previous armor types; it was opened in the back.
➢ **Hanran:** Rebellion

- **Hari ken** also called **shikan ken:** extended knuckle fist
- **Hasami** also called **Basami:** to scissor
- **Hasami tsuke:** scissoring punch; done often as an **Irimi** with **Jumonji No Kamae.** This strike is used in modern arts very differently.
- **Hasso:** to attack, wood
- **Hatamoto:** "Bannerman"; retainers close to the **Daimyo** or **Shogun** and accorded certain privileges and special status.
- **Heian**: un-effected; peaceful mind
- **Heian** Period: from the year 794 to the year 1192.
- **Heiho** also called **Hyoho:** battlefield strategy methods
- **Heimin:** commoner, non-**samurai**
- **Heishi:** Term applied to conscripted infantry of the **Yamato** Period.
- **Hensohokoho:** Drunk stagger method used by **Ninja** as a disguise
- **Hensojutsu:** the martial art of disguise and impersonation
- **Hensojutsu shichiho:** seven disguises
- **Hi:** secret; to fly
- **Hibi:** normal, everyday, first intention
- **Hicho:** flying bird
- **Hicho no kata:** flying bird form
- **Hidake:** Short lengths of **bamboo** filled with gunpowder
- **Hidari:** Left or left side.
- **Hiden:** secret traditions
- **Higeki:** sorrowful drama; Japanese term for tragedy.
- **Hiji** also called **empi** and called **shuki:** Elbow. **Hiji** is specifically (unlike the others) used as a term when

describing motion in the elbow.

> **Hiji ate:** modern way of saying **Shuki ken** *elbow strike*
> **Hiji dori:** elbow seizure
> **Hiji ori:** elbow break
> **Hijo:** Gunpowder filled Ball of paper with a sharp stick stuck through it to be thrown like a dart.
> **Hikan:** A retainer/attendant of lowly rank; a personal retainer of the **Ashikaga shogun** who filled an ostensibly low-ranking post.
> **Hiki:** To draw or pull
> **Hiki wake:** A draw. (Sport martial art term **judo, sumo, kendo** and **karatedo**)
> **Hikitate geiko:** practice to improve someone's technical skill and level
> **Hikyu:** Fire Balls
> **Himo:** string
> **Hineri:** wrench, twist
> **Hinin** also called **Chori:** literally "non-man"; for example, beggars, minstrels, panderers, prostitutes
> **Hira:** flat, even, level
> **Hira basami:** "tiger's mouth." A strike in which the first knuckle of the first finger is used like in **haito ken**; but the area between the thumb and the first finger is formed as a fist as the hand opens into the shape of a "C" just before impact. Widely used DIFFERENTLY by **Karatedoka**.
> **Hira shuriken** also called **shaken**: flat wheel blades
> **Hiragana:** phonetic script used for writing in Japanese within combination along with writing **kanji**
> **Hirajiro:** "Castle on the plain"; a castle built on flat ground
> **Hirayamajiro:** "Flatland Mountain Castle"; a castle

built on a rise surrounded by plains.

➤ **Hiriki no yosei:** elbow power; a thought to describe the movement from the elbow within **Aiki**

➤ **Hishigi:** to crush

➤ **Hito tobi:** flying man attack

➤ **Hiya:** Gunpowder filled tubes attached to an arrow

➤ **Hiza** also called **Hittsui:** Knee or sometimes lap.

➤ **Hiza guruma:** knee wheeling throw

➤ **Hiza gashira:** kneecap

➤ **Ho:** method, direction

➤ **Hobakujutsu:** martial art for restraining an opponent.

➤ **Hodoki:** "method way to the energy", free, loosen, unbind

➤ **Hoi:** encircling

➤ **Hojo:** Rope, clan an important military house that dominated the **Kamakura shogunate** by acting as regent for the **shogun**

➤ **Hojo Undo:** traditional body conditioning exercises done during class. They consist of any exercises, strengthening drills, stretches and movements.

➤ **Hojojutsu:** The martial art of tying people up. Advanced techniques used to tie and immobilize a victim by means of a cord.

➤ **Hojutsu:** The martial art of firearms or gunnery.

➤ **Hokashi:** street peddler

➤ **Hoko:** Bear, encircling tiger, walking, Military service, especially after 1590.

➤ **Hokode** also called **nekkote:** Finger Claws

➤ **Hokucho:** The Northern court.

➤ **Hombu** or **Honbu:** "Headquarters." This term can be used to define any headquarters-**Dojo** for a **Ryu**.

➤ **Hon** also called **Yubi:** fingers, **Hon** (not **Yubi**) can also mean the root; from the root.

- **Honjin:** The headquarters of a **daimyo** or general on a campaign.
- **Honjin hatamoto:** A **samurai** responsible for the guard of a field headquarters; commander of a headquarters' staff.
- **Honjo:** A primary castle mutually supported by satellite castles (**Shijo**).
- **Horagai:** Conch-shell horn used as a signaling device on the battlefield and for ceremonial purposes.
- **Hori:** Water moat.
- **Horo:** Large cape-like armor accessory worn mainly in the **Heian** Period whose exact purpose is unknown.
- **Hoshi:** Arrowhead, Battle formation; arrowhead formation.
- **Hyakusho:** Farmer, villager, cultivator.
- **Hyobusho:** Ministry/Minister of War; court rank/office established as part of the **Taiho** Code (702) and later a ceremonial title.
- **Hyojo hoko:** slippery surface walking
- **Hyororyosho:** Council of State; head administrative body under **Kamakura Bakufu**.
- **Hyoshi:** Timing, rhythm

I

- I also called **shin:** mind, heart, spirit; will, intention
- **Iai:** motion of sword drawing, can mean drawing cut
- **Iaido:** martial way of drawing a sword and re-sheathing it, a non combat art aimed at leading the practitioner to intellectual and spiritual awareness.
- **Iaidoka:** one who trains in **Iaido.**
- **Iaito** also called **keikoken:** an unsharpened practice

sword.

- **Iaijutsu:** Martial art which **Iaido** was taken, a battlefield art which requires the practitioner to draw his sword rapidly and strike to kill, and then replace it in its scabbard.
- **Ibuki:** lie, Dynamic tension breathing, breathing method common to many martial arts.
- **Ichi:** one, use to mean market, marketplace.
- **Ichi kyu:** 1st ranked student (brown belt)
- **Ichiban:** first, best
- **Ichimonji:** the written character of one (1) in Japanese, used by us to mean straight line.
- **Ichitaita:** one against many
- **Ie:** House, household; family.
- **Iga:** Remote region of Japan famous as the home of the **Ninja; Mie** Prefecture.
- **Iga mono: Iga** region **ninjutsu gumi** (**ninja** clan)
- **Ihen:** emergency, change
- **Iie:** No!
- **Ikebana:** the art of traditional flower arranging.
- **Iki:** will power
- **Ikki:** league or alliance. Can mean, a rebellious or riotous peasant group, from the 15th Century into the **Edo** Period.
- **Ikko-ikki:** Militant league consisting primarily of commoners, "village **samurai**", and religious adherents-especially one associated with the **Honganji** sect of **Jodo Shinshu** Buddhism which was prominent in the 15th-16th Centuries.
- **Ippon:** Full point awarded in sport martial arts competitions for the flawless execution of a technique.
- **Ippon ken:** one knuckle-fist

- **Ippon kumite:** one step exercise
- **Ippon seoi nage:** what **Judo** called **seoi nage**
- **Imayo:** a singing style popular in the late **Heian** Period.
- **In:** yin, used to mean a retired emperor
- **Inyo:** yin-yang
- **Inashi gata:** the form of polishing the body, form of skillfully avoiding and upsetting opponent's attack.
- **Inazuma:** Lightning
- **Inka:** Certificates awarded by a **Zen** master to a student that signified the holder had achieved some degree of enlightenment in their practice.
- **Inro:** Medicine carrier, literally, "seal basket"; small decorated box.
- **Insei:** An old **Soke** that still runs the **ryu and**/or **kai.** This term came from an old meaning describing a system whereby retired/abdicated emperors continued to rule from behind the scenes. Once commonly translated as "government by cloistered emperors", the term "cloistered" is now considered misleading. Emperor **Go-Daigo** officially abolished this system in 1321.
- **Inton:** concealment and camouflage
- **Intonjutsu:** the martial art of disappearing
- **Inu Omono:** Archery **Samurai** sport in which live dogs were chased and shot from horseback.
- **Inyo:** yin and yang
- **Inyoho:** the in interaction of all things
- **Ippon nukite:** One finger spear hand
- **Ippon shobu:** One point contest (sport martial arts)
- **Iri:** to enter
- **Irimi:** entering
- **Irimi nage:** entering throw

- **Irogome:** Colored Rice **ninja** Code
- **Isagi yoku:** "without regrets"; dying after all obligations have been fulfilled; the hope of every **Bugei**.
- **Isoku itto no maai:** One move forward, one cut distance.
- **Ishiki:** energy of intention
- **Ishigaki:** castle walls made of stone.
- **Ishiku:** a stonemason.
- **Ishizuki:** An iron tip located at the other end of the blade of a **Yari** or **Naginata**.
- **Issho kemmei:** a desperate striving; never stopping in life; even unto death, for a place in the world; many of the earliest **samurai** or mercenaries labored under this principle.
- **Itami:** pain
- **Itami jime:** painful choke
- **Itami nage:** pain throw
- **Izanagi:** In **Shinto**, along with **Izanami** one of the creators of Japan; **Izanami** is the lover, and the father of **Amaterasu**
- **Izanami** also called **Izanami no kami:** In **Shinto**, the Creator of Life; with **Izanagi** the creator of the Japanese Islands. **Izanami** is said to have retired to a castle in the underworld after the creation of the world.

J

- **Jakkin**: A secret nerve point in the upper arm.
- **Ji**: character; letter; word; handwriting, used to be a suffix indicating a temple

- ➢ **Jiai**: Affection and benevolence
- ➢ **Jibusho:** ministry/Minister of Civil Affairs; court rank/office established as part of the **Taiho** Code (702) then later a ceremonial title.
- ➢ **Jigoku:** hell
- ➢ **Jikan:** "Time"
- ➢ **Jime** also called **shime:** Choke or strangle
- ➢ **Jin:** man
- ➢ **Jinai:** temple complexes that included religious, militant, and economic dimensions; mostly those associated with the **Jodo Shinshu** sect.
- ➢ **Jinbaori:** sleeveless jacket, (big shoulder thing) worn over armor, often by important **samurai**, especially in the 16th Century.
- ➢ **Jindachi zukuri:** a relatively older type of sword-mounting in which the scabbard is tied around the waist with a long **seigio**.
- ➢ **Jingaijutsu**: **ninja** martial art of signaling
- ➢ **Jingasa:** simple iron helmet used by foot soldiers in the 16th Century that doubled as a shallow pot for cooking rations in the field.
- ➢ **Jita kyoei:** mutual benefit and welfare
- ➢ **Jito:** a lower-level official charged with the collection of taxes and the enforcement of laws on an estate level. The **jito**, created by the **Kamakura Bakufu**, answered to the **Shugo**
- ➢ **Jishaku: ninja** magnet used as a compass
- ➢ **Jissen gata:** real fighting; true fighting forms
- ➢ **Jiyu:** free, freedom; liberty
- ➢ **Jiyu kumite:** free sparring (sport martial arts)
- ➢ **Jo** also called **Shinbo:** a four foot long wooden staff.
- ➢ **Jo awase: Jo** exercises
- ➢ **Jo suburi**: Practice strikes of the **Jo**

- **Jodan:** "upper level", used to be a room with a raised floor-used by important figures
- **Jodo:** "Way of the stick" The Japanese method of stick fighting using a **Jo**
- **Jodori**: defense against a **Jo**
- **Jogai:** "Out of bounds" (sport martial art term) used by a referee to denote that either or both contestants are out of bounds.
- **Jogeburi:** straight up and down **suburi** with a **Jo**
- **Jojutsu** also called **Shinbojutsu:** the martial art of the **Jo**
- **Jokamachi:** the castle town, especially one of the late16th-17th Century and beyond.
- **Jokyusha:** advanced student, with a higher **kyu** grade
- **Jonin:** high level **ninja**; "grandmaster **ninja**", a **ninja** leader.
- **Joseke:** upper seat or high place; under the **kamiza** on the **shomen**
- **Joshu:** castellan; a castle keeper-a prestigious posting for the retainer of a **Daimyo** in the 16th Century.
- **Josokutei**: Ball of the foot
- **Jowan:** upper arm
- **Ju:** "giving", "gentle", ten
- **Judan:** 10th degree black belt; as high as you can go in martial arts (anything further is fake and silly)
- **Judo:** "Gentle way" A Japanese art of sport with Olympic recognition. **Judo** is a method of turning an opponent's strength and overcoming by skill rather than sheer strength.
- **Judogi:** The **judo** uniform, a baggy jacket and loose trousers colored off white or sometimes (rarely) blue.
- **Judoka:** A practitioner of **judo**.
- **Juji:** cross

- **Juji gatamae:** crossing limb lock
- **Jujutsu** also spelled **jiujitsu** and spelled **jujitsu:** "Art of gentleness" the martial art of suppleness, gentleness in which one is applying a technique using the body as a weapon in unarmed combat. Where **Judo** came from
- **Jujutsuka**: a practitioner of **jujutsu**
- **Jukendo:** Way of the Bayonet, a Japanese Martial Art that has recently adopted a sporting format. It consists of fighting with a bayonet fixed to the end of a rifle and developed primarily from spear and staff arts.
- **Jukenjutsu:** the martial art of the bayonet; where **Jukendo** came from
- **Jukyo**: theory of moral and governmental ruling that came from China.
- **Jutaijutsu**: martial art of grappling, locking, entangling, strangling and throwing
- **Juji Kumite:** Free Exercise
- **Juji Nage:** Crossed Arm Throw
- **Jukijutsu:** martial art of exploitation of an opponent's strength against himself. The name means soft or flexible and the art contains both armed and unarmed techniques.
- **Jumbi Undo:** Warming up Exercises
- **Jumon**: secret chant
- **Jumonji:** the written character ten in Japanese
- **Junshi:** act of following one's late lord in death through suicide. Generally applied to peacetime incidents of such suicides, **junshi** was expressly outlawed in the **Edo** Period.
- **Jutai:** soft body, smooth training
- **Jutsu:** "martial art" fighting method of the **bugei**, or

martial disciplines of war, rather than with the sporting or aesthetic practices of modern Japan.

➢ **Jutte:** A forked iron truncheon that can parry an attack, mostly used in arresting. Also displays one's rank by color.

➢ **Juttejutsu:** the martial art of the **jutte**.

K

➢ **Ka:** fire, practitioner (as in **Karatedoka** or **Judoka**).

➢ **Kabuto:** The helmet worn by **samurai**. It was made of iron or lacquered leather, and was secured to the head by a series of silk cords. The traditional helmet of the **samurai**, often decorated with an elaborate **mon** *crest*. The most common sort of **kabuto** by the 16th Century was the so-called **hachi mai bari**, or "eight applied plates". This cheap, conservative design was a descendant of the often ornate **kabuto** worn by earlier **Heian** and **Kamakura samurai** that were designed for using a **kyu** *bow* and protecting against **ya arrows**.

➢ **Kaburaya:** "Turnip head" bulbous **ya** *arrow* head that produced a distinctive noise in flight.

➢ **Kachi:** "Win", "victory"

➢ **Kachidoki** also called **kachi no kiai:** victorious shout

➢ **Kachinuki:** a training drill where a trainee faces consecutive opponents until defeated his last opponent taking his place until he too is defeated.

➢ **Kachinuki shiai:** a contest in which a contestant takes on each opponent in succession without rest between matches until he or she is defeated. Each win counts as one, and a draw counts as one-half but eliminates

both contestants. (Sport martial arts)
> **Kado:** way of reciting poetry
> **Kaeshi** also called **gaeshi:** from **kaesu**, spinning, counter-attack
> **Kaeshi waza:** spinning countering techniques
> **Kagami biraki:** Japanese new year celebration, held on different dates on our calendar every year
> **Kage:** shadow
> **Kage geri:** shadow kick
> **Kage no kiai:** shadow shout (throwing your voice)
> **Kage tsuke:** shadow punch
> **Kage uke:** shadow reception strike
> **Kage zuki:** shadow punch
> **Kagemusha:** "Shadow warrior"; an individual who acted as the double for a **daimyo** when his appearance on the battlefield or elsewhere needed to be feigned. Sometimes used as another name for a **ninja**.
> **Kagi:** hook
> **Kagi yari:** "Key spear" a hooked spear used for parrying and hooking an enemy's weapon; it was useful in policing.
> **Kaginawa:** grappling hook and rope
> **Kagoshima:** Town in **Satsuma**. **Kagoshima** acted as the seat of power for the **Shimazu** family from the early **Kamakura** Period onward, and was the scene of a Western naval bombardment in 1863 following a misunderstanding (murder of a British diplomat).
> **Kaho** also called **Kakun: Daimyo** house law, the set of guidelines and/or rules by which the **daimyo** and his retainers operated. The earliest **kaho** may have been the "Wall Writings of the **Ouchi**", some of which dates from 1440.

- **Kai:** association, organization
- **Kaicho:** The head of an organization
- **Kaiden:** master's certificate
- **Kaiken:** "Short knife" six-inch knife used by women of the **samurai** class.
- **Kaiki:** breaking in / opening **ninja** tools; collective name given to all tools used for breaking and entering
- **Kaishaku:** "A second"; an assistant to the act of **seppaku** *suicide*, whose job it was to behead the **samurai** committing suicide after he had cut his belly and leaned forward, so as to minimize the suffering he would have to endure.
- **Kaisho:** open hand
- **Kaiso:** founder
- **Kaiten:** roll, spin, turn, wheel round, revolve
- **Kaiten ashi** also called **Tenkan**: pivoting around on one foot so as to turn up to 180 usually 90 degrees
- **Kaiten gari:** wheel reap with the leg
- **Kaiten nage:** open and turn throw
- **Kaiten waza:** rolling and flipping techniques
- **Kajo Chikusei:** Bearing and respecting the qualities of the flower and the spirit of the **bamboo.**
- **Kajo Waraku:** Having a heart as peaceful, joyful and lovely as that of a flower.
- **Kakato:** Heel of the foot.
- **Kakato geri:** heel kick
- **Kakarigeiko:** attackers in line, one after the other
- **Kake:** application of a technique
- **Kake uke:** hooking reception strike
- **Kakejin:** Exercise in which the **ninja** trainee hangs from a branch for hours while weighted with sacks of stones
- **Kakemono:** vertical hanging scroll

- **Kaki:** fire tools
- **Kakie:** sticky hands
- **Kakiwaki uke:** reverse wedge reception strike
- **Kaku:** angle; horn
- **Kakudo** also called **nanamae:** angle
- **Kakunin in:** hand gestures (**mudra**) of the **Nyorai**
- **Kakushi Buki:** hidden weapons
- **Kakushi geri:** hidden kick; crescent kick
- **Kakute:** Finger Ring with a spike or hook that could be used to strike a deadly blow, Sometimes attached to the other end of **hojo** (rope for tying an enemy up)
- **Kakuto ken:** bent-wrist strike
- **Kakuto uke:** bent wrist reception strike
- **Kakuyoku:** Battle formation; "crane's wing"; Used by certain **daimyo** in the 16th Century; such as **Takeda Shingen** at **Kawanakajima** in 1561), the **kakuyoku** was intended to envelop a retreating or surprised enemy.
- **Kama:** sickle
- **Kama yari:** spear to which a single edged sickle (or two) is/are also attached.
- **Kamae:** "Attitude", transitory position; reflection of heart
- **Kamae naotte:** return through from one **kamae** to another
- **Kamae no kata:** posture transitions
- **Kamakura** Period: 1192 to 1334
- **Kamari:** name once given to a group of **Ninja**, meaning scout.
- **Kami kaze:** "Divine wind", the winds that came and opened up the sea and stopped the Mongol invasion destroying the Mongol fleet twice, World War II suicide pilots

- **Kami samurai**: those who serve; aka the two sword man, since only **samurai** were permitted to carry more than one sword or to possess a sword more than two feet long.
- **Kamishimo:** Formal **samurai** attire consisting of a **Kimono**, **Hakama**, and **Kataginu**. During the **Edo** Period, **kamishimo** became everyday wear.
- **Kamiza:** "upper seat" The area at the front of the **dojo;** the center of respect under which the instructors and honored guests sit.
- **Kampai:** cheers, toast
- **Kan:** Organization, a unit of cash-equivalent to 1000 **Mon**
- **Kana:** the Japanese phonetic syllabic writing system
- **Kancho:** master of the house, the person in charge of the **dojo,** a much older term for spies
- **Kane sute:** flying sacrifice throw
- **Kangeiko:** mid-winter training
- **Kani**: crab
- **Kani sute** also called **kani basami:** crab sacrifice
- **Kanji:** Chinese ideograms as used by the Japanese
- **Kanjo:** A letter of commendation, often issued by a **daimyo** to a valued retainer, especially one who had performed some meritorious deed or service.
- **Kanku:** viewing the sky
- **Kanmi hen:** method of observing the enemy's strategy and positioning
- **Kanrei:** sub leader of a **Ryu** second in command under the **Soke** or **Sodenke**. Came from the deputy or Vice **Shogun**; established in the late 14th Century. Two **Kanrei** positions were ultimately established: the **Kyoto Kanrei** and **Kanto Kanrei**, the latter acting as the **shogun**'s executive office in the **Kanto**

region. The last individual to hold the post of **Kanto Kanrei** was **Uesugi Kenshin** the famous **samurai**.

> **Kanren:** linked, connected
> **Kanren waza:** linked techniques, one technique followed by another
> **Kansetsu:** twist and lock
> **Kansetsu waza:** joint manipulation restraining techniques
> **Kanshi:** suicide to admonish an overlord for his erratic behavior.
> **Kanzashi:** "hairpin" an ornamental hairpin used for self-protection by the women of feudal Japan.
> **Kappo:** resuscitation
> **Kara:** empty
> **Karami** also called **Garami:** entanglement; entwined
> **Karami waza:** entanglement techniques
> **Karate:** "Empty hand", "China hand" (misused term for **Karatedo**)
> **Karatedo**: an unarmed method of self-defense or sport which many parts of the anatomy are used to punch, strike, kick or block.
> **Karatedoka:** A **karatedo** practitioner. Accepted now, but derived from a misspoken term, **karateka** is used to state the same.
> **Karatejutsu** also called **Dakentaijutsu** or called **Todejutsu**: the martial art of striking and kicking
> **Karoku:** the stipend (a monetary allowance) paid to a clan retainer, room, board.
> **Karu waza:** acrobatic techniques
> **Kashin:** Retainer
> **Kashindan:** A **daimyo's** retainer band.
> **Kashira:** "pommel cap", "ferrule" a metal cap covering the tip of the hilt of the **katana, wakishashi,**

tanto and so forth.

➤ **Kasugai:** a large iron staple used to bind a header (two large boards above a doorway), used by a **ninja** to climb with and kill with

➤ **Kasumi:** mist, fog, temples

➤ **Kasumi no ho:** methods of the fog

➤ **Kasumi no ho no sekai:** realm of fog/consciousness

➤ **Kata:** "form", shoulder, also a series of prearranged maneuvers practiced in many of the martial arts

➤ **Kata gatame:** shoulder lock

➤ **Kata guruma:** Shoulder wheel throw

➤ **Katadori:** shoulder seizure

➤ **Kataginu:** Stiff shouldered sleeveless jacket worn by **samurai** over a **kimono** along with **Hakama** in formal circumstances, especially in the **Edo** Period.

➤ **Katame** also called **gatame:** joint lock

➤ **Katame waza:** joint lock techniques

➤ **Katana:** "Sword" a Japanese sword, with a curved, single-edged blade twenty-four to thirty-six inches long. A traditional long sword of the **samurai** constructed through the folding and refolding of a bar of hot metal thousands of times. Renowned for its toughness and cutting ability, the **katana** or **tachi** replaced the bow as the primary weapon of the **samurai** during the later **Kamakura** period, although it was often secondary to the **Yari** *short spear* in battle.

➤ **Katana bukuro:** Cloth cover for the **Katana**

➤ **Katana keibo:** wooden club used by the Japanese police.

➤ **Katanagari:** describing the confiscation of arms from all non-**samurai** at the end of the 16th Century.

➤ **Katanakaji:** Sword smith

- ➢ **Katate dori:** wrist grab with one hand
- ➢ **Katchu bujutsu:** martial techniques done while wearing armor
- ➢ **Katsu:** resuscitation methods
- ➢ **Katsu jin ken:** The saving of your enemy's life
- ➢ **Katsuhayabi:** "Victory right here, right now"; "speed which transcends time and space"; spiritual tenet of **Aiki**.
- ➢ **Katsujinken:** life-giving sword
- ➢ **Karo: Ryu** elders, came from those trusted retainers of a **daimyo** whose service is long and loyal.
- ➢ **Kawa** also called **Gawa:** River, side
- ➢ **Kayakujutsu:** the martial art of fire and explosives; demolitions
- ➢ **Kebiki odoshi:** A kind of close lacing used to construct armor.
- ➢ **Kegutsu:** Boots made with fur (often from bears) popular among high ranking **samurai** in the **Heian** Period but out of style and rare by the 16th Century.
- ➢ **Keika:** espionage strategy in which captured **ninja** reinforce misinformation
- ➢ **Keiko:** practice
- ➢ **Keiko shokon:** reflect on the old to understand the new
- ➢ **Keikoken** also called **Iaito:** practice sword
- ➢ **Keiseimachi:** Courtesan district; literally meaning "district of destroyers of cities"; otherwise known as "pleasure districts"; a place of prostitution, these areas were grudgingly allowed by the **Tokugawa bakufu** during the **Edo** Period and catered to all classes of men.
- ➢ **Keisotsu:** thoughtlessness
- ➢ **Kekomi:** penetrating, blade of the foot

➤ **Kemmu Restoration:**1333-1336, brief period in which full authority was restored to the Imperial house under **Go-Daigo**. **Ashikaga Takauji** a former ally of **Go-Daigo** who brought the Restoration to an abrupt end by seizing power and creating the **Ashikaga Bakufu**.

➤ **Kemmu Shikimoku:** Set of 17 injunctions composed by the monk **Zeen** on the order of **Ashikaga Takauji** in 1336 essentially acting as a representation of the **Ashikaga**'s authority. There were numerous additions made to the original 17 articles-a total of 200 by the year 1520.

➤ **Ken:** blade, fist (modern thinking), A unit of distance equal to 1.818 meters or 6 **shaku**.

➤ **Ken kudaki:** punch destroyer

➤ **Kenchi:** Cadastral study, land surveys conducted by many **daimyo** in the 16th Century to maximize the lands registered for taxation. **Toyotomi Hideyoshi** organized the greatest of the land surveys between 1587-1597. Land surveys were patently unpopular with the peasantry and local **samurai**, sometimes prompting riots, attacks and many forms of resistance.

➤ **Kendo:** "way of the sword" modern art and sport of Japanese fencing. The object of a **kendo** contest is to deliver scoring cuts to an opponent's predetermined target areas with a **shinai** while both participants are dressed in **Keiko yori**.

➤ **Kendoka:** a practitioner of **Kendo**

➤ **Kengata to seido:** fist form and accuracy

➤ **Kengeki** aka **chambara:** sword theater; a work of fiction.

➤ **Kenin:** "men of the house"; the term which the

daimyo might use to refer to his vassals.

➤ **Kenjutsu:** the martial art of the sword; an aggressive method of swordsmanship which **Kendo** came from.

➤ **Kenjutsuka:** a practitioner of **Kenjutsu**

➤ **Kenkyaku:** "fencer" one of many words used to describe those who lived by the sword, especially in literary usage.

➤ **Kenpo** also called **Kempo:** higher order of the blade, modern meaning "fist law" this modern term describing a modern martial art of combination unarmed striking

➤ **Kenshi:** expert swordsman

➤ **Kentsui uchi:** fist hammer strike

➤ **Keppan:** blood seal made with vow upon entering a **ryu;** the act of cutting the fourth finger on one's left hand with a knife and smearing the resultant blood on an oath, below the signer's signature or monogram important to all **samurai** and many **budoka**.

➤ **Kerai:** Retainer

➤ **Keri:** Kick.

➤ **Keri kudaki:** kick destroyer

➤ **Keri waza:** kicking techniques

➤ **Kesa:** A monk's ritual shawl, robe or cloak, sometimes worn over armor by **samurai** who were also Buddhist monks. Now the term is used for the top portion of a **Keikogi**.

➤ **Kettsuin:** ritual magic finger movements of the **ninja**

➤ **Ki:** energy, "Spirit" Ideally, the mental and spiritual power summoned through concentration and breathing that can be applied to accomplish physical feats. This centralized energy, possessed by every person, can be manifested through practice.

➤ **Kiai:** "spirit shout", "spirit meeting." A toned shout

pointed at attacking the enemy energetically, modern **budoka** yelling

➤ **Kiaijutsu:** the martial art of the spirit shout, focus life energy

➤ **Kiba:** horse

➤ **Kicho**: "curtain of state"; a portable curtain that protected people from looking in; it stopped prying eyes

➤ **Kihon:** the basis for the art; the foundation , "basics" or "basic training" modern thinking -fundamental techniques.

➤ **Kihon dosa:** basic movements

➤ **Kiiro obi:** yellow belt

➤ **Kikenshiso:** "dangerous notions"; notions of rebellion.

➤ **Kime:** focal point, focus

➤ **Kimono:** Standard everyday wear throughout Japanese history, designed in part to keep its wearer cool during the summertime and warm in the winter. **Kimono** were made from cotton, hemp, or silk, depending on the station of the wearer, and changed styles frequently over the centuries. Formal **kimono** as a court noble or important **samurai** might wear was made of fine silk and was bilious, with especially long sleeves and reaching to the floor. Peasants and foot soldiers often wore half **kimono** which allowed easy movement and more importantly were cheap; it is a long wide-sleeved robe; often elaborately decorated and usually belted with an **obi,** worn by both men and women as an outer garment; frequently in layers; one over another.

➤ **Kimusubi:** tying one's **ki** to that of the partner

➤ **Kinai:** The provinces around **Kyoto**, especially

Yamashiro, **Yamato**, **Kwatchi**, **Izumi**, **Settsu**, **Iga**, **Tamba**, and **Omi**

➤ **Kinagare ki no nagare:** streaming **ki**, flowing training
➤ **Kindai:** modern
➤ **Kinnyu hen:** method of locating agents after a war breaks out
➤ **Kinsei:** Early Modern period in Japanese history; the time between the **Momoyama** and **Meiji** Periods.
➤ **Kinteki:** Testicles
➤ **Kinton:** using metal
➤ **Kirigami menjo:** classical license on a simple piece of folded Japanese paper
➤ **Kirishitan:** Christian
➤ **Kirisutogomen:** the noble right of any **samurai** to kill instantaneously and without warning any low caste person whom he thought had given him insult. (**Edo** Period)
➤ **Kiritsuki:** cut and thrust
➤ **Kiseru:** Long handled wooden pipe popular among **samurai** in the late 16th Century after the European introduction of tobacco to Japan.
➤ **Kisho: ninja** surprise attackers
➤ **Kishomon:** a vow made on entering a classical tradition
Kizami tsuke: a jab
➤ **Ko ashi: ninja** stealth walking with small, stabbing steps
➤ **Ko soto gari:** minor outside reaping throw
➤ **Ko uchi gari:** minor inside reaping throw
➤ **Koan:** riddle in **zen;** used to assist **Zen** meditation
➤ **Kobaya:** A small ship without a roof; found in medieval navies, manned by 20 oarsmen.

- **Kobo itchi:** attack and defense as a continuum of response in combat
- **Kobudo:** classical martial ways; Old martial arts, modern martial arts use this to mean weapons way; it became a generic term coined in the 20th century, which can be used to describe collectively all **Okinawan** combatives. This more accurate to specify "**Okinawan kobudo**" in order to distinguish them from "Japanese **kobudo**."
- **Kobujutsu:** classical warrior arts
- **Kobutowari:** helmet splitter
- **Kocho:** butterfly
- **Koda yari:** spear with a sleeve
- **Kodachi:** short sword; backup sword; a forerunner of the **wakizashi**, a blade between twelve and eighteen inches.
- **Kodachijutsu:** the martial art of using the **shoto** (or now) **wakizashi**
- **Kodan:** prose tales of warriors and heroes
- **Kodansha:** a high-ranking black belt of fifth degree and above.
- **Kodoha:** "Imperial Way" military faction
- **Kodokan:** The world headquarters of **judo,** in Japan, a seven-story building that includes a 100 by 100-foot hall with 500 mats. Named after the **Kodokan: Samurai** school established by the **Mito Tokugawa** house that became well-known and controversial.
- **Koe:** small place where the leg meets the trunk of the body
- **Koga kubo:** Rank by which the **Kanto Ashikaga** branch was known for
- **Koga mono: Koga** region **ninjutsu** clan
- **Koga ninja:** a **ninja** whose history is derived from

the **Koga** region
- ➢ **Kogeki:** Attack, offensive dominating action
- ➢ **Kogusoku:** an ancient method of unarmed combat mentioned in connection with **kumiuchi** and **sumo** in the oldest records of the Japanese martial arts.
- ➢ **Kohai:** junior leader in a **dojo**
- ➢ **Koho:** rear, back
- ➢ **Koho geri:** back kick
- ➢ **Koho tobi:** backward leap
- ➢ **Koho ukemi:** backward breakfall
- ➢ **Kojiri:** the end cap of the **saiya** (scabbard) of a **katana**
- ➢ **Komi:** inserted, crowded, mixed
- ➢ **Komuso:** mendicant flute playing monks/ priest
- ➢ **Konidatai:** Supply train for an army in the field
- ➢ **Kojiki:** "the record of ancient matters"; quasi-mythical history compiled in the first millennium.
- ➢ **Kokei:** A successor
- ➢ **Koken uke:** rounded arm reception strike
- ➢ **Kokka:** A **daimyo**'s realm, his direct sphere of influence; the land a **daimyo** ruled.
- ➢ **Kokon:** old and new
- ➢ **Kokoro:** retained spirit, heart, or mind
- ➢ **Koku:** An important unit amount of rice (44.8 gallons/180 liters) that was used to measure an individual's wealth and a place's theoretical productivity. In the 16th Century, a simple **samurai** might be awarded a stipend of 100 **koku** a year, while in the **Edo** Period an income of 10,000 **koku** was considered **Daimyo** status. One **koku** was held to be enough rice to feed one man for a year.
- ➢ **Koku ryo-sebai:** double guilt; concept by which a **daimyo** or magistrate may arbitrate a quarrel without

declaring either party in the right.

> **Kokudaka:** The value of a holding expressed in **koku** of rice
> **Kokujin:** "Man of the province", "provincial"; term used to describe locally powerful **samurai** families during the **Muromachi** Period. As they were often not far removed from the peasantry in terms of priorities and concerns, **kokujin** were much like **jizamurai** if not the same, for all intents and purposes.
> **Kokutsu:** backwards leaning
> **Kokyu:** breath, breathing
> **Kokyu nage:** breath throw
> **Kokyu ryoku:** breath power
> **Kokyu ryoku taiso:** deep breathing from the **hara** breath power
> **Kokyuho:** breathing methods
> **Koran:** agitators **Koku:** empty space
> **Koroshi:** to kill
> **Koryu:** classical or old warrior martial arts family tradition
> **Koryu bujutsu:** classical or old tradition of warrior arts
> **Kosa:** cross over, pass
> **Koshi:** midsection, the hip(s), can mean ball of the foot
> **Koshi guruma:** Hip wheel throw
> **Koshi jime:** Hip choke
> **Koshu: Kai** province and things of **Kai** province.
> **Kosode:** "small-sleeved garment"; an early version of **kimono.**
> **Kote:** forearm
> **Kote gaeshi:** spinning the forearm

- **Kote hineri:** wrenching the forearm
- **Kotsu:** essence
- **Koyo gunkan:** History of the **Takeda** clan in the **Sengoku** Period possibly compiled in part by **Kosaka Masanobu** sometime before 1578 but more recently attributed to **Obata Kagenori**; interesting that it is one of the first texts to mention the term **Bushido** (the warrior code)
- **Kozuka:** "blade"; a small knife or dart used for cutting food and for throwing at an enemy; a throwing dart
- **Ku:** Nine, void
- **Ku no sekai:** void realm, empty realm, field of all possible realities; place where things are born from
- **Kubi:** neck
- **Kubi bukuro:** Head bag; a netted bag used to carry home the heads of defeated enemies.
- **Kubi nage:** neck throw
- **Kubisuji:** nape of neck
- **Kuda bashigo:** tube ladder
- **Kudan:** 9th degree black belt
- **Kuden:** direct transmissions
- **Kufu:** discipline; de-localizing the mind to guard against over concentration
- **Kuge:** Court noble(s)
- **Kugyo:** High placed court nobles
- **Kuhi tobi:** sacrificial flying leap
- **Kuji:** Dues levied in labor; a requirement to send men for provincial work.
- **Kuji in:** nine syllable seals, energy channeling
- **Kuji kiri:** "Energy channeling" a hypnotic movement of the fingers used by **ninja**
- **Kukyu:** 9th degree student

- **Kumi:** group, set
- **Kumi tachi:** paired sword practices with the sword
- **Kumite:** sparring, fighting
- **Kumiuchi** also called **kumigata:** a beginning grip used in training to teach and learn in which one hand grips the **uke** (man who receives) under the elbow (modern- at the elbow) and the other hand grips behind the **uke**'s neck (modern- at the collar).
- **Kumon:** chest
- **Kun:** Motto or oath
- **Kunai:** trowel-like gouging device **ninja** weapon; knife with a metal ring at the other end of the handle
- **Kuni:** Province
- **Kunoichi:** female **ninja** "nine holes and one more" or "nine plus one"
- **Kuro obi:** black belt
- **Kurogo:** prop-handler in **Kabuki** theater
- **Kurorokagi:** ice-axe-like devices used by **ninja**
- **Kuruwa:** a castle compound
- **Kusa:** Grass, a name once given to the **Ninja**
- **Kusari fundo:** chain with weighted ends
- **Kusarigama:** chain-sickle; noted for its efficiency in neutralizing the sword at long range then quickly closing the distance and killing at close range.
- **Kusarifundojutsu:** the martial art of the short chain with weighted ends
- **Kusarigamajutsu:** the martial art of the sickle and chain
- **Kuton:** using all elements and combining their forms
- **Kukan:** "space" and the timing within the space
- **Kukyu:** 9th degree student (yellow belt)
- **Kutsu:** lean, bend
- **Kuzure:** broken, collapsed

- ➤ **Kuzushi:** off balance
- ➤ **Kyo:** principle, learning, unpreparedness; false
- ➤ **Kyodai:** brother
- ➤ **Kyojutsu:** the martial art of integrating truth and falsehood
- ➤ **Kyojutsu tenkan:** the martial art of alternating appearances of reality
- ➤ **Kyokaku:** a sword-carrying commoner
- ➤ **Kyokei:** strong tendons
- ➤ **Kyoketsu shoge:** sickle blade weapon with weighted cord
- ➤ **Kyokotsu:** the sternum, breastbone
- ➤ **Kyoman:** observation and perception
- ➤ **Kyomon:** religious understandings
- ➤ **Kyosei:** A student teacher equivalent to **shodan** in some **ryu**
- ➤ **Kyoshi:** sixth- or seventh-degree black belt rank.
- ➤ **Kyoto:** "capital city" A city which held the Imperial Capital from 794AD and was originally known as "**Heian kyo**" ("the capital of peace and tranquility") until 1868. **Kyoto** also acted as the seat of **Ashikaga** power from 1333 until 1573, and was the scene of the **Onin** War (1467-77). Throughout, **Kyoto** was the largest city in Japan, and may have numbered as many as 150,000 citizens in 1550.
- ➤ **Kyu:** student; student rank designation signifying a level of achievement below black belt (**dan**) rank.
- ➤ **Kyuba:** archery and horsemanship
- ➤ **Kyuba no michi:** way of mounted archery, bow and horse; old name for the warrior arts, a term for the **Heian** and **Kamakura** era martial values.
- ➤ **Kyudo:** "Way of the bow" modern practice of archery as a discipline of coordinated integration of clarity of

execution, the poise, and the control over the bow, done in order to find **zen**.

> ➤ **Kyujutsu:** the martial art of archery. **Kyudo** came from **Kyujutsu**
> ➤ **Kyusho to kiai:** targeting and focus of the spirit
> ➤ **Kyushojutsu:** the martial art of striking pressure points.

L

The older Japanese language does not have any words that begin with the letter "L"

M

> ➤ **Machi:** communities within a city; a large town; a division (a city block).
> ➤ **Machi bugyo:** city magistrates that handled many civil tasks for their **daimyo**, especially when he was away serving in **Edo**. **Edo** itself counted two **machi bugyo**.
> ➤ **Ma ai:** distancing, the distance between two opponents, indicating the measured distance just out of reach of any/ all extended limbs. The distance between **Uke** and **Tori**. The distance of time and space between two forces. Fighting Method in which the **Ninja** uses close-in moves against a fighter who specializes in distance movement.
> ➤ **Mae:** Front
> ➤ **Mae Geri:** Front "snap" Kick
> ➤ **Mae Kekomi:** Front blade Kick

- **Mae no sen:** taking the initiative, attacking the instant the opponent thinks about attacking
- **Mae Tobi Geri:** Jumping Front Kick
- **Mairi:** tapping with the hand to signify submission
- **Majutsu:** the martial art of invisibility
- **Makeru:** To lose or to be defeated.
- **Maki:** to scroll, volume, book, twirling
- **Maki geashi:** Wrapping reversal
- **Maki komi:** wrapping dropping
- **Makibishi:** Almost like **Tetsubushi**, Small pointed objects usually scattered on the ground in order to stop or slow down an enemy
- **Makimono:** scroll
- **Makiwara:** a training post designed for toughening various striking
- points.
- **Makko Karatake Wari:** A way to cut an opponent vertically in half
- **Makoto:** Sincerity, pureness of intention
- **Maku** also called **jinmaku** and called **tobari:** Camp curtains enclosing a leader's headquarters while on campaign or on an outdoor excursion. **Maku** were essentially silk walls and did not have a roof.
- **Mandala:** Sacred diagram; cosmic map
- **Mandokoro:** The chief governing body of an important family or a complex; in the **Kamakura** Period, primary executive branch of the **Bakufu**
- **Manrikigusari:** ten thousand power chain; weighted chain. Sometimes used as another term for a **Kusari Fundo** (almost the same thing)
- **Maru:** circle
- **Masakatsu Agatsu:** "True victory is self victory"
- **Mata:** Groin

- **Mawashi:** around
- **Mawashi Geri:** Round Kick
- **Mawashi Tsuke:** Round Punch
- **Me:** eye
- **Meiji** Period: 1868 to 1912
- **Meijin:** Expert. One who has mastered an art far beyond the boundaries of physical prowess. Martial geneses.
- **Meiso:** meditation
- **Mekiki hen:** method used to observe the geographical layout of the enemy's territory
- **Mekugi:** A **bamboo** pin used to secure the handle of a **samurai** sword to the blade.
- **Mempo:** Face mask or plate worn with armor; a mean face often including a lot of hair. Popular from the mid-16th Century and progressively more elaborate as time went on.
- **Men:** Head, The name of the head protector used in **kendo**
- **Men buton:** Cushion on the top part of the **men**
- **Men gane:** Metal grill on the face mask of the **men**
- **Men uchi:** Strike to the head
- **Menbu: kyusho**, the face or forehead area
- **Menjo:** The name for the formal ceremony at which rank promotions are given, "diploma"
- **Menkyo:** license, teacher's certificate
- **Menkyo kaiden: "all things passed", "keeper of the scrolls" this person will become** A certificate of full proficiency in a Japanese martial art, usually awarded to an advanced student deemed more suited to carry on the translation of the art to the next generations.
- **Menuki:** ornaments of a **samurai** sword found under

the wrapped cord of the handle.

> **Metsubushi:** Twisted paper, eggshells or paper bags filled with sand, pepper, and metal shavings and thrown at an opponent's eyes.

> **Metsuke:** "all seeing eyes" Lesser officials who in the **Edo** Period appear to have handled under-cover police work "**ninja**" and acted as spies for the **Tokugawa** government. spies, roving eyes, point of focus for observation.

> **Mezashi:** A **bamboo Jo** with an arrow tip concealed in one end

> **Mi:** the body; one's self, The blade of a knife or sword

> **Michi:** way

> **Michinoku: Mutsu** province, often poetic (**Heian** Period).

> **Michiyuki:** a journey and the emotions that accompany it in a song, poem, or book

> **Midori obi:** Green belt

> **Migi:** Right or right side

> **Mikazuki Geri** also called **Hari Geri** and called **Kakushi Geri:** Crescent Kick

> **Mikkyo:** An esoteric secret knowledge teaching

> **Mikoshi:** Buddhist shrines that were carried to **Kyoto** when warrior monks rioted and made demands on the Court.

> **Mimi:** ear

> **Minatomachi:** town with a river port.

> **Minbusho:** a man that held the posistion of Ministry or Minister of Popular Affairs; court rank/office established as part of the **Taiho** Code (702) and later a ceremonial title.

> **Minka:** House/houses of the people, a broad term for

402

a variety of residential housing.

- **Misogi:** Purification of mind, body, and spirit. These practices for the purpose of purification are **misogi** *sweating,* **misogi** *cleaning* and **keiko** is **misogi.**
- **Mitsu kujiku:** the higher level of **kiaijutsu,** silent **kiai** used to break an opponent's spirit, technique and body.
- **Mitsumono:** Spies
- **Miwake hen:** method used for the observation of enemy force, numbers and capabilities
- **Miyako:** artsy term for **Kyoto** and occasionally **Nara**
- **Mizu no kokoro:** "Mind like water." A psychological principle of the martial arts emphasizing the need to internally calm the mind, much like the surface of undisturbed water, while facing an enemy.
- **Mizugumo:** "Water strider (spider)"; Flotation devices that allow a **ninja** to walk on water. These were composed of four carved pieces of wood fastened together to form a circle with a hole in the middle.
- **Mizukaki:** A web-like shoe device used by the **ninja.** They were placed on the feet during swimming. Similar to present-day flippers. Sometimes called **Mizukakigeta**
- **Mo ikkai:** do again
- **Mochi** also called **dori:** hold/grip
- **Mochikata:** gripping attacks
- **Modotte** also spoken to mean the same is **Motonoichi:** A command for returning to the original position, used in competition (sport martial arts).
- **Moguri:** sinking not ducking (never duck)
- **Moguri gata:** crouching/kneeling forms

- **Mojirijutsu:** imitation
- **Mokpyo:** Striking point or target. Weak areas of the body that can be effectively struck or kicked.
- **Mokuroku:** catalog of techniques; transmission scroll or license
- **Mokuso:** Quiet thought. A quiet form of meditation usually performed before and after a training session in the Japanese martial arts.
- **Mokuton:** using plants and wood for concealment
- **Momo:** Thigh
- **Mon:** Family emblem or family crest, often displayed on flags, formal clothing, and armor. Used especially after the 15th Century
- **Mondo Zen:** question and answer
- **Monogashira:** captain, leader
- **Monouchi:** one sided blade
- **Moro:** both
- **Morote:** two hands grabbing one arm or wrist
- **Morote gari:** A throw in which the attacker wraps his arms around the opponent's legs and pushes his shoulder into the opponent's abdomen to take him down backwards.
- **Morote tsuke:** Double Fist Punch
- **Motodori:** Topknot, hairstyle of a warring **Samurai**
- **Mu:** "Nothing." The **Zen** concept of nothingness or emptiness. This principle is often used in the Japanese martial arts to make one clear in the mind of all thought so the body will respond instantly to any situation.
- **Mudan:** "no high level" a term sometimes used to describe a long time **budoka** whose **sensei** has died; not being able to attain further rank from his **sensei** and no longer wanting to go by the past rank

received, because he feels he moved far beyond it; not desiring to be ranked under any other **sensei**; also being truthful as to not self promote (decide what rank he wants to call himself); then they adopt this title to mean "unknown level".

- **Mudansha:** A martial arts student who has not yet attained the rank of black belt.
- **Mudo:** practiced stillness for the **ninja** lying-in-wait
- **Mudra:** Hand Gestures
- **Mujo daimyo: Edo** period **daimyo** who held an income of 10,000-20,000 **koku** but no castle
- **Mukei bunkazai:** intangible cultural assets
- **Mukyu:** no belt, no rank
- **Mune:** Chest or abdomen
- **Munen muso:** no desires, no thoughts
- **Mura:** Village
- **Murasame: kyusho** (village rain), notch between clavicles
- **Muraski obi:** Purple belt
- **Muromachi** Period: 1394 to 1603
- **Musan:** scattering fog
- **Musha:** warrior
- **Musha shugo:** itinerant training in martial arts
- **Musha shugyo:** warrior quest
- **Mushin:** no heart, no mind; original mind, a mind not fixed on anything and open to everything
- **Muso:** without thought
- **Muso shinden:** knowledge transmission of the dream or a vision
- **Musubi:** Art of Knots and Tying people up
- **Musuko:** Son
- **Musume:** Daughter
- **Muto:** no sword

> **Muto dori:** unarmed defense against a sword

N

> **Nafuda kake:** Name and rank board indicating hierarchy of the **dojo fuku** (members)
> **Nagako**: tang of a sword; where the hilt is fastened to the handle; on which is placed the signature of the maker
> **Nagare** the modern term being **Nagareru:** to flow, streaming, water fall
> **Nagashi uke:** Sweeping reception
> **Nagashi tsuke** also written as **Nagashi zuki:** Flowing punch
> **Nagaeshi uke:** deflecting reception strike
> **Nage:** Throw
> **Nage waza:** throwing techniques
> **Nagedeppo:** old world-classical grenades
> **Nagimaki:** halberd-like weapon similar to the **naginata** designed for horse mounted use
> **Naibakuken:** telepathy, **Jin** (a part of **mikkyo**)
> **Naiwan:** Inner arm
> **Naka:** center
> **Nakatsukasa:** Ministry/Minister of the Central Office; court rank/office established as part of the **Taiho** Code (702) and later a ceremonial title used by warrior houses.
> **Namban:** Southern Barbarians, term applied to Westerners, especially in the 16th century-presumably in reference to the fact that most arriving the Spanish, Dutch, and Portuguese ships came from ports south of

China.

- **Nambuchuko** Period: years 1336-1457, sub-period within the **Muromachi** Period referring to the years in which two separate imperial courts existed at the same time. They vied for power. The Southern Court, established after **Ashikaga Takauji** defeated **Go Daigo** in 1336, and was finally forced to submit in 1457.
- **Nami gaeshi:** Avoiding a leg sweep by raising the leg
- **Nami gaeshi geri:** Rolling wave kick
- **Nami juji gatame:** half cross strangle
- **Nana** also called **shichi:** 7
- **Nanadan:** 7th degree black belt
- **Naname:** Angled (implies a 45° angle)
- **Naname giri** also called **keisa giri:** Diagonal cut
- **Nanane buri:** Side to side **suburi**
- **Nanban do -** Armor inspired by Western examples, especially that of a Spanish Conquistador, popular between 1580 and 1600. **Tokugawa Ieyasu**, for instance, wore a suit of **nanban do** at the Battle of **Sekigahara** in 1600.
- **Nanushi:** village elders
- **Naga bishaku:** A farmer's implement consisting of a pole about six feet long with a cup attached at one end which was used to spread human feces around the fields as fertilizer.
- **Nagamaki:** sword blade attached to a pole; (**naginata** variation)
- **Nagashi:** receiving flow; parry; deflect
- **Naginata:** Halberd "Reaping sword". A curved-blade spear, once used by Japanese monks and **samurai**. It is approximately seven feet in length including the blade. Many women of the **samurai** class became

adept at the use of this weapon. Made popular in the **Heian** Period. Originally the weapon of a foot soldier, the **naginata** came to be known as the favored weapon of the **Sohei**. The **naginata** was not otherwise in general use by the 16th Century.

> **Naginatajutsu:** the martial art of the **naginata**
> **Nakadaka ippon ken** also called **ippon ken:** middle finger one knuckle fist
> **Nakago:** The tang; that portion of the sword blade to which the hilt is attached
> **Nakaima:** the here and now
> **Nakayui: shinai**'s Middle leather string
> **Nashi:** none
> **Nawabari:** the placement of the outer walls; the planning of a castle's defensive layout in particular.
> **Nawanuke no Jutsu:** Techniques for escaping from bindings; often by dislocating one's joints.
> **Ne** also called **Za**: ground, root, base
> **Ne waza:** seated grappling [for us, for other groups use this term to mean groundwork]
> **Nejiri:** torque
> **Nekkote:** A type of finger claw
> **Neko:** cat
> **Nekome:** Telling time by observing dilation of a cat's pupils
> **Nekote:** finger tip "cat claws" weapons made of steel
> **Nen:** purity and unity of the mind
> **Nengu:** An annual land tax for the surfs or rent.
> **Netane:** Espionage Tactic of planting agents in situations months to years in advance
> **Netsuke:** intricately carved toggle
> **Ni:** two
> **Ni jigen no sekai:** 2 dimensional world; meaning that

the fifth dimension is very much a part of this existence. [1 height, 2 length, 3 width, 4 time, 5 field of all possibilities]

➢ **Nichirin in:** understanding the elements of nature, **Zai (mikkyo)**

➢ **Nidan:** second degree black belt

➢ **Nidan geri:** two level double kick

➢ **Nidome:** A policy in which the **Sengoku daimyo** would refuse to allow certain commodities to cross their borders; essentially a form of economic warfare

➢ **Nigite:** Shrines papers cut and folded in a zigzag manner; found in the **Kamidana**.

➢ **Nihon** also called **nippon:** Japan

➢ **Nihon-gi:** chronicle of Japan; companion volume to the **kojiki**.

Nihon nukite: two finger spear-hand

➢ **Niju:** twenty

➢ **Nikyu:** second degree student maroon belt

➢ **Nin:** perseverance, endurance, stealth, blade, heart. Can also mean man or person. The first part of **ninja, ninpo, ninjutsu**…

➢ **Nin yaku: Ninja** medicine a part of the study of **Yogenjutsu**.

➢ **Ningu: ninja** tools

➢ **Ninja** also called **shinobi** and called **shinobuka, rappa, suppa, kagemitsu:** A warrior assassin who has mastered the art of **ninjutsu;** said to take 20 years of training. "Stealer in" Japanese warriors most associated but sadly stereotyped with spying, infiltration and assassination. They became legends in their time, supposedly capable of disappearing into thin air and turning into animals. A term often loosely applied to irregular forces, spies, and assassins in the time of the **samurai**. According to legend, the services of **ninja** clans, especially those of **Iga** and **Ise** provinces, were highly sought after by the **sengoku daimyo**.

➤ **Ninja juhakkei:** eighteen skills of the **ninja**

➤ **Ninja no hachimon** eight fields of knowledge

➤ **Ninja Shoku: ninja** food

➤ **Ninja Yashiki:** A **ninja** house.

➤ **Ninjakenpo** also called **Ninjatojutsu**: Martial art of trickery **ninja** swordsmanship.

➤ **Ninjato** also called **Ninja katana** and called **Ninjaken, Shinobito, Shinobi katana, Shinobiken:** commonly thought of as a straight-bladed sword, but it need not be. A square **Tsuba sword guard** is common to this sword. Often equipped with hidden compartments for poisons, knives, and blinding powders. The sword of the **ninja**.

➤ **Ninjo**: human emotions; man's will; the personal or conscientious inclination which is often opposed or constrained by **giri** or duty.

➤ **Ninjutsu:** The skills and techniques practiced by **Ninja**

➤ **Ninindori** also called **futaridori:** two attackers

➤ **Ninpiden**: Translated as secret teaching of **ninjutsu**

➤ **Ninpo:** way or path of perseverance. Can mean endurance and stealth. Many take it to mean the higher order of **ninjutsu**. Some historians, such as myself, believe the term originated outside of the realm of **ninjutsu** and at that time had nothing to do with **ninja**.

➤ **Ninpo mikkyo:** a new term used to describe **ninjutsu** secret principles of the universe.

➤ **Ninpo Sanjurokkei:** 36 main parts of the **ninja**'s

training.

- **Nintai Seishin:** The ability to pocket insults and humiliation then later throw it away together with all traces of resentment; so that nothing is harbored.
- **Nitto** or **nito:** two swords
- **Nitojutsu:** The martial art of using both the **daito** and **shoto** or **wakisashi** at the same time.
- **No:** "of", "is", possessive particle, Traditional form of theater popular among the court and **samurai** that makes use of dance, costumes, music, and a chorus to portray an often-complex tale; **No** was developed 1350 and 1450 by **Kanami Kiyotsugu** and his son **Zeami Motokiyo**. The term is derived from the phrase **sarugaku no no**.
- **No bori:** Long, vertical flag popular in Japan after the 15th Century; carried by the retainers of a **daimyo** in battle by the **daimyo** himself. **No bori** Displayed the individual family crests, patterns, or written characters.
- **Noboriki:** Climbing Tools
- **No dachi:** Field Sword; Huge two handed sword fairly popular in the 15th and 16th Centuries, essentially an over-sized **Tachi katana**. Surviving examples from the **Muromachi** Period include **no dachi** about 6 feet long. **Samurai** are said to have brought them to Korea in 1593, in great numbers, to use as a psychological weapon against Korean soldiers.
- **Nodo:** Throat
- **Nodo tsuki:** Throat punch
- **Nokizaru:** "Rooftop Monkeys", commandos
- **Noren:** dark blue banners/flags marked with the merchant's **mon**.

- ➤ **Noson:** Farming village.
- ➤ **No Suke (nosuke):** Deputy Lord of...; another honorific title common especially in the 16th Century.
- ➤ **Noto:** proper way in placing the blade back into the **saya**
- ➤ **Nuki:** draw; pull out
- ➤ **Nuki Ashi:** sweeping step **ninja** use in stealth walking
- ➤ **Nuki tsuke:** Drawing strike
- ➤ **Nuki waza:** Avoidance, dodging techniques
- ➤ **Nukiuchi:** drawing cut
- ➤ **Nukite:** fingers bunched together; spear-hand
- ➤ **Nukitsuke:** Drawing the sword from the **Saya** (its scabbard)
- ➤ **Nunchaku** slang term "Nunchuck": a modern weapon of **Karatedo** made of two short rods joined by a rope or chain
- ➤ **Nushi:** Lacquerers
- ➤ **Nyoibo:** huge battle club.

O

- ➤ **O:** "Big" or "great."
- ➤ **O goshi nage:** basic hip throw.
- ➤ **O guruma:** big wheel throw, on which the opponent is slung vertically around the side of the attacker's waist.
- ➤ **O sensei:** Great teacher; The honorific prefix "o" attached to the word **sensei** indicates respect and acknowledgement of the chief instructor of a **ryu**. Most commonly associated with **Morihei Uyeshiba Osensei**, founder of **Aikido** [his students being the

first to use the term specially for him.]

> **O soto gari:** major outside reaping throw
> **O tsuke:** stepping, lunging punch
> **O uchi gari:** major inside reaping throw
> **O Yoroi:** "great harness"; a box-like sheath with a paneled skirt that hung from the shoulders with broad straps and fastened around the waist. This elaborate suit of armor was in general use during the **Heian** Period. Also worn among important figures into the **Sengoku** Period. Often constructed with many thousands of strips of laminated bamboo, the **O Yoroi** was expensive and hard to produce. The armor was boxy. **Samurai** while on horseback intended this for use. It was impractical for fighting on foot and therefore fell out of favor as the **samurai** went from bowman to spearman and then swordsman. **Daimyo** continued to wear variants of the traditional **O Yoroi** up until the 19th Century.
> **Obi:** Belt
> **Obi goshi:** throwing the opponent by grasping his belt, sash, top of pants.
> **Ocha:** tea
> **Odachi** also called **Otachi**: Large sword
> **Ofuro:** A Japanese style bath
> **Oji waza:** Defensive techniques
> **Okegawa do:** A more simple suit of armor very common in the 16th Century, constructed by riveting together strips of metal. Probably introduced sometime around 1555. The **Okegawa do** could be produced cheaply, easily maintained, and was well suited to **Sengoku** period warfare. Like most armor of the period, **Okegawa do** was tapered to allow the wearer's waist to support most of the armor's weight.

- **Oki:** Big, large
- **Okuden:** inner or hidden transmissions of a **ryu**
- **Okugi** also called **ogi:** secret teachings or principles
- **Okurasho:** National Treasury; court rank/office established as a part of the **Taiho** Code (702) and later a ceremonial title.
- **Okuri:** Sliding
- **Okuri ashi harai:** sliding or gathering foot sweep
- **Okuri eri jime:** sliding collar throw
- **Ometsuke:** the Inspector general in the **Tokugawa Shogunate**
- **Omote:** Front side, standard or obvious
- **Onaka:** Stomach
- **Onchi:** reward of land given by a **daimyo** to a **Samurai** for exceptional service
- **Ongyo:** concept used by **Ninja** for concealment
- **Ongyo in:** enlightenment, **Zen**
- **Ongyo no Jutsu:** leaping and concealing techniques
- **Ongyoho:** Invisibility methods
- **Oni:** An Ogre, demon, devil, monster or slang for a particularly violent and brutal person
- **Oni ken** also called **shikan ken:** Extended knuckle fist.
- **Oni kudaki:** demon crusher
- **Oniwaban:** Secret Service position for **Ninja** serving the **Shogun,** name of the **Ninja** whose undercover job was as castle guard
- **Onmitsu:** Spy or Detective
- **Onmyoshi:** an astrologer
- **Onnagata:** female impersonators; in **kabuki**, men who acted women's roles **osho** an instructor of **budo,** a monk.
- **Onshin no Ho:** methods for attaining invisibility

414

- **Onshin Tongyo no Jutsu:** Techniques for concealment and escaping
- **Onshinjutsu:** the martial art of invisibility
- **Orei:** Respect, etiquette; An expression of formal greeting in **budo**.
- **Ori:** to break, fold
- **Orun:** Right
- **Osaekomi waza:** techniques of immobilizing and pinning the opponent.
- **Oshi:** push, press
- **Oshiro:** castle
- **Oshu:** Northern **Honshu**
- **Otagai:** together; as one, partner
- **Otemon:** castle's main gate
- **Oten:** martial arts cartwheel
- **Otoko no michi:** "the manly way"; for the **samurai**, living according to the demands of **giri** a part of **bushido**
- **Otonashi no Kamae** also called **Ushiro No Kamae:** Standing upright with a **buki** behind one keeping it horizontal and hidden
- **Otoshi:** Drop.
- **Otoshi hiji ate:** downward elbow strike
- **Otoshi uke:** dropping reception strike
- **Otoshi zashi:** a way of wearing a **daisho** *matched pair of swords* so that the scabbards are tucked into the **kimono obi**
- **Outai:** stature or place in a company, also used to mean belt rank
- **Oya yubi** also called **Oyubi:** Thumb
- **Oyagoroshi:** killing the parent, thumb crush
- **Oyo:** application
- **Ozutsu:** Cannon, in limited use in the **Sekigahara**

Campaign 1600 and the **Osaka** Campaigns 1614 and1615. Japanese cannon were generally inferior to their European equivalents, and saw most of their use as **siege** weapons.

P

- ➢ **Pinan:** Peaceful Mind
- ➢ **Po:** direction, higher order, way; side

Q

The older Japanese language does not have any words that begin with the letter "Q"

R

- ➢ **Rai:** thunder
- ➢ **Raigo in:** reasoning / teaching it can be a **mudra**
- ➢ **Rakachu:** name for **Kyoto** used until the **Edo** Period.
- ➢ **Randori** freestyle practice, random attacking and defending, a practice for application of the art and awakening the mind
- ➢ **Rango:** a game women played where they tried to balance the most **go** stones on a finger
- ➢ **Ransen:** a confused; wild battle, chaos battle
- ➢ **Ransetsu:** blizzard
- ➢ **Rappa:** Brigand, name given to **Ninja** meaning guide
- ➢ **Rei:** bow, salute
- ➢ **Reigi:** Etiquette, good manners

- **Reigisaho: Dojo** methods of etiquette and good manners
- **Reishi sen:** A lifeline between God and all living things
- **Reishiki:** histories message, etiquette displayed
- **Renga:** Linked verse poetry, often composed of 31 syllables in two parts
- **Renmei:** A federation, league, or union of Japanese martial arts
- **Renshi:** title for a 4th, 5th or 6th **dan**
- **Renshu:** Practice or training period.
- **Renwaku waza** also called **renzoku waza:** techniques used in combination, consecutive techniques, a series of techniques
- **Renzuki:** Continuous attack.
- **Ri:** measured distance. a **Ri** is equal to 4km or equal to 2.445 miles
- **Ri ken** also called **Ura ken:** Backfist
- **Rikishi: Sumo** wrestler
- **Rinji:** An emperor's personal edict
- **Ritsu rei:** standing bow
- **Rokkyu:** 6th **Kyu** red belt
- **Roku:** six
- **Roku Kanon:** 6 **Kanon** to protect all sentient beings in the 6 planes of existence
- **Rokudan:** 6th **dan**
- **Rokuhara:** District of **Kyoto** that functioned as the headquarters in that city for the **Taira** (modern day **Heike**) from 1156 until 1183. **Rokuhara** also acted as the headquarters for the **Kamakura Bakufu**'s deputies in **Kyoto** until 1333
- **Rokuhara** Period: 1156 to 1185
- **Rokushakubo** also called **bo:** a six foot staff

- **Romaji:** Romanization of Japanese **kanji**
- **Ronin:** "wave man" Masterless, unaffiliated **samurai,** warrior unattached to a feudal lord, Many **samurai** were made **ronin** by the vicissitudes of the **sengoku** Period, and so formed the basis for many bandit groups and outlaw bands that plagued the countryside into the **Edo** Period. Though not employed by a **daimyo**, a **ronin** was still entitled to wear his swords. It was this thinking that later gave rise to the **Yakuza**.
- **Roto:** Common term applied to both civil and military servants
- **Rozeki:** rioting
- **Ryaku:** strategy
- **Ryo:** both; two, back in the times of the **samurai** the term **Ryo** was used to mean gold currency
- **Ryoashi:** both feet
- **Ryobu Shinto:** "the two ways of the gods"; a combining of **Shinto** and Buddhism
- **Ryogoku:** Domain, Province, a **Daimyo**'s territory
- **Ryote:** two handed
- **Ryotemune dori:** two lapel grab
- **Ryotedori** also called **ryotemochi:** two-hand grab (hand to hand)
- **Ryoude jime:** two-arm choke
- **Ryu:** dragon, flowing, school, tradition, martial family, (modern thinking is) a style, chain of thought
- **Ryufu:** "willow wind" larynx, Adam's apple
- **Ryugi:** an emotional and spiritual concept to mean wearing the beliefs, emotional connection and support of one's **Ryu** as a uniform
- **Ryuha:** style, school of a certain art
- **Ryuha daihyo:** representative of the tradition

- **Ryuka** also called **yaku:** "dragon under" **kyusho** point the calves
- **Ryukyu:** older term for **Okinawa**
- **Ryumon:** "dragon gate" **kyusho** point the hollow point in between the bones of shoulder
- **Ryutai:** flowing body, fluid training
- **Ryutai undo:** flowing body movement

S

- **Sabaki:** evasion, footwork
- **Sacho:** The bridge of the nose
- **Sado:** ceremonial preparation of tea
- **Sageo:** A cord fitted on the **saya** by the **kurikata**
- **Sageonana no jutsu: ninja** technique for using the **Sageo**
- **Sai:** a modern martial arts weapon (we do not use), A three pronged truncheon about fifteen to twenty inches long, said to be used as a defensive instrument against various weapons such as the sword. This is not believable from a historical or technical standpoint. It was said to have been developed from an **Okinawan** farming tool.
- **Saihai:** Baton carried by leaders to aid in the direction of troops; worn at the waist when not in use.
- **Saiminjutsu:** the martial art of hypnosis and mind control
- **Sakayaki:** Describes the portion of the head shaved by many **samurai**
- **Sake:** Rice wine. **Sake** was traditionally produced in the winter months by brewers and created through a process of the breakdown of rice grains by a fungus

and fermentation.
- ➤ **Sakigawa:** Leather cap on top of the **shinai**
- ➤ **Sakki:** "The force of a killer", Killing intentions, a psychic emanation of malice
- ➤ **Sakotsu:** Collarbone (**koppo** point)
- ➤ **Samurai: bushi**, Japanese warrior, "One who serves", the traditional warrior class of Japan until 1876. While of obscure origins, the **samurai** emerged as a powerful force by the 10th Century and after 1192 acted as the rulers of Japan. Until the 1590s, the status of **samurai** was somewhat fluid, and within the grasp of those born in the lesser classes- especially in times of war. In the 16th century, many **samurai** worked alongside the peasantry until they were called to service. After **Toyotomi Hideyoshi**'s clampdown on social mobility, all men who carried arms were considered **samurai** (but varying ranks) and made to live in the castle town of their **daimyo**. With no more battles to fight, the **Edo samurai** refined their ways of thinking and in many ways shaped the romantic way in which **samurai** history is now perceived.
- ➤ **San:** three
- ➤ **San jigen no sekai:** 3 dimensional world
- ➤ **Sanbon Yari:** A three bladed **Yari**.
- ➤ **Sanbyo no Imashime:** The law of three illnesses.
- ➤ **Sandan:** 3rd dan
- ➤ **Sanjaku tenugi:** three foot hand towel used to cover the face
- ➤ **Sankaku:** triangle, triangulation
- ➤ **Sankyu:** 3rd **kyu** grey belt
- ➤ **Sannin Jinba:** Three-Man jumping technique used to launch a **Ninja** over a wall

420

- **Sanpo:** three directional natural walking
- **Sanpo gata:** collective name given to certain techniques of **Hensojutsu.**
- **Sanpo geri:** walking kick
- **Sanshakubo** also called **Hanbo:** three foot staff
- **Sanshin no kata:** movement form of the body, mind and spirit
- **Sanshin gogyo no kata:** movement form of the body, mind and spirit. Uniting the three hearts with the five principle forms: earth, wind, water, fire, void
- **Sanshitan ken:** three fingertip fist
- **Sanzuri:** A radical or part of a **Kanji** meaning water
- **Saoto Hikigane:** Listening device of the **ninja** similar to an ear trumpet
- **Sappo:** A method of attacking vital points of the body in order to cause a
- coma or death
- **Saru:** A radical or part of a **Kanji** meaning going forth
- **Sarugaku:** Dancers and Entertainers, a common disguise of the **ninja**
- **Sarugakushi:** performer, actor, singer
- **Sasae:** propping and supporting
- **Sashi:** Stone training weights
- **Sashimono:** Small banner, their flag; affixed to the back of a suit of armor, for battlefield recognition purposes. Common in and after the 16th Century.
- **Satori:** Comprehension, enlightenment, sudden realization of truth
- **Saya:** scabbard
- **Sayu Yoko Buri:** Spinning the chain/rope of a **Kusarigama**
- **Sei ken:** twisting fist

- **Seiki:** one's life energy
- **Seiryaku kekkon:** a political marriage
- **Seishin:** Mind, soul, or spirit
- **Seishin teki kyoyo:** spiritual refinement
- **Seito:** Pupil, student
- **Seiza:** seated posture, correct sitting
- **Seki bune:** Medium sized ship common in 14th to the16th Century navies, operated by a 40 man crew.
- **Seki Hitsu:** "Stone Brush", a writing kit of the **ninja**
- **Sekisho:** Toll barriers. One of the ways **sengoku daimyo** gathered income especially in the provinces around Lake **Biwa**, Tollbooths were particularly unpopular. **Oda Nobunaga**'s abolition of toll booths in the **Kinai** brought him considerable acclaim from the people.
- **Sekkojutsu:** the martial art of scouting including techniques on surveillance and how to employ an army
- **Seme no kiai:** attacking shout "Buououo"
- **Sempai** or **senpai:** student senior leader
- **Semui in:** fear not, a **mudra**, fearlessness
- **Sen i:** Fighting will, fighting spirit
- **Sen no sen** also called **tai no tai**: taking the initiative for attack
- **Senban** also called **sinban:** formal judge
- **Sengoku** Period: Japan **Samurai** war time **Sengoku Jidai**, The Country at War. From 1477 to 1600. The term **Sengoku jidai** is taken from a roughly comparable episode in Chinese history
- **Sengoku jidai:** warring states period
- **Senjutsu:** the martial art of becoming super human
- **Sennin:** mystic, a practitioner of **Senjutsu**
- **Sensei:** "one who has gone before" teacher or

instructor
- **Sensen no sen:** pre-active, preemptive initiative for attack
- **Seoi:** Shoulder
- **Seppa:** The washers above and below the **tsuba** of a **katana**
- **Seppuku** also called **hara giri:** Ritual suicide, the act of killing one's self by slitting open his belly. Possibly first carried out by **Minamoto Yorimasa** in 1180, **seppuku** came to be the official manner of suicide for a **samurai**, and was prohibited for all other classes. In time, **seppuku** came to take on spiritual connotations, but in essence the exceedingly painful manner of dying it brought was a mark of grim pride to the **samurai,** a final showing of his bravery. By the 16th Century a **Kaishuku** *second* had been added to the ritual, to limit the amount of suffering the **samurai** who was to die would experience. When a female member of a **samurai** house committed **seppuku,** she almost always did so by folding her neck around the knife and pulling to slit her own throat.
- **Sessho:** Regent of the empire
- **Setsu:** snow
- **Shaken:** wheel blade, throwing stars
- **Shako ken:** claw strike
- **Shaku:** A measurement of length 1 **shaku** = 33cm
- **Shakuhachi:** bamboo flute often associated with traveling musicians.
- **Shi** also called **yubi:** finger, **shi** (not **yubi**) can also mean four
- **Shi no ko sho:** the four major classes/castes of feudal Japan: warriors, farmers, artisans, and

merchants

➢ **Shiai:** matches or contests

➢ **Shiatsu:** massage

➢ **Shibari:** to tie

➢ **Shibire Gusuri:** Poisons that produce a numbing or parlaying effect

➢ **Shibu:** training location

➢ **Shibucho:** The head of a branch group

➢ **Shibum:** Demonstration

➢ **Shibumi:** elegance

➢ **Shichi:** seven

➢ **Shichi dan** also called **nanadan:** 7th **dan Shidoshi:** teacher of the warrior way; **shodan** or higher

➢ **Shichi kyu** also called **nana kyu:** 7th **kyu** blue belt

➢ **Shidoin:** An instructor that is not the head

➢ **Shidosha:** A leader; a teacher 1st **dan**

➢ **Shidoshi-ho:** assistant teacher of the warrior way

➢ **Shihan:** honorary title of master teacher; **hachidan** and above

➢ **Shihan Cho:** A title of Chief Master in the **Dojo**

➢ **Shihandai:** student teacher

➢ **Shiho:** four directions

➢ **Shiho geri:** four directional kicking drill

➢ **Shiho nage:** four-corner directional throw

➢ **Shikan ken:** extended knuckle fist

➢ **Shikaku:** square, dead angle

➢ **Shiki:** element beyond **ku** a teaching of **mikkyo**, pure consciousness, wisdom, determination, can also mean courage

➢ **Shikko:** the method of walking on one's knees

➢ **Shikomi jo:** A **Jo** with a concealed weapon

➢ **Shikomi zue:** a walking stick with hidden weapon normally a sword

424

- **Shikoro:** Saw with a triangular blade
- **Shikoro:** Neck guard comes from the bowl of a **samurai**'s **Kabuto**
- **Shime:** to choke, constrict, tighten
- **Shime ashi:** squeezing feet **ninja** stealth walking maneuver
- **Shime waza:** constricting techniques, choke holds, strangulation techniques
- **Shimeki:** Iron Bars with wedged ends used to jam doors
- **Shimoseki** also called **shimoza:** "Lower seat" In a traditional Japanese **dojo**, the area where students line up and face their **sensei**
- **Shimoza: Dojo** rear wall
- **Shin:** heart, mind, spirit
- **Shin shin shin gan:** mind and eyes of god
- **Shinai:** practice sword made of split bamboo so as not to injure in practice
- **Shinchu:** a **kyusho** point at the center of the heart, middle of the chest
- **Shinkokyu sanaun:** spirit breath meditation 3 "ohms"
- **Shinken:** live blade, a real sword, real combat
- **Shinken gata:** real fighting form a practice to get a real feeling
- **Shinkyo:** Mirror placed in front of or inside the **kamiza**
- **Shinobi** also called **ninja:** used to refer to agents of espionage
- **Shinobi iri:** stealth and entering methods, infiltration
- **Shinobijutsu** also called **shinobi no mono** and called **ninjutsu:** the martial art of stealth, evasion, assassination and perseverance

- **Shinobi aruki: ninja** stealth walking
- **Shinobi ho** method of stealth
- **Shinobi Kumade**: Collapsible sectioned **bamboo** device that the **Ninja** used to put a rope or hook over the wall
- **Shinobi no juhappan:** eighteen **ninja** skills
- **Shinobi shozoku: ninja** uniform of war
- **Shinobi zue:** staffs and canes of varying sizes with hidden weapons inside
- **Shinobibune:** Collapsible **bamboo**-and rope stepladder
- **Shinobigatana** also called **ninjato:** short **ninja** sword
- **Shinodake:** thin **bamboo** under water breathing tube
- **Shinpan:** High ranking **dan** official judge, a **sinban** that is a black belt
- **Shinpi:** concepts of mysticism
- **Shinren:** Heart training
- **Shintai:** "Stopped mind" A condition in which one remains exclusively defensive (modern thinking)
- **Shintaiho:** spirit-body methods of movement
- **Shinzen Rei:** A ceremonial bow
- **Shisei:** posture
- **Shishin ken:** finger needle strike
- **Shitage:** Uniform Pants
- **Shitan ken:** thumb pressure strike
- **Shizen:** natural, in accordance with all that is
- **Shizen gyo un rysui:** moving naturally like flowing water a concept used in the practice **Suwari waza** during **rendori**
- **Shizen ken:** natural weapon, using any and all parts of the body to strike, anything you can think up
- **Shizen nobori:** natural climbing

- **Shizen tai** also called **shizen no kamae:** natural body transitory position
- **Shizoku:** Term used after 1869 to refer to former **samurai**
- **Shobo:** A wooden or steel ring with a small projecting stick that can be used to target pressure points
- **Shodai:** A title given to one who founds a **ryu** in the martial arts. The first generation
- **Shodan:** 1st **dan**, black belt
- **Shoden:** basic level of training, initial transmission
- **Shogo:** The three classical **Samurai** ranks of **Renshi, Kyoshi** and **Hanshi**
- **Shogun:** ruler of Japan, commander-in chief
- **Shogunate:** Term used to describe the government of a **shogun**
- **Shoji:** A paper sliding door, also an old term for Japanese chess
- **Shokunin:** Craftsman, a term that at first had a general connotation to include almost everyone; but eventually came to mean one who worked with their hands
- **Shomen:** the front wall
- **Shomen uchi:** forehead strike
- **Shonin:** Head of **Ninja** Clan
- **Shosen:** The first attack in a battle or war
- **Shoshin:** first intention
- **Shoshinsha:** Novice, beginner, All **Mukyu**
- **Shoten no jutsu:** climbing to the heavens going where they can't fallow
- **Shoten no jutsu to nobori gata:** vertical running and climbing methods
- **Shoto:** short sword

- ➤ **Showa** Period: 1926 until present day
- ➤ **Shozuku:** the **ninja**'s uniform for war
- ➤ **Shu:** hand; arm
- ➤ **Shu Ha Ri:** an expression referring to the 3 stages of training from simple imitation to personal development in the martial arts
- ➤ **Shudo:** art of the written characters, Japanese calligraphy
- ➤ **Shu ken** also called **tesho ken:** palm strike
- ➤ **Shuki ken** also called **empi ken** and called **hiji ken:** elbow strike
- ➤ **Shuko:** hand claws
- ➤ **Shukojutsu:** the martial art of using the **Shuko**
- ➤ **Shumatsu undo:** Cool down exercises
- ➤ **Shuriken:** throwing knives, spikes, darts, axes, blades, stars, and grenades
- ➤ **Shurikenjutsu:** the martial art of throwing weapons
- ➤ **Shushigaku:** a belief that a person's life is governed by the circumstances of his or her birth.
- ➤ **Shuto ken:** knife hand strike
- ➤ **So** also called **yari**: spear
- ➤ **Sode:** sleeve
- ➤ **Sodedori:** sleeve grab above the elbow
- ➤ **Sodegarami:** "sleeve entangler" a long pike with hooks at the end facing in all directions
- ➤ **Sodenke:** a scroll inheritor, used to describe the position of a **Soke** of an offshoot branch of an established **Ryu**. **Sodenke** is a title given to the head of the offshoot **Ryu**.
- ➤ **Sodezutsu:** A small hand held cannon 1 **shaku** 1 **sun** long
- ➤ **Sohei:** defenders of the truth, Warrior monks; relatively modern term describing the armed warriors

that acted as military muscle for major religious establishments from the 9th Century until the 1580s. In particular, the warrior monks of the **Enryakuji** (Mt. **Hiei**) were an important political force for centuries, and their support was often sought after in times of war. At the same time, the **Sohei** were destabilizing elements, and clashes between riotous **Sohei** and **Bakufu** and Court forces was reasonably common until 1571. In that year, **Oda Nobunaga** destroyed Mt. **Hiei**'s monastic complex and Hideyoshi's later forays into the **Kwatchi Kii** area marked the beginning of the end for the **Sohei**.

➢ **Sojutsu:** the martial art of the **yari** *spear*
➢ **Sokki geri** also called **hiza geri:** knee kick
➢ **Sokki ken** also called **hiza ken:** use of the knee to strike as if doing **shikko** on the person
➢ **Soke:** head of family, grandmaster, as far as one can go in a Japanese derived martial art. A man who has attained the level of **menkyo kaiden**
➢ **Sokim:** Fake, feint
➢ **Sokodo:** Speed
➢ **Sokotsu biro:** Carelessness, indelicacy, impoliteness
➢ **Sokotsu shi:** The act of committing suicide to make up for an offense or failure
➢ **Sokuho geri:** sideways kick
➢ **Sokuho kaiten:** sideways roll
➢ **Sokuho tobi:** sideways leap
➢ **Sokuji in:** mirror like wisdom a **mudra.** A teaching that converts anger and aggression into a mirror. An attempt to pass on wisdom "that which we dislike in others is the same thing we dislike about ourselves" "in the face of your enemy resides a reflection of yourself"

- **Sokushi ken** also called **sokugyaku ken:** toe strike
- **Sokuto geri** also called **kekomi geri:** foot edge kick
- **Sokutoki:** A small container that filled the air with **metsubushi**
- **Sokutsu shi:** suicide in honorable expiation for a crime
- **Sonbu:** Japanese pronunciation of Sun Tsu, author of the book **Sonsi**
- **Sonshi:** The Chinese book of strategies Sueng Tsu
- **Soshi:** Grandmaster
- **Soto:** outside
- **Sotojishi in:** submission to the way of the universe, a teaching of **mikkyo**
- **Suburi:** Single broken down movement using a **buki** done as a solo practice
- **Sugoroku:** Backgammon, popular in medieval Japan
- **Sui:** water
- **Sui no kata:** water form
- **Suihei:** horizontal
- **Suijutsu:** the martial art of swimming combat
- **Suiki:** Water crossing tools
- **Suiren:** water training
- **Suiton:** the using of water
- **Suki:** a momentary opening in guard, Opening, A gap in an enemy's defense or technique, "the space between which something can enter"; a fatal inattention engendered by self-consciousness.
- **Sukke:** beggar, common **ninja** disguise
- **Sumi:** corner
- **Sumikiri:** sharpness of body and mind
- **Sumo:** A basic and modern Japanese form of grappling in which the participants are of gigantic proportions. Victory is either achieved by forcing the

opponent out of the ring, or by forcing him to touch the floor within the ring with any part of his body above the knee. Traditional form of wrestling that was once part of religious festivals, particularly popular in the **Edo** Period. **Oda Nobunaga** enjoyed **sumo** and in February 1578 held a lavish **sumo** tournament at **Azuchi** Castle involving as many as 1,500 wrestlers.

➤ **Sumotori: Sumo** wrestlers
➤ **Sun:** A measurement of length, 1 **sun** = 3.3cm, 10 **sun** = **shaku**
➤ **Sunamochi:** Strengthening exercise involving holding clay pots filled with sand at arm's length
➤ **Suntetsu:** A small oval piece of wood fixed to the finger with a strap
➤ **Suri ashi:** shuffling, sliding feet **ninja** stealth walking technique
➤ **Sute:** sacrifice
➤ **Sutemi waza:** sacrifice techniques, giving up balance to control an opponent
➤ **Suwari waza:** laying down techniques

T

➤ **Tabi** or **tabbi:** traditional footwear of the Japanese **budoka**
➤ **Tabidatsue:** "setting Out", first phase of a **Ninja** operation
➤ **Tachi:** standing, long **katana**; can be a general term. worn hanging from the belt edge down
➤ **Tachi rei:** any "Standing bow"
➤ **Tachijutsu:** the martial art of using the **Tachi**

431

- **Tai:** large, big, great; the body
- **Tai kai:** "body of the organization" a great party; annual seminar
- **Tai ken:** body fist
- **Tai no kurai dori:** positional body management
- **Tai otoshi:** Body drop throw
- **Tai sabaki:** body evasion; natural movements for evading attacks
- **Taibumi:** Travel Bow
- **Taihenjutsu:** the martial art of the body; rolling, leaping, silent movement, tumbling, breakfalls
- **Taiho:** A cannon
- **Taihodoki:** body method way to energy
- **Taijutsu:** The martial art of unarmed combat
- **Taijutsu no kamae:** transitory positions of the martial art of unarmed combat
- **Taikyoku:** first cause
- **Taisho:** General, captain, commander
- **Taisho Period:** 1912 until 1926.
- **Taiso:** flexibility exercise; stretches; body conditioning
- **Take: bamboo**
- **Takemusu:** improvised Martial art
- **Takemusu aiki:** improvised Martial art through the principle of **aiki**
- **Takezutsu:** Breathing Pipe
- **Taki** also called **nagare:** waterfall
- **Tama:** ball; sphere
- **Tameshiai:** mutual testing; competing against one's own self
- **Tameshigeri:** test cutting with the sword
- **Tameshiwari:** test breaking, tile, board, wood, bricks and ice

432

- **Tanbo:** 6 to 9 inch stick
- **Tanbojutsu:** the martial art of 6 to 9 inch stick
- **Tanden:** the center of the **hara**; center of **ki**
- **Tani otoshi:** Valley drop
- **Taninzugake:** several attackers
- **Tanren:** Conditioning training
- **Tanto** also called **tanken:** knife, dagger, dirk
- **Tantojutsu:** the martial art of knife fighting
- **Taoshi:** to throw down, take down, to fall, knocked down
- **Tare nagare:** hanging flow, dropping into a roll
- **Tashi:** "Expert" An expert of Japanese martial arts who is of third to fourth degree black belt. All belts within this category, however, do not receive this title.
- **Tatami:** straw mat
- **Tatami do:** armor common in the 16th Century that could be folded up for easy of storage
- **Tatamiya:** rice straw mat makers
- **Tate:** erect, standing, vertical
- **Tate Tsuke:** Vertical Fist Punch
- **Tatehiza:** Half-seated position with right knee raised, what the **samurai** would sit in instead of **fudoza** when wearing their **yori**.
- **Tatsujin:** fully developed, enlightened human being
- **Tatsumaki:** "dragon roll" tornado, whirlwind
- **Tatsumaki jime:** "dragon roll choke" dragon choke
- **Tawara:** straw rice bag; bale
- **Te:** hand
- **Te nagashi Uke:** Hand Sweeping reception
- **Te yari:** A very short **Yari** between 3 and 4 **Shaku** in length.
- **Tehodoki:** hand method way to energy

- **Teisatsu:** Scouts
- **Teisho Tsuke:** Palm Heel punch
- **Tekagi:** iron hand claws like **shuko** but worn over the outside of the hands.
- **Tekatana:** Hand Sword; using your hand like you would slice with a sword.
- **Teki:** enemy
- **Tekki:** Iron Horse
- **Tekubi:** wrist
- **Tekubi dori:** wrist grab
- **Ten:** heaven, sky; top; celestial beings; 7th level of existence.
- **Ten chi jin ryaku no maki:** heaven, earth, and man strategy scroll.
- **Ten ryaku no maki:** heaven strategy scroll
- **Tenbourin in:** turning of the wheel of law a **mudra**
- **Tenbu:** divine beings
- **Tenchi:** a single **waza** for some, a "heaven and earth" **aiki** principle for us
- **Tenchi Buri:** Spinning the chain or rope of a **Kusarigama** above the head.
- **Tengu:** folk lore winged demon, similar to a griffin
- **Tenkan:** Circular withdrawal
- **Tenmon:** astronomy / astrology
- **Tenno:** The emperor
- **Tento:** The crown of the head.
- **Tenugui:** A towel.
- **Tensen:** To fight in various battles
- **Tenshin:** evasive and counterattacking body movements
- **Tensho:** rolling hand; fluid hand
- **Teppo:** Gun, rifle, musket.
- **Teppojutsu: Teppo:** the martial art of the gun, rifle

or musket
- **Tessen:** iron fan
- **Tessenjutsu:** the martial art of the iron fan
- **Tetsu:** iron
- **Tetsubo:** the iron and wooden club/staff
- **Tetsubushi:** caltrops
- **Tetsu Yari:** An all steel **Yari**.
- **Tettsui** also called **Tsuki ken** or **kentsuki:** Hammer fist downward strike with closed fist, little finger end as the striking surface. Just **Tettsui** can also mean iron hammer.
- **To:** and, door, drop, fell; gain an overpowering will; head; sword
- **Tobi:** leaping and jumping
- **Tobi ashi:** leaping feet
- **Tobi Kaiten:** Jumping rolls.
- **Tobi keri:** leaping kick
- **Tobibashigop:** Throwing Ladder
- **Tobu:** Jumping Training
- **Todajutsu:** Japanese term for Chinese martial arts.
- **Togime:** Door-Jamming device
- **Tojutsu** also called **kenjutsu:** the martial arts of using a Daito
- **Toki:** top of foot, climbing tools, the highest position of a member of the government
- **Toki kudaki:** toe/foot destroyer
- **Tomoe:** large u; u-like pattern
- **Tomoe nage:** dropping "U" throw
- **Tonfa:** A modern **Karate** weapon. Said to be originally the handle of a grinding wheel that was used as a weapon by **Okinawan** peasants. The **tonfa** is most often used as a whirling instrument, swung by its handle, but the handle itself can also be used for

attack. Its "use" includes stopping a **katana** should you choose to believe that.

> **Tonyu hen:** method for continuous observation, agents always placed even during peaceful times
> **Tori:** to seize, catch, a generic term for the person performing a technique
> **Torinoke:** Birds' eggs; blown eggs filled with gunpowder
> **Torite:** arrest, hand trapping
> **Toritejutsu** can be another term for **hojojutsu:** the martial art of arresting with binding restraints.
> **Totoku hiyashi:** avoiding **shuriken**
> **Tozama:** "Outer lord"; term used in the **Edo** period to describe those lords who had joined or submitted to **Tokugawa Ieyasu** only after his victory at **Sekigahara**
> **Tsuba:** sword guard; hilt
> **Tsubokiri:** Gouging and wedging device
> **Tsugi ashi:** Shuffling step
> **Tsuka:** The handle of a sword
> **Tsukaito:** Handle wrap of **katana**
> **Tsukami uke:** Grasping reception
> **Tsuke:** straight punch
> **Tsuki:** to thrust, to attach, fix
> **Tsukubo:** A long staff with one end having another piece of wood perpendicular to it and full of spikes. It was used for restraining.
> **Tsukuri:** stepping into the throw
> **Tsumasaki:** Tips of toes
> **Tsune no ashi:** pinching feet
> **Tsuno yubi:** finger nails
> **Tsunobito:** peasant
> **Tsuri:** Lifting, fishing

- **Tsuri goshi:** Lifting hip throw
- **Tsuri komi goshi:** Lifting pulling hip throw
- **Tsutsushimi Bukaku**: Modesty, discretion and carefulness
- **Tuite waza:** Grappling techniques, Using pressure points for joint manipulation

U

- **Uchi:** inside, to attack, defeat, destroy, conquer, strike
- **Uchi gake:** striking hooking leg throw
- **Uchi gari:** inner reaping-throw
- **Uchi mata:** inner thigh throw
- **Uchi mawashi geri:** inside roundhouse kick
- **Uchi uke:** inside reception
- **Uchi waza:** striking techniques
- **Uchideshi:** Special disciple that lives with the **sensei** full time, live in students who dedicate themselves to the art.
- **Uchijishi in:** healing **mudra** related to the **kujiin, sha**
- **Uchikata** also called **Dakengata:** striking and hitting attack forms
- **Uchikomi:** Repeated practice of **Nage Waza** *throwing techniques*
- **Uchitake:** A **bamboo** tube used as a waterproof container
- **Udaijin:** Minister of the Right; one of the imperial ranks held by **Oda Nobunaga**
- **Ude:** arm
- **Ude garami:** coiling arm entanglement
- **Ude gatame:** whole arm lock

- **Ude kime nage:** arm focal point lock throw
- **Uijin:** One's first military campaign
- **Uji** also called **gumi:** Clan, family
- **Uke:** receive; one who receives the technique
- **Uke nagashi:** receiving and deflecting the attack; receiving flow
- **Ukemi:** receiving a fall; breakfalling
- **Ukemi waza:** breakfalling techniques
- **Uki goshi:** Floating hip throw
- **Uki otoshi:** Floating drop
- **Ukimi no Justu:** Techniques for walking on ice especially with **Geta** *old world Japanese wooden clogs*.
- **Ukidaru:** Flotation device
- **Ukiyo:** "Floating World"; a cultural movement focused on pleasure and entertainment
- **Uma** - Horse.
- **Uma I:** Horse physician, veterinarian.
- **Uma Jirushi:** "Horse standard"; large rectangular flag/banner often used to mark a **daimyo** or important general's presence on the battlefield
- **Undo:** drill, exercise
- **Ura gyaku:** opposite side overturn
- **Ura kimon:** "inner demon gate" a **kyusho** point in the ribs under pectoral muscle between ribs 4 and 5.
- **Ura nage:** opposite (back to back) throw
- **Ura shuto:** opposite side sword hand strike
- **Uraken:** backfist strike
- **Urakimon:** inner spirit gate **koppo** point ribs under chest.
- **Ushin no shin:** consciousness of oneself
- **Ushin no shin sunyata:** "emptiness"; voiding the body of conscious thought, which in swordsmanship

guards against over-concentration
- **Ushiro:** rear, back
- **Ushiro geri:** back kick
- **Utsu:** To attack.
- **Utsubo:** Arrow quiver
- **Utsuri:** shift, switch, transition, change
- **Utsuri goshi:** switching hip throw
- **Uwagi:** jacket worn for martial arts training

V

The older Japanese language does not have any words that begin with the letter "V"

W

- **Wa:** "Accordance" An ancient Japanese term for harmony, accord
- **Waka:** the classic Japanese poetic form, severely elegant in style, typically consisting of only 31 syllables
- **Waka sensei:** young teacher
- **Wakare:** separation
- **Waki:** armpit, the side, lateral
- **Waki gatamae:** elbow lock done with the armpit
- **Wakizashi:** short sword
- **Wako:** Japanese pirates who ravaged the coasts of China and Korea between the 13th and 16th Centuries, in some cases attacking hundreds of miles inland. The activity of the **Wako** (which often included pirates from any number of nations in

addition to Japan) was one of the factors that contributed to the Mongol Invasions. The **Wako** were largely suppressed by 1587.

- ➤ **Wan:** arm
- ➤ **Wanto:** arm sword
- ➤ **Waraji:** Straw sandals
- ➤ **Ware:** break, split
- ➤ **Wari ashi:** split **bamboo** toes, wearing special footgear
- ➤ **Washide:** eagle hand
- ➤ **Waza:** techniques
- ➤ **Waza ari:** (sport martial arts term) "half point" used in competition

X

The older Japanese language does not have any words that begin with the letter "X"

Y

- ➤ **Ya:** arrow, dart
- ➤ **Yabusame:** A form of archery practice conducted from horseback
- ➤ **Yagen:** poisons and curatives, part of the study into **Yogen**
- ➤ **Yajiri:** heavy bladed saws
- ➤ **Yakuza:** Japanese Mafia.
- ➤ **Yamabushi:** mountain warrior ascetics
- ➤ **Yamashiro:** Hilltop fortification, castle, especially one prior to the 17th Century

- **Yamikeigo: ninja** practice in the dark
- **Yari:** spear
- **Yarijutsu:** the martial art of the spear
- **Yasha:** warriors of fierce stance
- **Yasuyoshi Fujibayashi:** compiler of the **Bansenshukai** in the summer of 1676, in the time of the fourth **Tokugawa Shogun**
- **Yawara:** old term for **jujutsu,** can be another term for a **Tanbo** *wooden stick*
- **Yo:** hard, positive, light, male (yang)
- **Yogan in:** welcoming **mudra**
- **Yoi:** ready
- **Yojimbo:** Bodyguard, especially in the **Edo** Period
- **Yoko:** side, to the side
- **Yoko aruki:** sideways walking part of **shinobi aruki waza**
- **Yoko gake:** side leg hooking sweeping throw
- **Yoko geri:** side kick
- **Yoko tobi geri:** jumping side kick
- **Yoko ukemi:** side breakfall
- **Yokoha:** the hook of a **jutte**
- **Yokomen:** the side of the head
- **Yokomen uchi:** lateral strike to head, strike to side of head
- **Yoko nagare** also called **yoko kaiten** and called **yoko nagare kaiten:** sideways flowing roll
- **Yon** also called **shi:** four
- **Yondan:** 4th **dan**
- **Yonkyu:** 4th **kyu** green belt
- **Yoriki:** law enforcement official in the **tokugawa** period
- **Yoroi:** a suit of **samurai** armor
- **Yoroi hitatare:** Set of silk shirt and pants worn under

armor, primarily in the **Hiean** period

> **Yoroi kumiuchi:** battlefield grappling in armor
> **Yoroidoshi:** dagger-like thrusting blade for use against armor
> **Yoshin:** raising spirit, raising heart
> **Yubi:** finger
> **Yudan:** Title for someone who has passed one or more **dan** grade examinations in a **ryu**
> **Yudansha:** those holding black belt rank, two or more **Yudan,** plural of **Yudan**
> **Yudansha kai:** the organization of Black Belts in a **ryu**
> **Yuga:** Graceful, elegance
> **Yugake:** archer's glove
> **Yugamae:** proper posture for shooting a bow
> **Yugasumi** also called **dokkoden:** "evening mist" a **kyusho** point found at the hollow point behind ear
> **Yugen no sekai:** the field of all possibilities, world of the subtle and profound, the fifth dimension, unmanifest realm
> **Yuki waragi:** snow sandals
> **Yumi:** Japanese archery bow
> **Yumiya no Michi** the old term for **Kyujutsu:** the martial art of the bow and arrow
> **Yuyo Semarazu:** A sincere, calm and well composed attitude.

Z

> **Za:** seat, use to mean a trade or craft guild. **Toyotomi Hideyoshi** outlawed merchant **za** in 1585.
> **Za gata koho ukemi:** seated backward break fall

- **Za gata zenpo ukemi:** seated forward break fall
- **Za rei:** any kneeing or seated salutation (bow)
- **Zankanjo:** a note of explanation left at the site of an assassination
- **Zanki:** The perception of a cutting intention
- **Zanshin:** increased awareness of events in a fight, state of cautiousness, remaining mind
- **Zarei:** kneeling salutation
- **Zazen:** seated meditation done in **seiza** very uncomfortable
- **Zekken:** name tag, made of cloth or leather and attached to the **gi**
- **Zempo:** forward, front direction
- **Zempo geri:** forward stomp kick
- **Zempo kaiten:** forward roll
- **Zempo kaiten katate:** one handed forward roll
- **Zempo kaiten mute:** no handed forward roll
- **Zempo kaiten ryote:** two handed forward roll
- **Zempo kitten** also called **Zempo tenkai:** forward handspring
- **Zempo tenku:** forward flip
- **Zempo tobi:** forward leap
- **Zen:** Considered both a philosophy and a sect of **Buddhism**, **Zen** became popular in Japan among the **samurai** after its embrace by the **Kamakura Bakufu** in the 13th Century. By the 16th Century, **Zen** was almost universally studied by **samurai** and **daimyo** alike.
- **Zengo:** around, forward and back, front and rear
- **Zenjou in:** meditation or contemplation **mudra**
- **Zeoi:** to carry on one's back
- **Zokusei:** Attribution
- **Zori** sandals

- ➤ **Zu tsuki** also called **kikaku ken:** head butt
- ➤ **Zubon:** trousers, the modern term for **Gi** pants
- ➤ **Zui:** The old Japanese name for China
- ➤ **Zuki no kokoro:** having a mind like the moon
- ➤ **Zukin: ninja** hood

For years, my students have asked me for a greater list of terms. This glossary represents 17 years of jotting down terms. Most of the terms I wrote down were things I figured I would not remember. So, the list is kind of strange because it jumps back and forth through a great many centuries. It is in no way complete. I did do a lot of digging through all of my notes and this is everything that is not in the belt manuals with some stuff that is. Its intent was merely a reference guide for some common and some obscure terms too. Hope you enjoy it and learn from it.

444

Index

Sogobujutsu

curriculum. *See* Kyoka

R

S

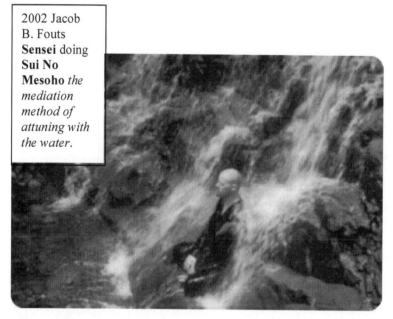

2002 Jacob B. Fouts **Sensei** doing **Sui No Mesoho** *the mediation method of attuning with the water.*

Bibliography

Aiki News / Aikido Journal.
www.aikidojournal.com/images/catalog/back_issues_index.h
tml.
Aikibujutsu, The International Society for the preservation of
Daito Ryu. *Daito Ryu Aikibujutsu Kenkyukai.*
www.daitoryuaikibujutsu.com.
Ellerbe, Jamie. *Nagano Ryu Heihou.* www.naganoryu.org.
George Sansom, Sir George Bailey Sansom. *A History of
Japan to 1334.* Stanford University Press, 1958.
Kando, Katsuyuki. *Daito-ryu Aikijutsu Headquarters.*
www.daito-ryu.org.
Koryu. www.koryu.com.
Samurai Archives. www.samurai-archives.com (accessed 08
01, 2010).
Takenouchi Ryu. www.takenouchiryu.com.
Tanemura, Shoto. *Genbukan.* www.genbukan.org.
Triplett, Stan. *Stan Triplett Bio.* www.stantriplett.com.
Wikipedia. en.wikipedia.org (accessed 7 4, 2010).

Falcaro **Sensei**'s 2006 Interview
Interviewed by his **Sensei**, Edward J. Smith **Sensei**

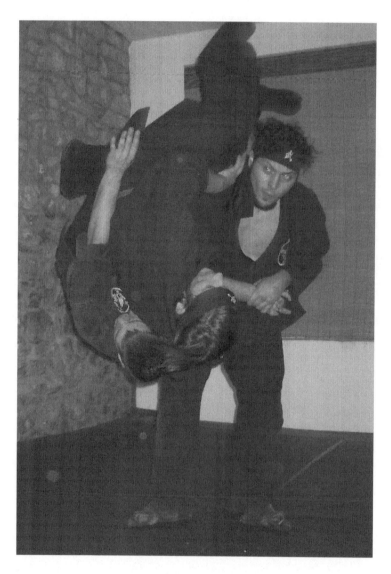

The reason I have included this interview is because I wanted to share some of my training experiences in the past. It is a part of our shared history. As a member of our martial family, you are now adding your experiences to our tradition. Please enjoy reading this interview and let it inspire you to document your own journey for our future. I am asking you to do for others what I have done for you, document to help us leave a beautiful legacy to the next **Bugeisha** *warriors* that eagerly awaits our story.

An interview with David C. Falcaro, **Sodenke**

* Please describe your earliest training experiences.

1984 This is the only photo of me at a young age wearing a **Gi**. Taken with my sister Jen, my brother Mike and cousins.

In **1984**, at age seven, I started my training in an American blend of **Karate**/ Kung-fu. This class was offered at Lehigh

Carbon Community College. It was taught by a police officer. He worked well with kids, but even at a young age I knew that I wanted something else from the martial arts. I can vividly go back into my memories and recall a week of practice. I was told to squat as low as possible in a deep "Horse Stance" with my arms in a cross-block above my head. I was to hold that position. I remember feeling my thighs burning as I attempted to remain steady. I asked my instructor after class what the purpose of the exercise was. He told me that if I lasted another week he would grant the answer. A week later (with larger thighs) I walked up to my instructor to get my long awaited answer. He quickly began with the response, "You see, now that you are stable with your overhead X-block and Horse Stance, when someone attacks you by swinging a bat at your head, you can absorb the impact." Being a child, one of the greatest insights I gained from my early experience in the martial arts was that I was not interested in modern martial arts.

In **1990,** I started training in authentic **Ninjutsu**

1992 The day I received my **Hachi Kyu**.

and have done so diligently ever since. I started training under Stan Tripplet **Sensei.** He was once a member of the **Genbukan** (a large **Japanese Ninjutsu** organization) and also trained under some of the top guys in the **Bujinkan** in the 1980s (a rival **Japanese Ninjutsu** group). He had his falling outs and so forth. He also trained me in aspects of **Shotokan Karate**, **Isshin Ryu Karate** and a little bit of Southern Shoalin Kung-Fu. We spent about three years on Pentjak-Silat. He is now the Grandmaster of his own **Ryu**. On the other hand, I felt a desire to train hard in traditional **Japanese**-derived martial arts. Rank was never important to me. Knowledge was and is to date.

Also, in my journey to remain open and experience different aspects of the martial arts, I studied **Kodokan Judo** for one year and also spent a year studying

2006 **Aiki Nage**

Kokikai Aikido.

To enhance my well roundedness as a practitioner, I studied the **Japanese** art of healing known as **Reiki** with

457

Reiki Master Lance Isakov and with my wife, **Reiki** Master Jody Falcaro.

* What were your primary reasons for studying Budo *martial arts*?

　　As a child, I was brought up in a strongly Christian household. My father was one of the pastors at our church. I was taught as a young child to be kind and loving, always praising the word of God. When I went to school, I presented myself as the helper or peacekeeper type of person, which did not go over well. Kindness was taken as a weakness and children can be cruel. Picked on, outcasted, messed with, made fun of and bullied, I turned the other cheek.

　　When I first heard of martial arts, it was the generic American slogan of "defense and honor" that piqued my interest. I was attracted to the idea of "secrets of combat" that I would be able to subdue an attacker that was larger and stronger than me. As a seven-year-old kid, I just wanted to be the hero. I was named after King David in the Holy Bible; as a boy, I thought martial arts could help empower me to live up to the "David vs. Goliath" legacy.

* What led to you first meeting Edward J. Smith Sensei and please tell us about that meeting.

My sister met a kid at the local mall, they started

1992 **Tantojutsu** demo

dating, and after a few years they became a close couple. I just got my driver's license and my sister had asked me to drop her off at her boyfriend's house. When I got there, I was asked to come in. My sister always pushed me to get to know her boyfriend better. She spoke of how we had so much in common since we were both martial artists. As I walked into the apartment, I did not feel like having another conversation about martial arts with him.

In the past, at every meeting, he spoke highly of his **Sensei** and the martial art he was learning. He attempted many times to impress me by showing me joint-locks, strangulations, throws, and strikes. But because he was somewhat of a beginner (and because of my past and current training in **Budo**) I remained unimpressed. The way I was accustomed to studying was learning everything I could from my teacher (at that time I studied **Ninpo**) and cross checking it with every book and video I could find on the topic. I spent most of my free time on the further pursuit of a greater

2006 **Aikijutsu** demo

understanding of **Budo**.

So it was time to once again talk martial arts with my sister's boyfriend. I never minded these talks. They just never seemed to go anywhere. They went something like, "Oh yeah, well did you ever see this one?" I'd reply, "Yes, it's called **Waki Gatamae**." So, sitting in the upstairs apartment deep into our compare and contrast argument/discussion, my counterpart says, "Okay! We are not getting anywhere." I nod. He then presumes to go downstairs to the apartment under his to bring back his instructor. I remember feeling setup. I had no idea that his **Sensei** lived there.

Seemingly reluctant, his instructor engaged the conversation. We spoke about martial arts and I attempted to impress this instructor by dropping names of (whom I thought were obscure) **Budoka** and terms that I was sure he could not know.

Before getting too far into the conversation that changed my life, I feel I should mention where my mindset was at this point in my seventeen-year-old life.

I had many encounters prior to this one with would-be instructors. I took it as a challenge to "get one up" on them. History, philosophy, Japanese terminology, and form and function of technique--I hit martial arts instructors up on each field. It proved as good practice for me, I did not see any harm in it. The worst I figured people could label me as a "know it all".

I knew who was in the area as far as martial artists and the knowledge I gained from my studies in the **Genbukan Ninpo Bugei** was unmatched. It's not that I believed myself as such a great scholar, I did not, just compared to what little was available (as far as knowledge of **Nihon Budo**) to the Lehigh Valley, well I was looking pretty good. I knew where I stood; I was studying real **Budo** where it seems others were trapped (as I was as a child) in "cookie-cutter money-making **karate** fitness centers". They were learning very little and being charged a lot. After years of searching, I found the "in" into "real" **Japanese** martial arts and was confident about it. There were not many martial artists in the area that had this opportunity, so I put forth the

2006

effort into knowing the craft as much as I could at a young age.

This brings us back to the conversation I was having with Edward J. Smith **Sensei**. From the beginning of the meeting, he remained reserved and did not speak much, which threw me a curve. When you meet a martial arts teacher, all they want to do is talk about themselves. He did not. Instead, he just sat and simply answered my questions. This was crazy to me; he answered every question, no matter how I tried to stump him. I quickly got the notion that he was merely toying with me. I loved it, but it scared me. I had many questions for him. Who are you? Where did you come from? Are there others like you around here? I believe he knew then that he piqued my interests. He did not answer; he just smiled, shook my hand and turned to leave. I scrambled to get him to hold on. I asked, "Please, could you tell me how you have come to know so much?" He smirked and turned to my sister's boyfriend to shake his hand and leave. Just then, with some sort of small quick jerk, Smith **Sensei** cast the man airward, he flew across the room and was tossed with impacting force into his bed. I had no idea how this could happen and I never saw anything even close to that type of movement. Immediately, I blurted out: "WHAT!?" and then, "but…What the heck?"

I remember feeling as if something was amiss and I had to know why and how this man was thrown across the room into his bed.

Smith **Sensei**, as he walked down the stairs, extended an invite to his **Dojo** the next night.

463

* Can you describe the first time that you went to the Takishin Dojo?

The **Takishin Dojo**, at that point in time, had just moved into the Allentown Boxing Gym. Smith **Sensei** set up an agreement to sublet a small room of the gym from the head boxing coach (at that time, Dave Barbosa). This room was in use by the gym as a closet.

My first encounter happened shortly after the students emptied the room. I showed up early and met some new faces. I helped as we moved some more things out of the new **Dojo**. We made more room to fold out another mat to add to the already set up floor.

I sat off to the side by the doorway in the seated position of **Seiza No Kamae** as a visiting student. The class began as the students did their warm up drills. It looked to me at that time as something close to what I was accustomed to within **Aikido,** but the movement was tighter and they were swinging their arms in differently changed-up fists. I made out the fists: **Shikan Ken, Fudo Ken, Age Ken, Happa Ken, Ippon Ken**. My thoughts were, "**Aikido** does not strike like this, this was **Ninpo**". I felt relaxed. I had a grip on what was being taught.

464

Smith **Sensei** called "**Yamae**" and students spread to the edge of the mat and the **Sensei** took the **Embusen** *center of the mat.* Just then, he called to his largest student to attack

and without warning, the student swung. I saw the way Smith **Sensei** evaded the attack and thought, "this is not **Ninpo**". I saw a recognizable jointlock, but then the jointlock seemed to go away and the large man went upside down. Smash! As he hit the mat, the floor shook and I could feel the impact. The student rose up again and attacked! He

465

folded as if he were the one being hit, but I couldn't see from where and then once again he flew upside down. Smash! Over and over, getting up and attacking fast and hard, this heavy-built 6'3" monster of a man attacked and was tossed. Smash! I remember thinking, "I can't understand why the joint lock disappears? Where is the power coming from? Why is this guy going upside down?" It was far too intense to be a hoax. I recognized every fourth or fifth entanglement and lock; they were being used in a way I had never dreamed, used to wield this guy through the air and into the ground. Sometimes no jointlock, no entanglement, the guy just was thrown. *Must be some unknown power!* My interest was overwhelming and my legs were screaming for relief from **Seiza No Kamae**. Smash. Smash. Smash. The vibration from this was starting to draw onlookers. The door to the **Dojo** was left open and people gathered to watch. One guy poked his head in and asked me how this guy was being "chucked like that". I responded, "I have no idea."

Every student had his turn attacking the **Sensei** and ending with the same result. After this, they were given something to work on and Smith **Sensei** walked over to where I was seated. He asked me to relax (which I was grateful for) and asked for my thoughts. I replied with nothing but questions. How? Why? He asked again what I thought and I told him that I did not understand what I was seeing but it looked so very impressive. He then offered for me to feel it. Of course I said, "Yes!"

He was very kind to me that day, I took a hold of his wrists and then I flew off backward to the ground. Again and again, I tried to hold on--different ways of grabbing, different stances-- nothing worked. I just couldn't hold on and I kept

466

falling, with force, to the ground. As far as I could tell, there was no technique. I just kept getting thrust to the ground by nothing. I guessed that this same sort of "magic trick" was being used in replacement of a joint-lock in the throws I was witnessing before.

I did not know how or why it worked but it worked everytime. I kept finding myself on the ground.

When class ended, I felt myself tearing up, as I knew the choice that was in front of me: join under this **Sensei** (if he would have me) or quit the martial arts forever.

Taken during the presentation of my first two **Densho** in 2005. Edward J. Smith **Sensei** and David C. Falcaro **Sensei**.

<u>* How did this training differ from the other arts that you studied?</u>

It was hard. It tested me and **Sensei** tested me every day. It tested my body, the training days were every day instead of two days a week and they were mean. We tried to punch and kick **Sensei** and he punched, kicked, locked, choked and threw us. Pain, all sorts of new and interesting pain. Things I never felt before and more things I did not know existed. Mentally, I was tested to remember names and terms more than ever before. I had to deal with things that were not touched on by past instructors. Another aspect was the mind games that were impossible to win and I never knew when he was playing or not. Now, I tend to think all the time. Frustrations. More than I had ever known.

On a good note (not that all of training wasn't good, because it was), there was a neverending depth to this art. I am sure every martial art could claim this and they would be right in doing so, but what I'm speaking of is that this art and my **Sensei** offer countless techniques, countless knowledge and countless amazements.

* Why is **Reigi Saho** so important to your studies and why is it relevant today?

Reigi Saho, aside from its more simply put meanings and courteous attributes, is done in preparation of the martial artist. It molds the practitioner into moving correctly. It makes adjustments to the form of the martial artist. It sets in key components to the desired movements that will later enable the practitioner to grasp a greater scope of their martial studies. Its importance is difficult to measure; it is one of the most important parts of training, and to the beginner, it is essential for development. Simply put, it makes doing **Aiki** possible.

* Can you describe your efforts to learn **Aiki Myoden** and the various stages that you've experienced?

Ha! Frustration. It's been difficult and continues to be difficult. Stages, it seems that everything is a stage in getting one to **Aiki Myoden**. It has been for me. My **Sensei**

468

taught me that **Aiki** was combative and to get this in its truest combative nature, I had to study the hard forms of **Jujutsu**. For my studies, **Aiki** without **Jujutsu** is pointless. This may change as I grow, but for now, without a strong hold on **Jujutsu**, **Aiki** is nothing more than parlor tricks. With **Jujutsu**, **Aiki** makes jointlocks and throws effortless. It aids in more powerful strikes and makes use of the **Hara**.

I have experienced many stages. The first stage was finding **Kazushi**, how to balance and off balance. This is what brought my **Jujutsu** to the forefront in playing an active role in teaching me about **Aiki** principle.

From there, **Sensei** guided me into lessons that, when looked at, seem like magic, but when worked, became a mental and physical understanding of minimized movement.

I grasp some as others lose me. The process feels like chasing a pest through a maze. It is quite good at evading me. I get lost quite frequently until I finally eliminate enough possibilities to corner it in truth, thereby finding out what the teaching is all about.

* What does the future hold for you as a **Budoka,** husband, and father?

As a **Budoka,** I will never stop climbing, growing, learning and taking time out to bring others along with me.

As a husband, I hope to employ these skills where I can to allow for ease in my relationship with my wife.

As a father, I am building a legacy that one day my offspring will be able to call their birthright.

* What are some of your most memorable **Aiki Budo** training moments?

I have many fun stories about my training history that I frequently share with my students and I am making more memories every day. I think this is one great part of the journey. As my mind is strictly note-taking and encoding all of the material **Sensei** likes to throw at his students, I end up encoding social memories as well. I remember much of the older training as if it were yesterday.

Funniest moment.
Looking back on it, it is funny, but not so much at the time. I was a student of my **Sensei**'s for about a month. At this time, I was still feeling things out. It was just before class, I am dressed and walking by **Sensei** and Rivera **Sensei** as they were discussing something. As I was passing, **Sensei** asked me to stop for a moment. He asked, "Don't you need to go to the restroom before class starts?" I replied, "No **Sensei**, I just came from there." He told Rivera **Sensei** to watch and asked me on to the mat. It immediately grabbed the attention of the rest of the class. **Sensei** then asked again, "You sure you don't have to go?" I responded, "Nope, I'm good **Sensei**." Wham! **Sensei** struck me with both fists. "Aaaah!" Immediately, I was losing control of my bladder. I did not mean to speak loudly, but I blurted out, "**Sensei**, please! May I go to the restroom?" **Sensei** nodded, I bowed and ran!

Scariest moment.
Among many, this was a scary one. Maybe a year into training under **Sensei**, he spoke of stepping things up in my training. **Sensei** invited a Golden Glove champion boxer into the **Dojo** for the night. This was not that big of a deal as

470

Sensei often used different fighters to attack him so that he could show **Oyo** *applications*. I just about lost it when the boxer was given instruction to punch me.

Sensei says to the boxer, "If you can hit him, do it. It will be good for him." **Sensei** then says to me, "Dave, just **Irimi Waza** *entering techniques*, you will not be striking back." So, I got to enter in on a boxer, but most of the night, basically, I got punched a lot.

Taken at the moment I received my first two scrolls from my **Sensei** in 2005 at the Bethlehem **Godaishin Hombu Dojo.**

Most challenging moment, aside from learning **Aiki**. Throughout the early years of training (first 5), **Rendori** *the practice of random attacks, pitting two or more people against each other* was the most challenging. I came in the low man on the totem pole. The guys I was up against were more equipped than me. **Sensei** liked guys with different backgrounds: Judo champion, ex Special Forces trainer, Muay Thai Kickboxing champ, Marines, hardened police officers, black belts of **Karate**, **Jujutsu**, Hapkido. These guys were older with years more experience with **Sensei** and bigger 6'1" to 6'3" and outweighing me by a hundred or more pounds. It was widely known that some could bench 550lbs. So, I didn't really have much of a chance being that I was a High School student, 175lbs. I was knocked around on a nightly basis.

* Who were students of note and why are they memorable?
Martin Rivera **Sensei**--awesome guy. He would hangout with me before and after class and help to explain things. He knew where everyone was coming from; he did martial arts his whole life and was amazing at them. He had legitimate black belts in (I think) five arts. So when someone had trouble with understanding, he could relate it back to something we had already trained in another art. Also, he would just wreck anyone. I remember watching him box a boxer with one arm behind his back. This was without any martial arts, and he won. When he kicked you, you would fly at least 6', it was unreal! He practiced all of his striking on trees. He had muscles popping out all over, built like a brick house. I don't care who you are (aside from **Sensei**) he would walk through you.

Squire Douglas--fun guy, trained hard. He was originally a Hapkido black belt, and a good one at that. I remember him getting into street/bar fights. He would try out what we learned, break peoples' arms and toss them, hit them in nerve points and kick them in the throat. He would come to class and show us how he did it.

472

Dave Claudio--we were sort of at odds for much of our training together. I don't think he liked "little kids" messing around trying to learn the art. I think, for him, I was in the way. That is the feeling I got from him anyway. He would rather train with the bigger guys, being 6'3" himself.

2006

"Smaller guys were not challenging," is something I remember him stating many times. He was the ex-Special Forces trainer and one of the guys that could bench 550lbs. He spent much of his time, outside of training, being a bouncer at tough bars in Allentown. He got to use a lot of arresting techniques and I'm sure employed more. I remember, quite well, how hard he hit. One time during class, while we were in **Rendori** *the practice of random*

473

attacks / fighting, he would not submit to any of my joint locks. After getting punched in the ribs twice and feeling my innards shift, I pulled his ankle apart with **Ashikubi Gatame** *an ankle lock.* He was quite upset with me.

Craig Johnson--great guy. If you met him, you liked him. He was helpful and a good **Uke** *person that takes the technique, the receiver.* I would call him a "go getter". He trained hard and developed great technique. A career Armed Forces man, he trained the military in martial arts combat. That was his job until he outdid a superior in front of many high-up personnel. This was done during a large military martial arts demonstration. His superior was quite insulted when Craig received all the praise. After this, Craig was forced to be stationed in Alaska.

Big Gus--"the 7ft giant" collegiate wrestler. He never lost a wrestling bout. He was strong and huge. He never lost a fight either. Looking at him, you would not want to fight him. He was the largest man I have seen in person. Nice guy, but he did not stay long. Outside of wrestling, strength, and mass, he was not skilled. The rest of him made up for what he did not know. We used him as a beat up guy, we couldn't help it. It was so great to train with someone that huge. A fond memory of mine was when **Sensei** asked me to punch him with my **Hara**. I hit him once and he dropped back and said in his deep accent, "How does a little man like you hit so hard?" Another fond memory was when my student, Jacob B. Fouts **Sensei**, met him and got to train with him. I remember Fouts **Sensei** saying, "I never met a guy that made me feel small." Training on Gus really helped in instilling confidence in the art.

Matt Henderson **Sensei**--I don't really know him very well.

He is renowned for his **Gojo Ryu, Karatedo** background, as well as, so I am told, a strong **Hakko Ryu, Jujutsu** background. I met him a couple of times. The question was asked about students of note and for sure he is one. **Sensei** speaks of him highly. What little I did see him do, looked good. When I was thrown by him, he performed well. I know he trained a while before I was around. Henderson **Sensei** trained under **Sensei** back when **Sensei's Sensei** was still alive. He got to meet **Katsumi Tanemura Sensei**. He got the honor of training with **Tanemura Sensei** a couple of times. That is something I wish I could have done.

<u>* What do you feel about the political (online) problems that your group has faced?</u>
First off, I think it is a horrible thing that martial artists can be so petty. E-**Budo** (the online forum dedicated to making childish fun of martial artists) is a cruel joke. Members of E-**Budo** whom engage in such witchhunts should be ashamed of themselves. E-**Budo** was the first (as far as I know) but is in no way the last. This bashing of fellow martial artists is a trend. This trend has really taken off and has become a widespread pastime for many. Any respectable person who has read these online threads would agree on the ridiculousness of the accusers.

Often, I have witnessed accusers make up background stories about people and then make up more stories in the way of some type of silly defense. Then they all gang up on tearing into the person for all of the things they made up about them. Another thing they make fun of are websites. This is their

Taken during a demo in 2007 while demonstrating a bone breaking **Kensetsu Waza** with Eric P. Fichter **Sensei**.

bread and butter. They pull text and photos off of websites, import it into online threads and rip it apart. They alter content, deface photos and even pick on grammar. All of this is done before getting a real understanding of whom it is they are picking on.

I understand the need to separate oneself from fakes and charlatans. That is only natural. What these people engage in is quite different.

I hold events every year since 2003; at these events, I invite people from different backgrounds to display their arts. My judgment of others is based off of personal experience. My judgment stems from seeing and feeling practitioners' technique. I interview them personally, so when I give my opinion on someone, it is based on something factual. I make every attempt to get the truth about someone before giving my opinion.

What I find funny is that because I make time to watch as others perform, I have been judged as being "with them". This is some sort of guilt by association. It seems no one is safe from their ridicule.

Something I found strangely comforting happened as my wife went on a cooking forum to find some recipes for new meals for dinner. She found one, made the meal, and it was great. Because we enjoyed it so much, she wanted to post about our thanks. What she found were many post-writers going back and forth with each other ripping into each other's ability to cook and give advice. Making fun of credentials, heckling and name-calling. It was a really nice meal, which got me thinking that people most likely did not even try it before bashing it.

The thing I find strangely comforting is maybe it is not martial artists acting the fool, it might just be an inherent human trait.

* How has your role as an instructor changed or evolved your **Bujutsu**?

Tons. A person can tell almost to the year how long someone has been training **Aiki**. Because of this, teaching really makes me train more on the finer points of **Aiki**, so that when viewed by my **Kyu** *students*, I am seen as someone who is telling the truth. Not just truth out of my mouth, but also through my movements.

 As long as my **Sensei** lives, I want him to be proud of what I am producing out of my students. Because of this, teaching takes on five main focuses for me: for my **Sensei**, for myself, for the students, for the art, and for the tradition. This is a heck of a lot to live up to.

I try my best not to let the business side of teaching affect my martial arts. It does, on occasion, poke its way in. I think this is a negative to teaching.

When teaching others, you get to see the art again for the first time through the students' eyes. That is magical.

Teaching yourself is one thing, but when trying to relate the art to another--wow. I really learn a lot more about the ins

Teaching an **Aiki Nage** to Eric P. Fichter **Sensei** in 2004 during a class at the Bethlehem **Godaishin Hombu Dojo.**

and outs of each little movement.

Having students on hand to practice on is a nice thing too.

* What do you teach in your **Dojo?**
I teach the **Waza** *Techniques*, **Gata** *Forms*, **Ho** *Methods* and **Undo** *Drills*, but I focus on the principles and concepts behind the movements. I feel working toward attaining them is of the utmost importance.

The principles I speak of here could be described as the reoccurring systematic emphasis that is placed behind every movement within the art. This is the backbone of all movement in **Sogobujutsu**. When one is trained by this principle-based system, the reoccurring emphasis becomes apparent to the individual. This opens one's mind to see the common thread that exists within everything in **Sogobujutsu**, i.e. the cut is the same as the throw. In this way, the art is not a whole bunch of scattered mismatched pieces. Instead, the commonality becomes so apparent that one comes to the realization that there is but one technique to train. This technique is guided by universal principles and inspired into creation by universal law.

Of course, all of this cannot be taught. Much of it is self-discovery. Through pointing out principles and concepts behind the movements, I hope to further the process.

* Is there anything that you would like to add?
I have always loved the martial arts as a whole. I have truly found my niche in the **Japanese** warrior arts. I am determined to remain humble and steadfast to the methods I study and teach. I hope to embody the true spirit of **Budo**.

About the author

David C. Falcaro **Sensei** was born in Bethlehem
Pennsylvania, USA. David has, to date, over 29 years in the
Martial Arts experience. The last 22 of which were spent
training in **Koryu**-based Japanese Warrior Arts. David is a
Sodenke. This means that he has received scrolls after

attaining levels of proficiency. Aside from these, he holds many titles, ranks, and positions in the martial arts. He feels that humility is lacking in the martial arts of today; therefore, he asks humility of himself and of his students. If you require a more complete resume of titles, ranks or positions, please ask him personally.

David is the head instructor of the **Godaishin Dojo**, **Neji Gekken Ryu**, **Sogobujutsu** as well as the **Kaicho** of the **Jihi Bujutsu Kai**.

David was knighted in 2008 under the order of the Esteemed Knightly order of the Redcross, defenders of the faith. He has since, in 2009, been passed and accepted as a Sir Knight of the order of Malta. Sir David, in 2009, was then raised and passed as a Sir Knight of Templar- Allen Blushant Commandery #20. David is happy to proclaim that he is a Christian. He is a big fan of Eastern philosophy and, at times, practices Buddhism as a philosophy.

He is an avid animal lover, as well as passionate for all things in nature.

David is a martial arts historian; he enjoys sharing his knowledge through his lectures and demonstrations as he tours high schools and universities many times a year.

Not shy to construction, he enjoys working for his father's remodeling business part-time. David has been known to construct things for the betterment of the **Fuku** and to ensure the prosperity of the **Neji Gekken Ryu**. Many **Fuku** have aided and continue to aid in the further production of the **Ryu**'s combined dream. For this, David remains grateful and excited for what the future will bring. He cares deeply about his journey in the martial arts and presents himself as a friend, brother, teacher and student. Falcaro **Sensei** has a loving, beautiful and supportive wife, as well as a young son and daughter. The most important things in his life are family and friends. **Sogobujutsu** is his passion, a life work.